Leaving Emmaus

A New Departure in Christian Theology

Anthony D. Baker

BAYLOR UNIVERSITY PRESS

Unless otherwise stated, Scripture quotations are from the New Revised Standard Version Bible, copyright 1989, Division of Christian Education of the National Council of the Churches of Christ in the United States of America. Used by permission. All rights reserved.

Cover and book design by Kasey McBeath
Cover art: Unsplash/Taneli Lahtinen

Library of Congress Cataloging-in-Publication Data

Names: Baker, Anthony D., 1975- author.
Title: Leaving Emmaus : a new departure in Christian theology / Anthony D.
   Baker.
Description: Waco : Baylor University Press, 2021. | Includes
   bibliographical references and index. | Summary: "Explores doctrinal
   systematics through the lens of contextual experience and language
   theory to depict Christian faith as an ongoing series of encounter and
   testimony"-- Provided by publisher.
Identifiers: LCCN 2021025020 (print) | LCCN 2021025021 (ebook) | ISBN
   9781481316040 (paperback) | ISBN 9781481316057 (pdf) | ISBN
   9781481316644 (epub)
Subjects: LCSH: Theology, Doctrinal--Popular works. | Spiritual formation.
Classification: LCC BT77 .B25 2021 (print) | LCC BT77 (ebook) | DDC
   230--dc23
LC record available at https://lccn.loc.gov/2021025020
LC ebook record available at https://lccn.loc.gov/2021025021

Printed in the United States of America on acid-free paper with a minimum of thirty percent recycled content.

For Stephanie

CONTENTS

PREFACE

On Losing and Finding the Faith

Perhaps Christians have, in various ways, always failed to live up to our biblical and theological vision in one way or another. Still, the twentieth and twenty-first centuries seem particularly replete with such failures.

For example: the ancient branch of the church that has spoken most loudly and most consistently about protecting the vulnerability of unborn children has proved itself astonishingly untrustworthy when it comes to protecting young people in its care after they have come into the world outside the womb. The Roman Catholic Church is not the only Christian institution guilty of sexual abuse and other abuses of power, of course. At the same time, the depth of Catholicism within world cultures, alongside many cases of reluctance to issue hierarchical condemnations, make these abuses the most visible public witness to the failures of Christianity in our times.

Or again, many churches fail to protect those whose nontraditional relationships to their own bodies or the bodies of others make them vulnerable to social alienation and hate crimes. Some Christians have organized or made common cause with violent protests against persons who identify as queer or who embody nonnormative genders or sexual desires; others have simply failed to note the vulnerabilities of these communities as the sort of human voices that call for Christian habits of justice and compassion.

Further, baptized Christians around the world openly refuse to welcome orphans and widows seeking asylum from violence in their countries of origin, a violation of one of the clearer mandates of the New Testament (Jas 1:27). In his pastoral letter "The Church's Mission amid the National Crisis," Archbishop Oscar Romero once wrote about the temptations to idolatry that draw Christians away from faith in God toward an absolute valuing of wealth, property, national security, or parties and organizations. The idolatry of wealth, he suggested, subordinates vulnerable lives to one's projected net value; the idolatry of political parties subordinates these lives to a strategy for achieving and maintaining power; and "the omnipotence of . . . national security regimes, the total disrespect they display toward individuals and their rights, the total lack of ethical consideration shown in the means that are used to achieve their ends, turn national security into an idol, which, like the god Molech, demands the daily sacrifice of many victims in its name."[1] The recent rise in the United States of an intellectual Christian nationalism is evidence of the success of all these idolatries, and the concomitant failure of a collective Christian imagination.[2]

This nationalism continues to have a devastating effect on the soil, water, air, and living things of the planet, as demonstrated for example in the recent—though brief—exodus of the United States from the Paris Accords, and the protectionist attitudes around the deforestation and run-away fires in the Amazon region.[3] A planet filled with fragile environments and vulnerable creatures is not, currently, finding a safe haven among the followers of the one "in whom all things hold together" (Col 1:17). Pope Francis summarizes this modern Christian failure: "An inadequate presentation of Christian anthropology gave rise to a wrong understanding of the relationship between human beings and the world."[4] Far from defending the endangered creatures and dying places of our world, that is, Christians have understood our own humanity in such a way as to aid an acceleration of these beings' harm.

A quarter of a century ago, the largely Christian Tutsi people of Rwanda were being slaughtered by the hundreds of thousands in the towns, homes, streets, and even churches of Rwanda. And they were killed by the largely Christian Hutu people who were their neighbors and, in many cases, fellow parishioners. "Never before have Christians killed one another in the very spaces where they had worshiped together for generations. What makes such a crisis of identity possible? What story is powerful enough to make people forget their baptisms in the very places where they happened?"[5] The answer to these questions is complex, and no one has dug more deeply into these complexities than the author who asked them. At the moment, we can at least note this as an astonishing failure of Christianity, and one with effects that will continue for generations.

Rowan Williams has written that there can come a point when the language of faith that is developing at any point in history "can provoke a degree of crisis: is what is emerging identical to or at least continuous with what has been believed and articulated?"[6] Though he meant this in reference to new paradigms of theological writing, we might extend the point to the broader life and culture of the entire faith community. We have come to such a point in Christianity now, when the terrorizing actions of Christians seem to suggest that a completely different religion is emerging. It is indeed a crisis.

We might call this a crisis of witness. Christianity is at its heart a life of testimony, a witness, a public proclamation. Today, the crisis is that it is in danger of becoming a proclamation of the predatory habits of priests and of the neglect of orphans.

Whether or not these are good reasons to turn from Christian faith (and though I hope they are not, I take that consideration to be one of pastoral theology, only answerable by individuals and communities who struggle to have hard conversations that take their experiences into account), I want to suggest that these are not reasons—or net yet reasons—to turn away from Christian theology. When Saint Paul wrote to the churches in Rome and Corinth, he wrote most often not in response to Christian successes, but failures. "For it has been reported to me by Chloe's people that there are quarrels among you" (1 Cor 1:11). There were public trials that showed Christians to be those who hate rather than love one another; rumors of gatherings in which they ignored the hungry among them; reports of Christians finding their fundamental identities in politicized parties rather than in their baptisms; stories of church members engaging in sexual practices that were destructive to families and the community.

Paul's response to these rumors was not simply to settle the disputes or call out the guilty. He did, in fact, turn to these epistolary admonishments, and there is plenty of ethical wisdom and practical advice to be found in these texts. But his letters open and often expend the greatest energy in the re-narration of the gospel. God has given Paul the task of "announcing the gospel of his Son" (Rom 1:9). "For the message about the cross is . . ." (1 Cor 1:18); "For just as the sufferings of Christ are abundant for us, so also our consolation is abundant through Christ" (2 Cor 1:5). We might characterize the form of many of Paul's letters like this: *The witness of your faith does not align with the story of the crucifixion and resurrection of Israel's messiah; perhaps we should start again at the beginning. What is this faith of ours?*

If I suggest that a return to the basic questions of faith might be relevant to the failures above, I do not mean to suggest that better theology will stop genocide or these other large-scale failures. Again: the roots of the Rwandan horror are deep, and, like the climate crisis and the abuse scandals and other failings, involve decades and more of political and economic abuses. But they *also* involve large-scale theological failure. I suspect the apostle never imagined that one or two letters would solve the problems around incest, hunger, and Christian division. What theology can do, at its best, is to invite what the New Testament calls a *metanoia*, or a turning of the mind and heart, so that people of faith—and people who take an interest in the faith—can begin to imagine that faith differently.

To put the matter simply: we Christians have, in more ways than we can give account for, failed to be people of "good faith." The failures are many, and they are dire. And perhaps these failures in the realm of action are corporeal symptoms of a disease within. The faith itself seems to be failing: perhaps what all this is telling us is that we have quite simply lost our faith. Before taking up questions about how to practice a more faithful witnessing to the faith of Jesus Christ—for which there are many excellent resources—perhaps we might turn again to the basic questions. What is this faith? What is the cross of Jesus the Palestinian Jew about? What do we imagine it is to be filled with the Spirit of the risen Christ?

It has been reported that we have failed to protect the most vulnerable among us and have even taken up weapons of violence and committed crimes against them. Perhaps we have not yet heard clearly the good news of the crucified one? In that case, there is no better time to turn, again, to Christian theology.

There is another reason, related to the first though in an oppositional tension, that this moment calls for theology. Theology, again, begins in witness, and if this is part of the disease, it is certainly also part of the healing. Along with being a time of great public failings of Christianity, the twenty-first century is also a time of remarkable witness to God's compassion, grace, and forgiveness. Christians are gathering to creatively name new practices of care for creation that do not ignore the needs of working-class families who depend on local industry.[7] Christians are serving refugees and protesting their inhumane treatment at detention centers along the world's troubled borders.[8] In the days before beginning the first draft of this book, I read about how members of the Greater Union Baptist Church in Louisiana, one of several historically Black churches recently burned in a spree of hate crimes across the state, gathered in a borrowed space to celebrate Easter. Their pastor, Reverend Harry Richard, led them in prayers for the white man arrested for the crimes, and reminded them in his Easter sermon, "You never give up on love."[9]

In many cases the witnessing act has gone beyond public action and words of forgiveness and has taken the ultimate form of Christian witness. On June 17, 2015, nine people attending a prayer service at Mother Emanuel African Methodist Episcopal Church in Charleston, South Carolina, were killed by an angry white man with a gun. Two years later, and closer to my home, twenty-six members of the First Baptist Church in Sutherland Springs, Texas, were killed by a young man angry with his mother-in-law. On the same Easter Sunday that the congregation from Union Baptist was praying for their enemy, suicide bombers killed more than 100 worshipers at St. Sebastian's Catholic Church in Negombo, Sri Lanka, part of coordinated attacks that claimed more than 250 lives, attacks timed to coordinated with the largest gathering of Christians in the year. Watching the news clips and reading these stories, we might recall the words of the apostle: "We are always being given up to death for Jesus' sake, so that the life of Jesus may be made visible in our mortal flesh" (2 Cor 4:11).

Praying for enemies, as Reverend Richard called his church to pray, is an act of Christian witness. But the act itself calls for something as well: it calls for theology. Who is the God, and what is the faith that could overcome hatred and the understandable desire for vengeance, and motivate such surprising words? Or at Saint Sebastian's: what is being made visible in the deaths of these new martyrs? To search for meaning in human violence of this sort is perhaps an unavoidable impulse. News sources will update readers and viewers on "what we know," tracing threads of racial, ethnic, and political turmoil, mental health, gun control, and more. Without detracting from these particular kinds of discursive accounts, theology can add something different. The earliest accounts of Christian martyrs focus not on the explanations of the violence, as those first Christians were taught from the beginning to expect to be treated something like Christ himself was treated. Rather, they focus on an experience of faith so saturated with transcendence that human threats and weapons become insignificant. Standing before an angry crowd armed with stones, Stephen "gazed into heaven and saw the glory of God and Jesus standing at the right hand of God." For Polycarp in the following century, eighty-six years of experiencing God's faithfulness led him to laugh at his executioners' flame, which "after a little while is extinguished."[10]

The implication in all of these accounts, from Stephen the Protomartyr to the Catholics of Saint Sebastian's, is that worshipers of the resurrected Christ take risks, lay down weapons, and go to their prayers because something that they encounter in the risen Christ motivates them to live—and perhaps die—differently. The members of Mother Emanuel may not have known a gunman was heading in their direction. Indeed, the gunman himself may not have known where he was heading when he left his home that day.[11] But those worshipers were aware that Black churches and Black Christians in the United States are targets of violence, and yet they gathered that Wednesday evening to say their prayers with no guards at the door. Even those worshipers at a relatively safe conservative white church in the U.S. South entered knowing that the world is unpredictable, filled with disproportionate rage, and there are certain risks associated with gathering and kneeling with backs to an unlocked door. Why would humans behave this way?

What I hope to show in the pages that follow is that it is precisely because of what they encounter when they encounter the risen Christ that humans might risk and make such radical witness as this. Their actions mediate this encounter: they make present, in limited ways, the great mystery of love that has caught hold of their lives. The witnessing act has been described by those more qualified to speak than I, for instance by the Amish families of Nickel Mines, Pennsylvania,[12] or the words of the pastor and parishioners of Mother Emanuel in solidarity with victims of the shooting at the Tree of Life synagogue in Pittsburgh,[13] or in Father Andrew Siboama's description of a group of once murderous Hutus and surviving Tutsis "drinking banana beer from the same jug."[14] Still, this witness and the account that the surviving church gives can motivate the question that theology must answer: what is this faith that, even failing in so many public ways, can motivate Christians to acts of vulnerability in times of terror? Theology follows such witness, as an attempt to gather it up, and to turn the act, the experience, into witness-made-discursive, the sharable substance of the faith. As Polycarp's biographer put it, "I, Pionius, collected these things, when they had almost faded away through the lapse of time . . ."[15] Collecting these things gives an account of the identity of the God and the substance of the faith that sustains these witnesses and these martyrs.

In the Holy Week before that same eventful Easter I spoke of above, stunning and heartbreaking pictures of Notre Dame de Paris in flames filled our newsfeeds. Perhaps the most significant response of the city of Paris, and of the world, was the heartbreak itself. This giant gothic space of worship, under construction when Thomas Aquinas first met Master Albert among the Dominican faculty at the nearby University of Paris, stands as a landmark and a reminder of something premodern, an aging memory of the faith that once mattered deeply to the city. Watching the fire, something seems to have shifted for a moment. "Notre-Dame de Paris is Paris itself," one Parisian put it. "It's our roots, our history, our civilization . . . I think of the generations of artists who spent all their lives working on this monument to God, to belief." Another noted that "Notre-Dame is not a relic but a living sacred place, the continuity of holy France" that in some ways still occupies the imaginations of Europeans more deeply than does the French Revolution.[16] I hesitate to draw too sharp a conclusion from statements such as this, motivated in obvious and understandable ways by the intensity of the moment. It does, however, seem to be worth asking, in light of the world-wide grief at the images of the great church in flames, whether the world still has some reckoning to do with the God of Moses, Mary of Nazareth, and Thomas Aquinas. Before we let it burn, or douse it with water as a historical preservation of our pre-enlightened innocence as a human race, is it worth asking again whether there might be something to the encounter that called up the remarkable witnesses of Stephen, Polycarp, and the people of Greater Union Baptist Church? Perhaps a general cultural readiness to give up on this faith, like the readiness to defend incoherent versions of it, is a sign that, like the church at Corinth to whom Paul wrote, we have not yet heard the full message, not yet encountered the breadth and depths of story of the risen Christ?

In these times, as this ancient faith fails, as it lives, and as we stand in confused grief watching it burn, we might pause for a moment, hold back any conclusive evaluations, and try once more to give an account of God's reclaiming of the world in the sending of the Son and Spirit to be with us. What was it, again, that came to pass in those days?

Advent, 2020

ACKNOWLEDGMENTS

This is a book about the theological language that can sometimes explode out of really good conversations, and it has its source, appropriately, in many such encounters. Most of them happened on the grounds of my theological home in Austin, Texas: Seminary of the Southwest. A student recently remarked that during her constructive theology course she's pretty sure we talked about Luke 24 every single day. Several cohorts of students have heard, reflected upon, and provided generously critical feedback on the ideas of this book. Two among them, Joe Williams and Brandon Haynes, gave me invaluable assistance in the editing and indexing of the final stages. My colleagues have likewise been generous with their theological gifts. I should especially mention Scott Bader-Saye, as the central idea was born out of some lectures we composed together. Jane Patterson's groundbreaking work on metaphor helped me encounter the cross in a new way. Steven Tomlinson intervened at a particularly apt moment to help me determine just what sort of book I was writing. A semester coteaching a course on liberation theologies with Rev. Melanie Jones helped me integrate some new material. Sharing life and language with you all is a gift, and I feel that gratitude every day.

The congregation at Saint Julian of Norwich Episcopal Church, where I serve as theologian in residence, gave valuable feedback to a spring forum on these ideas. Rev. Jonathan McManus-Dail, Rev. Miles Brandon, and Ashley Brandon have especially been generous with their time and insights. An invitation from Bishop Duncan Gray to give an address at the Gathering of Leaders led to some helpful conversations, and Alyssa Newton's critical feedback that day was especially important to me.

A wedding invitation from my friend Angel Méndez gave me the chance to hear a moving theological address from Carlos Mendoza-Álvarez, and Fr. Carlos' book came out just in time to be a dialogue partner within mine. Andrew Davison has been a cherished theological interlocutor for many years now, and I am always pleased when his wisdom manages to seep into my language. My own theology mentors show up in everything I say and write, and I could not begin to acknowledge my debts to them: Craig Keen, Gene Rogers, Peter Ochs, and John Milbank.

Finally, my family has been supportive with conversation and encouragement in countless ways. Walking through Laumeier Sculpture Park in Saint Louis with my sister Heidi while we talked about heaven and hell. Texts and calls from my son Lev about life, politics, and matters of faith as he encountered the wonders of the wide world. A drive across east Texas, discussing God and science with my daughter Anya. The day my daughter Lola talked me off the ledge about not writing anymore for a while. Mulling over questions of prayer with Steve Ramirez. My parents, who have been walking the road to and from Emmaus since long before I was born. And of course Stephanie, to whom this book is dedicated. You are my Cleopas, and I your unnamed companion, as we travel this road and feel the strange burn of revelation in our hearts.

INTRODUCTION

Thinking with the Witnesses

In the preface to his late thirteenth century *Summa Theologiae*, Thomas Aquinas complains about the way contemporary texts on offer bring students more "weariness and confusion" than clarity of thought. If I cite him here at the outset of my own brief *summa*, it is not because I consider my project to belong in the same sentence with that of the Angelic Doctor. Nor is it because I find theological writing today—much, though perhaps not enough, of which fills the pages and footnotes of this book—to be particularly worrisome or preoccupied with "the multiplication of useless questions."[1]

There is, though, something about the theological teaching of this age that does call for some attention, some redress, some correction even, and it is to this work that I hope the present book can make a contribution. To put it in a single sentence: it is time for theology to teach anew—so that students can learn anew—how to "think with" the testimonies it summons for its discourse.

Christian testimony or witness is the public acknowledgment of an experience—one with a certain discernible shape—of the God of Israel. The experience comes mediated, that is, through the life and death and resurrection of Jesus Christ, and is empowered by the presence of the Holy Spirit. This is the witness that lies at the heart of the historical church. The apostles put their experiences into words, wrote it down, passed around to their communities and other communities in letters; the lives of saints came to be seen as embodied proclamations of the truths God has revealed; martyrs became testimony without remainder, as the name implies.

Thomas wrote his own text when he was summoned from the University of Paris by his Dominican Order to teach theology at a *studium* for the Dominican Order in Rome. The style he adapted for the purpose was that of the *disputatio*, a remarkably generous method of argumentation in which various voices—witnesses—are summoned to present complex arguments from a variety of perspectives, including Jewish, Muslim, and pantheistic,

1

before the *magister* charitably sorts and orders and makes distinctions and clarifications on his way to providing a response. While he was not the first to adapt this style, he makes his own revisions, arranging the various voices with an obvious ear to the questions of students he had been called, late in life, to educate. Not all witnesses are present in his text, of course. In particular only those ancients with access to philosophy, and only those of his own era with access to university or monastic education, get a voice in his text. Still, the method seems to me to be among the most promising for structuring theological conversation.[2]

In terms of testimonial variety, theological methods altered and narrowed through the late Middle Ages and especially modern era. Now more strictly the discipline of university or divinity school curricula, theology became a univocally reasoned discourse, separated not only from the lives of saints but also of the lives of parishes and *scholae* far from intellectual centers. The questions and answers theology gave were thus alienated from the poor, the sick, and those who were in various ways isolated from the privileges of education. This is not exactly the same as separating theology from testimony, but rather of limiting testimony, since now the perspective of the theologian, attempting to speak for all, becomes the only testimony that counts. As Albert Schweitzer memorably put it in his study of the nineteenth-century research into the life of Christ, each era, and even each individual person, winds up creating a "historical" Jesus who is more or less the character of that era or author writ large. "There is no historical task which so reveals a man's true self as the writing of a Life of Jesus"[3] is his comic evaluation of the cottage industry. This is bound to be the case, though, if I am not engaging various testimonials that challenge and complexify my own. The Jesus I encounter will speak through my own experiences, and therefore with more or less my own voice.

A correction to this situation came in the latter half of the twentieth century in two directions at once. There was, first, an attempt to remarry the divorced disciplines of theology and spirituality, and so a reorientation of thought structures around Christian life and Christian practice. This involved, in the first place, a new reading of the premodern church for whom the modern divorce would have been inconceivable.[4] So it became possible to read premodern theologians in a more "constructive" way, which is to say as part of a community of testimonies for pressing theological questions. Maximus the Confessor, for instance, who in the early decades of the twentieth century would have belonged only on a syllabus for a course in "Post-Chalcedonian Christology" or "Spirituality of the Desert," might now find himself venturing out into new classrooms. Could there be material in Maximus for the contemporary priest preparing a Trinity Sunday sermon, or a layperson asking questions about the Incarnation? These new readings of classical material had various causes, but among them we should not ignore the migration of Orthodox theologians from eastern Europe and the initiation of dialogue with the western churches. For these theologians, unlike for the post-Enlightenment west, Maximus and others had never ceased being relevant to the needs of contemporary theology.[5]

The remarriage of theology and spirituality also manifested itself in the reconsideration of post-classical figures in Christian spirituality as theologically interesting, such as Julian of Norwich, John of the Cross, Thérèse of Lisieux, and Adrienne von Speyr. For names like these to show up on a theology syllabus would once have seemed like a confusion of genres, perhaps as though the rigorous intellectual discipline had been invaded by less serious "spiritual" pursuits. After a certain point in the latter half of the twentieth century, however, a loosening of categories and inclusion of witnesses became much more common, if not exactly taken for granted.[6]

These efforts brought a welcome change to the insulation of theology from the margins of its own language, in that now prayer and contemplation and Christian practice in general could become fodder for theological work.[7] During the same period a further development in attending to the cultural and economic margins of churches brought a much-needed critique to the perspective of the intellectual and ecclesiastical centers. Father Joseph Cardijn, for instance, developed a model of theology among the children and young adults working long hours at low wages in textile factories in Brussels. In this model the young workers began with the life situation that they saw in front of them, then reflected on the intersections of that experience with the gospel so that they could organize themselves for active responses.[8] Decades later, poor men and women in Solentiname, Nicaragua, saw themselves as empowered to provide interpretations of the gospel without mediation through the great universities of the West.[9] In such work, theology came to consider the social context of the theologian, and the theological community, as central to its testimonial perspective. In this they were surely recovering something fundamental to the early church, as I hinted above: Paul can rarely delve into the mysteries of Christology without mentioning contextual words like "Damascus," "Jerusalem," and "Tribe of Benjamin"—in other words, without bearing witness to the particular ways in which his very personal pathway intersects with the gospel of the risen Christ.

In both cases, then, we find a recovery of Christian witness for the task of theology: the testimony of Thérèse of Lisieux or Gregory of Nyssa as central to the preaching and teaching and living faith of churches, the testimony of poor and marginalized communities around the globe as a proper context for theological reflection.

The question that we are only now beginning to confront, even as we continue to discover experiences and testimonies excluded from the church's reflection, is how to *think with* these new testimonies. A brief glance at theology syllabi and introductory texts in Catholic and Protestant institutions[10] reveals some noteworthy features. It is common, in both denominationally specific and general theology courses, to find a syllabus offering "a range of perspectives," so that the student can survey the contemporary landscape and learn especially from emergent voices in global theology. It is likewise common in syllabi or texts that explore the frontier between theology and spirituality, or the related boundary between constructive and historical theology, to find chapters or units or assignments exploring the perspectives of premodern witnesses: like the "Christology of Saint Augustine," or the "Theology of Prayer in Teresa of Avila."

Both of these features mark an advance as well as an impasse. What they have in common is, on the one hand, a recognition of the need to multiply emergent voices that can "interrogate," to use Rebecca Chopp's term,[11] the denominational and other institutional centers of the discipline. On the other hand, they are also characterized by a lack of resources for approaching theology as a discipline of thought rather than, say, a survey of possibilities. Students are often asked in assignments to compare and contrast different perspectives, and perhaps, as a capstone exercise, to choose a perspective to call "their theology." At semester's end, one student prefers Barth, another the Minjung theologians, and a third tends to refer each question to Cyril of Alexandria. These students have clearly resourced their understanding with theological texts. But have they "done" theology?

To repeat, this resourcing is important work. Just as denominationally specific or para-denominationally organized theology is important for training students in particular patterns of Christian teaching (Lutheran confessional theology and Evangelical systems of theology, for example), texts and courses that survey new and old works, standard and emergent perspectives, can at their best provide a thick platform from which to reflect on theological possibilities. However, without the tools to sort what emerges from this field of possibilities into material for constructive or systematic thought, theology has not yet, at least in one important sense, begun. It is important to know what Cyril and Barth and Ahn Byung-Mu said, but to answer the question "Who is Jesus?" with "Barth says . . ." is to leave the question largely unanswered. It is to engage in a discourse that, as Jean-Yves Lacoste puts it, "leaves its object unthought."[12]

Theology, that is to say, is not just the amassing of testimonials, and Chopp's claim that now "the category for defining or ordering theology has changed from discourse in relation to reason to discourse in response to the moral summons in testimonies" risks leaving us without the tools to speak a common language about what it is these testimonies point to. If we imagine the theological discipline as a journey of encounter, the central metaphor throughout the present book, we might see that true encounter requires navigational tools to bring these disparate "travel narratives" into relationship with one another and with the aims of the journey itself. Without these tools, we encounter difference more like viewers of the Travel Channel during a global pandemic: we can take in various places and peoples without ever leaving our homes!

Critical theological reflection at its best is a way of "leaving home," as theologian Kathleen Fischer puts it. It helps us create a common language, so that we do more than notice and celebrate witness, and can also ask difficult questions about it.[13] Is Christian forgiveness possible across disproportionate levels of power? Or when contrition is lacking? No one could claim that public acts such as these are not powerful testimonies, but to say more than this we need a theology able to interrogate these testimonials as well as, and alongside, a collection of new witnesses capable of interrogating theological reasoning.

Christian witness, in this way, evokes a theological response, a response that can demonstrate the discursive links between the God of Scripture and the testimonies of the ever growing "cloud of witnesses." This task, in Sarah Coakley's words, is one of contemplative "unmastery" of these many witnesses, and ultimately a contemplative unmastery of the revealed God which their language is attempting to bring to expression. Theologians receive these witnesses, that is, not as if we were their evaluators and assessors, but as those called to contemplate the unity of what they offer, in and through–and occasionally despite–their various testimonies. Where this contemplation is at work we find ourselves attempting to present "the gospel afresh in all its ramifications, systematically unfolding the connections to the parts of the vision that is set before us."[14]

This necessary step into critical or discursive reasoning to help theological witnesses "leave homes" of contextual experience sheds some light as well on the "see-judge-act" methodology of Father Cardijn that was so influential on Vatican II and the early liberation theologians. The method begins in a kind of interrupted contemplation: what do we see of the gospel, and what in our surroundings is prohibiting the vision? By ending, however, in action—even a reflection on that action—the circle never completes itself, which is to say that the theological moment never returns to contemplation of God. This is something like answering the "Who is God?" question with "Barth says . . ." "Who is God in the factory in Brussels?" is an essential question for the church's gathering of testimony. For ongoing theological work, though, we also need to be able to ask, "In light of the witness of those workers in Brussels, and as that witness encounters Saint Augustine and Julian and the Minjung theologians, who should we say God is?" To answer this question, we need to learn to leave home.

It seemed, not long ago, that the multiplication of testimonies necessarily implied the end of "systematic" theology, which is to say a chartable course through theology as a thought-discipline. So a popular introductory text begins its first chapter with the line "All theological construction comes out of and is largely shaped by particular social, political, economic, cultural, and historical dynamics," and concludes that same chapter with "examples of the important differences that can ensue in theology even among theologians working closely together."[15] The opening statement is true as far as it goes, and the closing examples are useful for surveying the array of voices, but we can, it seems to me, go further into the construction of theology without ignoring this important observation. What we need, perhaps, is a working distinction between "contextual" and "systematic"[16] theologies, wherein the former takes shape as a gathering of witnesses and perspectives, and the latter as a bringing together of those witnesses into a common and coherent language of Christian faith.

The first chapter of the current book attempts to do some of this work by addressing what is commonly called theological source material. In particular, I return to the category of testimony to offer a new way of gathering voices *and* collecting them into a "system" or chartable path for the student. I provide here a method of "thinking with" the testimonies of faith. The chapters that follow attempt to carry out this method by moving through the various loci—my way of naming these loci, that is—of Christian theology.

There is much more to be said on this emergent challenge for theology. This is not a book of pedagogy—or andragogy—and most of what I have discerned in my life about how theology is taught and learned has come through the difficult and joyous work of the theological classroom.[17] It is, rather, my attempt to gather what I have learned, to think generously with these many witnesses, and then to offer a new departure point for Christian theology and see where this path leads. It begins, appropriately enough, with a new departure, and the story of two companions walking a familiar path that would take them into a brilliant and unfamiliar world.

1

THEOLOGY

The Life of Faith

"While they were talking and discussing, Jesus himself came near and went with them" (Luke 24:15). The cultures of Christianity and Judaism are built, first and foremost, on an encounter. Or, better said, they are built on a collection of encounters. "The Bible is not a textbook of philosophy or metaphysics, but the classical record of" the human "encounter with God in its most decisive phase in history."[1] The narratives, poetry, and all the various genres of biblical material serve, for Jews and Christians, as the canonized collection of the encounters that give shape to all others. The Bible is the textual icon of creation's confrontation with the God of Israel.

The Emmaus encounter, in which Cleopas and an unnamed companion walk with Jesus from Jerusalem toward their home, will serve for us throughout this book as the paradigm of the Christian encounter with the risen Christ. Here we read of how "the disciples came to recognize the Lord as the one whose Passion is spoken of by the scriptures," and then how it was that they "encountered him in the breaking of bread."[2] This encounter does not stand on its own, though; like every other narrative in the Bible in which God meets humans, this one sets itself against the background of Moses' encounter at the burning bush. Here the strange God of the forgotten ancestors reveals the name by which God will be known throughout the generations. The choosing of Moses and the liberation of Israel from slavery cast a light back upon early accounts of the calling of Abraham and his descendants, and even back to the encounter of God with Noah, and with Adam and Eve and creation itself. The God who self-identifies to Moses with God's own proper name in order to call Israel out of slavery is the same God who calls light out of dark, Adam out of dust, Noah out of destruction, and Abraham out of Ur. "I appeared to Abraham, Isaac, and Jacob as *El Shaddai*,

9

but by my name YHWH I did not make myself known to them" (Exod 6:3).[3] Similarly, Moses becomes the model of the prophet, or agent of encounter. Each figure who bears God's liberating word and calls on God's revealed name in the post-Exodus and post-exilic history of the people is "a prophet like Moses."[4]

To call these accounts textual icons, as I have, is to say something about what it is to be people of faith who read and hear these stories. We discover who we are, and how to make sense of our world, as we read ourselves into the narratives and poetry of the Israel and the church. Twentieth-century Jewish theologian Eliezer Berkovitz describes how this dynamic of textual iconography is already at work within Scripture itself. God's encounter with Moses at the burning bush, and then again at Sinai, is not simply a foundation story but a living reality, giving shape to every other encounter of God with Israel: "The revelation at Sinai never belongs to the past, it never ceases to be. It is as if the Divine Presence, never departing from the mountain, were waiting for each new generation to come to Sinai to encounter Him and to receive the Word."[5] This is the sense in which Jeremiah can identify himself as a new Moses, bringing a new covenant to the people of Judah that "will not be like the covenant that I made with their ancestors when I took them by the hand to bring them out of the land of Egypt." Not that the old Mosaic code is shipped off to the ash heap of ancient history; rather, it serves as the model for a surprising new revelation: "I will put my law within them, and I will write it on their hearts; and I will be their God, and they shall be my people" (Jer 31:33).

Moses is differently repeated in Jeremiah, and again, Christians say, in Jesus. The faith of Israel, and the shape of Israel's Scripture, gives shape and context to the New Testament. The centurion at the cross, Mary at the tomb, Cleopas and his companion, Paul on the road to Damascus: all become new Moseses, surprised in the midst of their ordinary lives to find themselves encountered by YHWH-El Shaddai.

To be a Christian, then, is not first of all to believe in the accuracy of Scripture, or to take the Scriptures as a model for a daily ethic, but rather to find oneself narrated, translated even, into these narratives of encounter through one's encounter with the risen Christ. Christian readers of the Gospels "encounter," as Carlos Mendoza-Álvarez puts it, "the performative force of the text." They live within "a praxis of continuation" of the text.[6] Such readers, further, hear their own voices singing Israel's hymns, speaking those prayers, and working out the ethical reasonings that all issue from these narratives. "Christianity is not an intellectual system, a collection of dogmas, or moralism," writes Joseph

Ratzinger, in what could be a commentary on Berkovitz's words quoted at the top of this chapter. "Christianity is instead an encounter, a love story; it is an event."[7] Thus the life of a Christian begins with an encounter with God, an encounter like enough to that of Moses or Jeremiah or Cleopas that these become containers, or shifting the metaphor, landscapes, in which my own experience has a place. I can describe an event or events of my own life as an encounter with God because these stories from Scripture have invited me to find a place within their world. "These [things] are written so that you may come to believe," is the way Saint John puts it (John 20:31).

What does "believing," or for the moment let's say "trusting that our lives can be shaped into the narratives of encounter with God in Scripture," look like? How could we flesh out and recognize a life of one in love, to borrow Ratzinger's language, with Moses' and Mary's God?

The primary way, for both Israel and the church, is through a change of habit. Aristotle, in this point following his teacher Plato, called habit, *ethos*, the way that all persons achieve either goodness or wickedness. *Ethos* is not the same as instinct, which describes an immediacy of relationship between external signals and embodied response, but rather the way that thinking, reflective humans form themselves and are formed by certain named goals and paths. Stones fall naturally to the earth, and no amount of effort will change this, "even if one tries to train it by throwing it up ten thousand times." Human ways of being in the world can change, though, by the mediation of external signals through thought, will, and new bodily practices. We change, he says, by practicing the thing we want to be able to do: builders become builders by building, harpists harpists by playing the harp.[8] We become believers by practice as well: practicing a life that manifests a trust in God.

Habit as a path to belief is an especially apt description of Judaism, formed as it is around a prayer-centered form of life. "Right living is," for Jews, "a way to right thinking," as Abraham Heschel put it. If the fundamental conviction is to know one's life to be "disclosed in moments of living in the presence of God," the fundamental question on the way to this conviction is not *how can we make ourselves believe that?* but rather "how can we live in a way which is in agreement with" this truth?[9] The ordering of life according to the *mitvah* is an embodied answer to the latter question. The way that Israelites farm their fields acts as a testimony to the plentiful God they serve: "When you reap the harvest of your land, you shall not reap to the very edges of your field, or gather the gleanings of your harvest; you shall leave them for the poor and for the alien: I am the LORD your God" (Lev 23:22). The way they rest on the Sabbath reminds them, their children,

and the nations around them that they were formed by their God for loving covenant, not for making bricks without straw in a life of Sabbath-less
enslavement: "Remember that you were a slave in the land of Egypt, and
the LORD your God brought you out from there with a mighty hand and an
outstretched arm; therefore the LORD your God commanded you to keep
the sabbath day" (Deut 5:15). The separating of foods reminds them of how
God separated them out as a people for the world's salvation. The offering of
sacrifices reminds them that their lives are not their own, and they continue
to exist only by the mercy of the God who chose them long ago.[10] These are
the habits through which God becomes intrinsic to their lives and communities: the habits of encounter, we might say.

Christians too demonstrate their love for God through the shaping of
new habits. Primary among these is the gathering for worship, where we
both "proclaim the Lord's death until he comes" (1 Cor 11:26) and celebrate
the resurrection of the first day of the week. From this primary liturgical
ethos, or *habitus* in the medieval Latin Catholic appropriation of Aristotle,
there issue the other habits or disciplines among those who discover themselves, through the iconography of sacred text, as the people formed by an
encounter with the risen Christ. "By this everyone will know that you are
my disciples, if you have love for one another" says Christ in John's Gospel
(13:35). Thus the care for the vulnerable poor, the orphan, the widow, and
even the intellectually weak, in Paul's idiom (1 Cor 8), has taken shape, in
Christianity's better moments, as the habits that form the bodily response
to the encounter with Christ the teacher. Like love, all the virtues that
accompany these embodied habits are themselves habits as well: joy, peace,
patience, and the rest, should not be understood as invisible qualities or dis-
positions of the mind or soul so much as ways of being bodily present with
God's fragile world. And ways that, like building and harp-playing, require
practice. They are, then, the Christian answer to Heschel's question, "How
can we live in a way which is in agreement with" the encounter with God?
These habits are the fruits by which the tree of Christian faith is known.

The Theological Life

If this is, at its most basic level, the form of the Christian life, what is theology? Etymologically, as is more or less obvious, it is the study of God,
the *logos* of *theos*. Without further context, though, this could be defined
in all sorts of ways. Is it the study of the divine being itself? The idea of
a divine being? The varieties of names and convictions about God? The

many ways the word God has been used (and abused), both within and beyond Christianity?

Let us imagine, first, that theology is a Christian *habitus*. Along with fasting and giving alms and singing Israel's psalms in worship, Christians put into carefully structured language what it is they encounter when they encounter God. Why would we do this?

The first reason, perhaps, is simply that humans enjoy thinking. We do not all enjoy thinking in the same contexts, and certainly many humans have no desire to take advanced courses in philosophy. Most humans though, from plumbers to judges to medical professionals to children making up stories, seem to take a certain joy in linking effects to causes, connecting actions to convictions and symptoms to analyses, or testing the implications of hypotheses.

While those who are deeply committed to the teachings of Christianity may enjoy a playful exploration of questions about their faith, there are also those who, without an existential commitment, find joy in reasoning through these mysteries. Argentine writer Jorge Luis Borges in one of his short stories describes a character, the narrator's uncle Edwin, as a playfully curious man who delights in toying with occult fiction and metaphysical theories of philosophers and geometers: an agnostic, "yet at the same time he was interested in theology the way he was interested in Hinton's fallacious cubes and the well-thought-out nightmares of the young Wells." The narrator recalls the exchanges between Tío Edwin and his Scottish Presbyterian friend: "His theological debates with my uncle had been a long game of chess, which demanded of each player the collaborative spirit of an opponent."[11]

In this sense, it is possible to engage in Christian theology in an agnostic mode, simply by assuming for the sake of exploration and discussion the hypothesis of the encounter with the risen Christ. We might imagine Tío Edwin making such a concession to his believing friend: *"Let's say for the sake of our game of chess that God is real, and that Jesus rose from the dead, and those Emmaus disciples actually met him on the road . . ."*

We can move a bit closer in, though: when those who *do* identify with the encounter in the stories of Scripture, and so profess Christian faith, engage in this intellectual activity, what are they doing? In Marilynne Robinson's novel *Gilead*, two preachers enjoy an exploration similar to that of Tío Edwin and his friend: "Boughton and I used to go through the texts we were going to preach on, word by word," Reverend Ames tells his son. "We had some very pleasant evenings here in my kitchen. Boughton is a staunch Presbyterian—as if there were another kind. So we have had our disagreements, though never grave enough to do any harm."[12] There is much to be said of friendships that grow from the pursuit of theology. For the moment, though, let us put some language to what it is that these friends are doing when they spend a pleasant evening "going through the texts."

Saint Bonaventure wrote that theology explores "how the manifold wisdom of God . . . lies hidden in all knowledge and all nature."[13] Anything hidden requires a search: what the old friends in Robinson's novel are doing, in this sense, is giving their minds permission to seek out the implications of the God they have encountered, the way that God has shaped and continues to shape everything that they know and experience about life, family, work, loss, and hope. And they are doing this by fusing the horizons of their own encounter with the many meetings between God and humans that occur in the pages of the Bible.[14]

The old friends, then, are coming to know God by naming what it is they have experienced. Notice, though, the way that knowledge and love are always related in human patterns of relationship. Pursuing what is hidden is an act of desire, whether we are talking about theology, hide and seek, or a search for a lost coin. I must want, desire, even love in some degree, the thing I pursue (the joy of the game of hide and seek, if not the person for whom I am seeking!). But to pursue it I must also have some knowledge of what it is I am looking for, no matter how fuzzy my concept is, as when we say something like, *I can't tell you what I'm looking for, but I'll know it when I see it*. For "who loves what he does not know?"[15] I cannot, in fact, do one without the other: I know the person or thing that I desire, and I desire the person or thing that I know.

This is of course especially true of a search for God, when my knowing always involves a greater degree of not knowing, and so of trusting. As we contemplate God, we find ourselves, like the Reverends Ames and Boughton, desiring to more deeply and fully describe "how the manifold wisdom of God lies hidden in all knowledge and all nature." Or, like Tío Edwin, how it *could*. We love the knowledge we discover in this contemplative search, insofar as it brings us nearer the one we seek to know and love. We love the contemplative unmastery[16] of the one we seek.

Testimony and Encounter

Contemplation: Christians care for orphans, and Christians also think about God. Sometimes they do these both at once, but most often the demands of orphans override any other considerations. When, in moments of quiet reflection or study, we consider God, this can sometimes lead us to silent awe, sometimes to frustrated sighs or flinging up of hands, and sometimes to language. When the latter happens, we are, theologically speaking, imitating the God who initiates the act of creation with speaking. "God's speaking is . . . an activity of bringing into being."[17] Theology begins in bringing into human language an experience with God.

There are, though, different forms of this language. When the contemplation of God leads us to speak, sometimes it leads to poems, the recitation of psalms, or the writing of hymns. Sometimes it is simply the bursting into language of an experience. When Cleopas and his companion get back to Jerusalem, excited to tell those gathered there about how they came to know the one they had been talking with when he broke the bread, they find that the expression of another experience greets them before they can even speak: "The Lord has risen indeed, and he has appeared to Simon!" (Luke 24:34).

Let us stay, for a moment, with this expressive "bursting forth" way of speaking. This is a theological expression, in that it is putting into words a divine encounter. We might call it a testimonial theology, or theology in a testimonial mode. If an encounter with God were like an encounter with a famous person, or an institution, or a work of literature, this might be enough. We could, without too much difficulty, identify the moment when we first encountered the person or text, and then begin talking and reasoning about the experience. In fact, we sometimes speak of an encounter with God in this way, though in doing so we risk making God into a bigger and stronger version of the sorts of people and things we encounter in our daily lives.[18] But if we take Scripture as our icon of encounter, a different picture emerges.

When the disciples on the way home to Emmaus first meet Jesus, they meet him only as a rather clueless stranger, since "their eyes were kept" by grief or actual tears or perhaps some even more ethereal energy "from recognizing him" (Luke 24:16). In response to his curiosity about their mood, they ask, "Are you the only stranger in Jerusalem who does not know the things that have taken place there in these days?" (Luke 24:18). As he begins to speak, interpreting Scripture to them, their sense of him shifts in ways that they find difficult to describe. He exegetes the Jewish Scriptures for them, explaining how it was "necessary that the Messiah should suffer these things" (Luke 24:26). The text suggests that at this point they are vaguely aware of a shift in mood, a shift that has not yet risen, perhaps, to their full attention. Whereas initially they "stood still, looking sad" (Luke 24:17), and speak of broken hopes, now they are eager to have this ignorant/wise stranger come home with them. It is in their home, as he breaks and blesses the bread, that they know him as the one they saw crucified. And then he is immediately gone from their table.

At what point in the narrative have these disciples encountered the risen Christ? At one level, the moment his path crosses theirs. But at another, it is not until the breaking of the bread, for it is only then that they know him, that they are, we might say, active participants in the encounter. If you ask me if I have ever encountered the teachings of Confucius, and my roommate has a series of notecards with these teachings taped to the wall in our apartment without attribution, I may answer "No." If so, I will be telling the truth, or at least not lying: I am not aware of any such encounter.

In this sense, it is only at the moment of their insight that they meet him. But even this final encounter is problematic, and on two levels. First, the moment of their awareness is the moment of his disappearance. Once they are finally "present" to the encounter, he is absent.[19] Secondly, even if, after the breaking of bread, they now are prepared to identify their guest with the crucified one, they are far from clear about who this man was, the man in which "they had placed their hope." For they must reinterpret every memory of him, from their initial meeting through the crucifixion and all the way to their recent journey alongside him, as memories of a risen friend whom they are only now realizing they have never yet fully "met." In fact, we might say that the Emmaus story is a narrative of nonencounter.

What changes, so that the experience of not quite encountering God in the risen Christ can become an experience of encounter? Here it is clearly the repetition of what happened on the way to Emmaus, as the friends prepare to leave home again. "They said to each other, 'Were not our hearts burning within us while he was talking to us on the road, while he was opening the scriptures to us?'" (Luke 24:32). They recount this story to one another, and then find the experience demands the company of others. Thus, disregarding the lateness of the hour and the dangers of the seven-mile journey,

> That same hour they got up and returned to Jerusalem; and they found the eleven and their companions gathered together. They were saying, "The Lord has risen indeed, and he has appeared to Simon!" Then they told what had happened on the road, and how he had been made known to them in the breaking of the bread. (Luke 24:33-35)

The introduction above referred to the centrality of testimony, or witness, for Christian faith, and here we are prepared to see it as a central category of the knowledge that initiates Christian theology, or as a category of revelation. If, as I said at the outset of this chapter, Christianity is a culture built on an encounter, we must recognize the way that the encounter itself is built on testimony. Why is that?

Testimony is, in fact, a basic element of human knowing. Though we often think of knowledge as cognitive units of information held by individuals, perhaps corroborated or supported by other sources, "testimony becomes a basic processing unit in a context where knowledge is not individually but collectively elaborated."[20] As it turns out, most of our knowing occurs in such contexts. Indeed, epistemology, the discipline that studies human patterns of thinking and gaining knowledge, is increasingly coming to consider ways in which all knowledge emerges through collective exchange. Suppose, for instance, a pilot "knows how" to fly an airplane, and takes this knowledge into a cockpit so that she can perform the task.[21] In fact, the knowledge "in" the pilot exists because of the testimony of teachers, books, and stories of successful and unsuccessful flights. So she herself is not simply a holder of knowledge, but rather a knowing agent who lives at the intersection of countless streams of knowledge. Further, even now the knowledge of how to fly exists outside of the pilot, in the words she waits to hear from the control tower, the signals from the mechanics and other members of the crew. Even the cockpit itself holds knowledge that the pilot must integrate before she "knows how" to fly the plane: what do the instruments say? What is the condition of the panel, the glass shield? What information is "held" by the weather systems that she observes, or whose observations she entrusts to others? Are there notes left from the previous flight? Even the integration of this knowledge requires a certain retelling, a repetition and adaptation of her prior experiences as a pilot. "I did this yesterday in the rain, on the south runway; I can do this today in the fog, on the east runway." She knows how to fly a plane, and not just abstractly: all that experience, wisdom, and gathered testimony has become knowledge of how to fly this plane on this day from this place. The pilot turns her gathered knowledge and even prior experiences into testimonials that make true the statement, "She knows how to fly."

Knowledge of God through encounters with the risen Christ is no different. The Apostle Paul seems largely unsure of what exactly has happened to him on the way to Damascus until he meets Ananias, recounts to him the story, hears it reinterpreted back to him (by the listeners who wonder how this could be the same man "who made havoc in Jerusalem," by Barnabas who eventually presents him to the apostles in Jerusalem), and the scales begin to fall away (Acts 9:17-27). He repeats his own story several times, altering the telling slightly by context and as his purpose in telling it shifts, perhaps even as his self-awareness grows, through the book of Acts and his own letters. The confusion of experience becomes the witness of testimony, and Paul now has something (quite a lot, in fact) to say. His odd and confusing encounter is still unmastered, still "appropriately apophatic,"[22] but has now nonetheless donated itself into human language.

A similar initial confusion reigns over all the resurrection experiences. Indeed, through Israel's history, encounters with God are strange, ambiguous, and repeated through speeches, apocalyptic imagery, or crafted writings that put them into new contexts as "call stories." Does Israel encounter God at Sinai? Or in the repetition of the story of the encounter to their children, the stories of encounter about which Deuteronomy (which is, after all, the "second law," or "Torah retold") says, "Recite them to your children and talk about them when you are at home and when you are away, when you lie down and when you rise. Bind them as a sign on your hand, fix them as an emblem on your forehead, and write them on the doorposts of your house and on your gates" (Deut 6:7-9). Perhaps the most accurate answer is "both." Or perhaps there is only one encounter, and yet it is the Sinai moment only as it is retold and reinscribed on doorposts.

Testimony is the repetition of an experience, and the theological encounter becomes an encounter in the layered retellings and integrations. If social knowing is essential for pilots in cockpits, it is even more so for those who wish to narrate their experiences as encounters with the Creator who dwells beyond sensory perception: the one who is present only, as at Emmaus, in absences. They see a bush, a wheel, a stranger on a dusty road. They hear thunder, or a strange voice, or Scripture interpreted in a new and unsettling way. Told in light of the witness of Scripture—and Scripture understood as the gathered testimony of others who have had unique but analogous encounters—perhaps those stories shift, and the tellers begin to hear themselves speak of an encounter with God. The repetition, strangely, becomes the "initial" encounter.[23]

This is why we often call theology, following Augustine and Anselm and many others up through Karl Barth, "faith seeking understanding." The knowledge of God and God's creation with which theologians work and play as we "go through the texts" is never a direct empirical knowing that issues from discrete cognitive units. We do not even begin with attempts to verify the existence of God. Rather, theology begins with the trust (real or hypothetical) that, as we listen to these gathered witnesses, the absence of direct encounter with God in the risen Christ can slowly emerge as itself an encounter.

Trust, Testimony, and the Sources of Theology

A reliance on testimony for theological knowledge implies a new importance of trust as a theological category.[24] Our pilot knows what she knows not only because she can recall what she has learned, but also because at the moment of takeoff she trusts the knowledge that exists around her as much as the knowledge that exists within her. Cleopas and his companion leave Emmaus to meet with the other disciples back in Jerusalem because they respect not only their own confusing experience, but also the testimony of these others. Perhaps they trust their own experiences as well, the burning of their hearts, along with the experiences told in the Scriptures that the stranger reinterpreted for them on the road. None of these postures of trust work in isolation from the others: they do not discount their experience because of the witness of the Law and Prophets, or the experience of Simon at the tomb based on their own at the table. Knowledge of the risen one "lives" in text, in experience, in Israel's traditions of interpretation, and the trust, along with the knowledge, is distributed in all these places.

A modern conversation about the sources of theology often gets tangled around various "sites" of revelation. Is it Scripture that gives knowledge? Is it the conciliar doctrines and the lives of the saints? Are normal human patterns of reasoning an adequate beginning, so that, for example, we might search for proofs of God's existence and faithfulness the way that we search for proofs in geometry? Or, seeking to allow theological language to spread like a pleasing aroma (2 Cor 2:12-17) to new peoples around the world, should we supplement all these with a separate source called "experience?"

The inclusion of experience at the "beginning" of theology seems to me to be essential, as I said in the introduction to this book, since this can allow us to include from the outset previously excluded voices and witnesses while also uniting the artificially split disciplines of theology and spirituality. Simon and Cleopas and Paul and Reverend Ames all speak of God not as an abstract idea they have come to, but as an event that has occurred to them through a variety of surprising and challenging circumstances.

But calling experience a source of theology seems not quite right, since this can make it sound as if an event, uninterpreted and "raw," has something to say. The passage into "something to say" is the movement from experience to testimony. It is, after all, not the presence of Simon at the tomb or Paul on the Damascus Road that is a "source" of the early church's understanding of the resurrection and all its implications, but rather the way that they themselves, and then their companions, interpret, describe, repeat, and eventually come to trust what happened, sometimes after a significant amount of time has passed. As Paul recounts to King Agrippa, "The Lord answered, 'I am Jesus whom you are persecuting. But get up and stand on your feet; for I have appeared to you for this purpose, to appoint you to serve and testify to the things in which you have seen me, and to those in which I will appear to you'" (Acts 26:15-16). Jesus' reply to Paul goes on, and is much lengthier than the brief address in chapter 9. We could say, returning to the language of repetition above, that it is only while standing trial before the king that Paul encounters Christ fully, or that his experience issues into the fuller testimony that supplies that key source of the early church's theology.

Theology, then, begins not with experience, but rather with testimony. As I have noted, the last half-century of theology has given rise to what we now call contextual theologies, or theological voices that identify them-selves with particular social and historical locations. These voices become new testimonies and thus a key to our gathered understanding of the God of Scripture, since they come from margins that were most often ignored in classroom teachings and published texts. How do poor Latin American Catholics describe their encounters? What about persons with physical or mental disabilities? Failing to attend to such testimony would be like writing an alternative ending to Luke 24, in which the disciples back in Jerusalem are so energized by the story of Simon that they pay no attention to what happened back in the distant and marginal Emmaus.

In a way, testimony is not even *a* source of theology, but *the* source of theology: I speak of God based on the witness of an experience formed by interpretation. My own testimony is important, but must be negotiated through and beside yours, Gregory of Nyssa's, Teresa of Avila's, Rev. Ames', the L'Arche communities',[25] the gathered witness of ecumenical councils, and the witness of Scripture. This latter holds a special place insofar as the gathered discernment of rabbis and councils has named it as the revelation of God filtered through the complex testimonies of humans. Scripture is the testimony through which all these other experiences are interpreted so that they too might become testimony. It is only by constantly gathering the many testimonies that we begin to put together a fully shared, "catholic" understanding of the Lord who meets us.

Kinds of Theological Language

How, though, do we "put together" such an understanding from the various testimonies of encounter? Left alone, would they not be potentially isolating and resistant to communal discernment? If "The Lord has risen and appeared to Simon" or "He was known to us in the breaking of the bread" become discrete units of theological revelation, then theology begins to look some-thing like a collection of various encounters, and no commonly discerned grammar of the language ever emerges. There is no real "language," in this case, just a forum for the presentation of multiple experiences.[26]

This is where reason functions in the discipline of theology. "The Lord has risen and appeared to Simon" is not yet what I am calling constructive or systematic theology; "If the Spirit of the risen Christ is alive in you, he will give life also to your mortal bodies" is. What is the difference? Before answering, let us sort out a few more definitions.

Whenever we speak (again, hypothetically or not) about the God encountered by humans in hymns, laments, or conversations, something theological is happening. A word (*logos*) about God (*theo*) is being spoken. So testimony is already theology of a certain kind, even before it is gathered up and united with other, perhaps even apparently conflicting, witnesses. This is, again, theology in a testimonial mode.

We sometimes say the word God without talking *about* God, but rather talking *to* God. Prayer is a mode of theological language, and again can include a range of expressions. "You were more inward to me than my most inward part and higher than my highest," Augustine says, reflecting on his lifelong search for God.[27] "Oh God, your will is hard/ But you hold every card," says Jesus in the Gethsemane scene from *Jesus Christ Superstar*. Some of the deepest insights into the character of God, from the Psalms to Anselm's *Proslogium* to the laments of weeping parents in a hospital chapel, come through prayer. This second person voice we might call orational theology, or theology in an orational mode.

On occasion, as the Christian contemplates God, she begins to put into words connected, carefully reasoned ideas about who this God is, and to put into words the implications of the encounters she recalls alongside the testimonies of others. She does this in a way that aims at a unity of the various experiences: for instance, "If the Lord is risen and has appeared to Simon, and was known to Cleopas in the breaking of the bread, what does this tell us about who our companion Jesus is?" Sometimes we refer to this as systematic theology, noting the way that a system is a coherent unity of parts. Alternatively, sometimes we refer to this mode as constructive theology, noting the way that the initial blocks of personal and communal testimony and prayer now become the material from which we build these unifying ideas. In this text, when I use the word theology without further specifying the mode, it will be this carefully reasoned, unifying, systematic or constructive theology I am speaking of.

In a passage from Alice Walker's *The Color Purple*, the narrator experiences a challenge to her own theological testimony by the critical reasoning of a friend. The novel consists almost entirely of journal entries by Celie, a

Black woman in the Jim Crow south. Celie addresses each entry to God, and God is clearly her primary source of strength through a lifetime of rape and abuse. "Never mine, never mine," she tells her sister, "long as I can spell G-o-d I got somebody along."[28] Two-thirds of the way through the book, though, she begins addressing letters to her sister instead of to God. She writes about the change in one of them: "I don't write to God no more. I write to you." Shug Avery, who perhaps catches a glimpse of her journal, asks about this change. "What God do for me?" Celie replies. "He give me a lynched daddy, a crazy mama, a lowdown dog of a step pa and a sister I probably won't ever see again. Anyhow . . . the God I been praying and writing to is a man. And act just like all the other mens I know. Trifling, forgitful and lowdown."

Shug then asks Celie to tell her what her God looks like. At first Celie refuses to answer the question, out of a combination of shame and surprise. Finally, though, she concedes. "Okay, I say. He big and old and tall and gray bearded and white. He wear white robes and go barefooted." Does he have blue eyes, Shug wants to know? "Sort of blueish-gray. Cool. Big though. White lashes." Shug laughs, and suggests that Celie has taken the most powerful being she knows, the white mayor of their town, and turned him into a god. "You mad cause he don't listen to your prayers. Humph! Do the mayor listen to anything colored say?"[29]

Celie's theological voice has undergone a shift, from orational to testimonial, in that her "prayed" journal entries become third person testimonials when she acknowledges her lack of encounter with the divine: "What God do for me?"[30] But then Shug's challenge motivates a new shift, one which only begins in this conversation and carries on through to the end of the novel: if your understanding of divine agency mirrors your experience of the power of white people, have you really been praying to or talking about the transcendent God? Shug's intervention is the challenge of constructive theology. Something is off about Celie's testimony, but it will take her some time and several new experiences and conversations to discover just what it is. Eventually, these new challenges will push back on her construct, and invite her to revise her language. The ultimate conclusion of this process, "Dear stars, dear trees, dear sky, dear peoples. Dear Everything. Dear God,"[31] brings us back to prayer, but now a prayer freed for new experiences through the liberative power of constructive theology.

This constructive mode of theology is not the only sort of theology Christians do. It is not even the main way that Christians use language. It is one intellectual *habitus* among many other habits of the Christian life and community. Calling it intellectual does not mean it is disembodied, in contrast, for instance, to the giving of alms, since as Celie's case shows us, the critical reflection is always in conversation with bodily experiences and communities in conversation. Constructive theology is a habit of the mind that is never disconnected from the places and encounters through which our bodies move. Theology, as I define it in this book, is the careful, critical reasoning that we do, surrounded by the pages of Scripture, the "cloud of witnesses" who have believed before or alongside us, and the philosophers, artists, and friends who challenge our imaginations every day, as we attempt to bring to unified expression our contemplations of the God who encounters us in the loving proximity of the risen Christ.

Theology as Leaving Home

The critical reasoning we employ in theology is the same human tool we use in other disciplines, from plumbing to astronomy. It is the discipline of putting one's own experiences and hypotheses up for the challenges not only of other testimony (of friends, of saints and other faithful witnesses, of Scripture), but now also of rigorous human reflection. When we take this step in our language about God we are moving from what two authors have named "embedded theology," defined as "the theology that is deeply in place and at work as we live as Christians in our homes, churches, and the world," to "deliberative theology," or "the understanding of faith that emerges from a process of carefully reflecting upon embedded theological convictions."[32] What emerges, through this process, is *connection*. Emphasizing the image of connective movement in critical thinking, I here call "deliberative" theology "discursive," a term with etymological connection with "running," the rapid movement of taking connected steps. Reason is a practice of making connections between experiences, between ideas, and between ideas and experiences. It is discursive in the same sense that writing which forms connections between letters is called "cursive." Constructive theology is the testimonial language of Christianity written in cursive.

This movement is key to the construction of a communal, engaged, engaging, hospitable language of the Christian faith. Shug's challenge to Celie is for her to make a new connection between the experience of power in the white mayor and the potential for a new kind of power in God: what if they are not univocal, but one is a twisted and depraved version of the other? Similarly, Paul, in Romans 8, asks us to make a connection between the way the Spirit works to bring life to the mortal body of Jesus and the way that the same Spirit will work to give life to us. In this way, he opens up the doctrine—which is to say the "teaching"—about the resurrection to the supplementation of new experiences. Paul gives the Christians at Rome a moment to wonder what encounters they might testify to that bear the marks of new life. What fruits has the Spirit borne in their life, in their community? What would others say they have seen in them? By bringing their experiences to Paul's discursive reasoning, these believers come to see a new implication of this fruit: they can look forward to a resurrection of the dead.

As I noted in the introduction, the risk and rigor of critical thinking can be seen as a "leaving home." Without it, with nothing but conviction formed from her own gathering of testimony, a theologian looks like "one who can politely but firmly argue for the irrefutability of personal opinion."[33] That irrefutability, Kathleen Fisher says, is precisely what keeps one from leaving home and moving, as in the Pauline example, to a new insight that conviction alone could not have provided.

The Emmaus disciples leave home in a double sense, in that their travel back to Jerusalem is also the journey of their own testimony toward the strange testimonies of others, and ultimately the risk of critical reflection that will attempt to make sense of all these encounters. We might even call "leaving Emmaus" the form of constructive theology: it is here that, first, experience becomes testimony; second, that it joins with the gathered testimony of a larger body; and, finally, that all this testimony offers itself for the construction of a critical and communal language.

Theology, then, is testimony of various sorts, with human reasoning to form discursive connections between these accounts, and between these accounts and their implications. (At a yet deeper level, to which we shall return below, we could say that theology is all of this and still nothing but testimony, since reason itself is, from a theological viewpoint, the passage of a word, or the Logic/Logos within God that is then shared with God's creatures, but let us not get ahead of ourselves.)

Luke reports, later in his account, Simon Peter's Pentecost sermon, in which Peter can reason his way from witness of the resurrection (Acts 2:32) to the working of the Spirit (2:33) and the need for repentance (2:38). Without leaving the home of his own inner witness, welcoming the testimony of others as to their encounters and their interpretations of Scripture, and without placing all of this within the challenging and risky framework of critical thinking, he could never have made this move. His sermon would have included only the repeated experience, "The Lord has risen and appeared to me!" He too has "left Emmaus," though, and so he can now lay out a path into the understanding of faith that others can walk with him.

2

SPIRIT

The Inception Problem

Theology is discursive reasoning about manifold testimonies of encounter with the risen Christ. To begin in theology is to leave home: to gather up one's experience, the doctrines embedded in my life through various mediums, and submit them to the risk of communal discernment, where, among other things, we employ critical thinking tools in order to construct a network of language.

Something odd begins to emerge here, as I have already noted, in the order of our discipline. On the one hand, it is called, like other disciplines, by the name of its object of study: *theos*. On the other, this object of study is nowhere obvious, apparent, or without ambiguity. Although the discipline begins with an encounter with God, this encounter is never immediate, but only filters through time, reflection, and the complexifying testimonies of others. We could even say that the various ways we receive and interpret this encounter become in a sense the encounter itself, as Paul encounters the risen Christ in his recountings of the encounter, which become new encounters themselves. We want to say that God coming to meet us is a gift, but the gift only ever arrives in the reception, since "what has not been received has not been given, merely abandoned."[1] And if the reception always takes shape as human language and human action, has a divine gift ever in fact been given?

It would seem that we have in place a language that is assured of only ever being a human language, and yet by means of this language we wish to speak of our meeting with the transcendent God. Do humans, perhaps human communities, "invent" the God that encounters them as a presupposition of their speech?

This is first of all an epistemological problem, in that we are attempting to know something that is beyond our sensory receptors. We are embodied mammals who come to know only as our bodies sense their environment and allow us to arrange concepts from the abstracted data. Saying we "know God" is always going to involve the paradox of knowing one whom we are not naturally equipped to know: the God who is something other than a material being with a temporal history. We wish to speak truthfully of the God we have encountered, and the tools we have are flawed and unreliable. The risk is unavoidable. No matter how much we wish to speak of God, we only ever speak of an idea of God bound within human language.

It is no way out of the bind to attempt to speak of God as the one who is unbound by our limits, who encounters us without mediation through our language, as theologians have on occasion tried to do.[2] In this case, we still have the problem of an act of giving that only manifests itself in the moment or moments of receiving. We could call this the *Inception* fallacy, invoking Christopher Nolan's 2010 film: we might attempt to "come up" a level, beyond human dreaming into reality, but then again we may find that we are only in another level of dreaming. If God is real, and God encounters us, how might we ever begin to trust that our shared testimony of this encounter is not just another layer of human invention?

To ask the question differently: if theology is the language of God, who is the one speaking it?

One way of focusing in on this question is to notice the way the Nicene Creed speaks of the Holy Spirit as the one who "has spoken through the prophets." *Through*: it does not say *instead of*, nor does it say *alongside of*. The preposition "through" invokes a certain hazy frontier of mediation—there are apparently words spoken by the Spirit that take shape only as they pass through other vocal media. The Creed seems to allow for the possibility of a complex relationship between agents of speech, in this case the prophets and the Holy Spirit.

This image gives us a hint, but only a hint, of our path forward in discerning how it is that embodied humans encounter the transcendent God. It has something to do, in classical Christian teaching, with the notion of human beings speaking the words of the Spirit who is beyond human voices. How can we imagine such a language?

Periperformative Speech

The challenge of this ambiguity is that we tend to think of speaking as tied to a single will and agency. However, just as knowledge is more often than not distributed among actors and objects within any given environment, language too is most often multivalent. Let us begin with an example from human conversation, before letting the analogy take us to the question of a divine act of speech.

Speech takes various forms, as philosopher J. L. Austin notes. On occasion it simply describes an act or situation, as when I say, for instance, "Her name is Annabelle." In more specialized circumstances, when contextualized by the appropriate rites and authority, speech can actually perform the thing it describes. A parent, holding her or his baby following the birth, or a priest at the baptismal font, might say, "I name you Annabelle." Now the speech act actually makes true what it describes: her name is Annabelle because the words just spoken named her, performed her naming. The descriptive act seems more or less passive, if we can set aside the activities of interpretation and remembering required to make the description, since I observe the state of affairs in which she has a name and simply put it into words. The second involves an agent whose speech performs that act, though in a certain sense she is also passive, in that the speaker, like the pilot of the previous chapter, inhabits the words and ritual context of others.[3]

These two possibilities, though, are not the only ways that speech can operate. A word more often acts with an uncertain and multilayered agency. There is "perlocutionary speech," where something new is provoked or invited by the speech act. I can speak in a way that neither describes nor performs but aims at provoking a response from someone else. Philosopher Stanley Cavell suggests that these often take the form of a "passionate utterance," noting the way that emotion especially causes a provocation.[4] When a child says, "I am bored," for instance, she is not really conveying information, but attempting to provoke a response from the parent or teacher. When a woman says, "You don't love me," she may be hoping for some charged, emotive reply.[5]

Indeed, to state these examples is to register certain perlocutionary connotations within much descriptive language as well. "Her name is Annabelle": if I say this to you in response to your asking what they named the baby, or your query about my relative or our classmate whose name you have forgotten, it will likely invoke some response on your part: "That's beautiful!" or, "Really?" or, "Oh, right! Please don't tell them I forgot." The perlocution or passion can lie within performative speech as well: the priest at the christening does not utter the name in order to see the tears of friends, grandparents, or godparents, but it is likely that the performance will summon these responses.

Some words, though, are intended, at a primary level, to provoke the passions that bring forth responses. In Mussorgsky's *Boris Godunov*, an opera based on Pushkin's play, and in turn based on the murky history of a battle for the throne of Russia in the sixteenth century, Tsar Boris enters Saint Basil's Cathedral to pray, racked with guilt over his secret murder of the boy who was the rightful heir to the throne. While he prays, a holy fool wanders into Red Square, only to have a group of boys taunt him and steal the coins that he has begged that day. When Boris exits out onto the Square, the fool calls out to him: "Those boys—they took my only coin away. Why don't you have them murdered, the way you murdered long ago our Tsarevich!"[6]

This is, to say the least, a provocation. A dare even, and it calls for some response. But what? Arrest the fool? Kill the fool? Admit Boris' own act of infanticide? Listen to the fool and kill the boys? There are here certain lateral possibilities that "cluster around" the prior speech act, in which case we have something like what Eve Kosofsky Sedwick calls "periperfomative speech."[7] Boris' response could run through a series of emotions and hesitations, depending on the blocking of the scene. In the end, though, his words come as surprise, perhaps even to himself: "Go, pray for your Tsar." The fool's prior words provoked or dared the Tsar to act, and in this sense they are active in the agency of the Tsar's reply. Still the Tsar receives—perhaps "overaccepts," to borrow the language of improvisational theory—the "dare" with an agency that is beyond the control of the fool.[8] He neither kills nor refuses to kill the boys; instead, he asks for prayer. Boris' response demonstrates a "crisis in the ground or space of authority,"[9] since with his periperformative reply he "forestalls and displaces"[10] the fool's initial parlay. While this provocation may be an extreme case, language often works in this way: provoking the kind of "rise" in the hearer that motivates a lateral, or surprisingly appropriate, response. The periperformative layer of speech thus "dramatizes the paths of uncertain agency."[11]

It is this uncertain agency that I wish to underscore as we turn back to our Emmaus disciples. The stranger on the road speaks. He interprets. He even insults the intelligence and/or faith of his new acquaintances. "Oh, how foolish you are, and how slow of heart to believe all that the prophets have declared!" (Luke 24:25). This language, couched in a narrative that concludes with his disappearance after breaking and blessing the bread, is certainly a confrontation; like the fool's "dare," Jesus' words demand some sort of response.

But what response? What is the appropriate reply? Denial? Defense? Acceptance? Cleopas and his companion respond first with a slow growth of interest and desire: "Stay with us" (v. 29). After he is gone this desire turns into an acknowledgment, and then into the radical act of running seven miles at night to tell their friends there that the crucified one "had been made known to them in the breaking of the bread" (v. 35).

There is a certain anarchy at work in their responses,[12] in that it both does and does not quite originate in those confrontational words of Christ. They have a freedom to respond, and, however chaotically they respond, they will in an important sense be receiving, even overaccepting, the passionate utterance of the stranger. Moreover, the anarchy of their answers will be itself a way of acknowledging their emotive response, their burning hearts.

In this way, the encounter with God invites, or demands, a response from those who hear it. Paul before Agrippa, telling his story differently, is still responding to the provocation on the Damascus Road. This is the same dynamic we see from Hagar, Moses, Jeremiah, and Cleopas to the lame man at the temple gate who responds to the command to be healed and walk by shouting and leaping all around the plaza: the response is free, whether it is studied or impulsive, silent and physical, or filled with words. Free, but not autonomous: the anarchic performance of the encounter's reception still dramatizes and responds to the "uncertain agency" within.

Analogy

We can conjecture for the moment that theology is the language, first of all and before we ever began speaking it, of God. It is God's language. Theo-logy is in this primary sense shorthand for *kai ho Logos en pros ton Theon*: "and the Word was with God" (John 1:1). Through John's prologue we hear echoes of every instance in the Old Testament of God speaking: "The word of the LORD came to Solomon" (1 Kgs 6:11), to Jeremiah, to Isaiah. The speaking that is proper to God's being—God's own language—came in a particular way to the prophet.

And what is the response from those to whom this word comes? Solomon builds a house, Jeremiah argues back. Hosea marries a prostitute. Isaiah proclaims that the spirit of the Lord is upon him, and so preaches, destroys, allegorizes, shaves his head, and runs around in his underwear. Even saying "the Lord said to me" is a way of responding, a way of reconstructing the mysterious encounter with a transcendent God in a dialogical format suitable for earthly communication.

The Lord who "speaks" through the prophets speaks in a way that is both like and unlike the speaking of friends and mothers and children. The like/unlike character here is important, because if we imagine God speaking only like others speak, we make God the sort of being we encounter in the world around us—limited, no matter how powerful, by the very medium of interaction. The fool's provocation of Boris—"Murder these boys!"—implies a complex interaction of layered human agency (the fool "dares" the Tsar, the Tsar's response "clusters" near the dare); it also bears, though, in context—because the fool is a *holy* fool—a suggestion that God is an agent in this act of communication. Is God (or, in fact, according to the fool, "the Virgin") saying what the fool says? Not exactly . . . but not exactly not, either. The phrase "God says" should always register to our ears as an analogy, which is to say as a device that affirms connection across difference. God is here speaking both within and beyond the speech of the fool, so that the latter's words, one might say, are human words "saturated" with an excess that is not their own.[13]

"The Word was with God . . . and the Word became flesh and lived among us." Theology is the speaking of God that comes mediated through human speaking, and, when heard by human ears, motivates unscripted and oftentimes lateral responses. Hence the question that hovers over every page of John's Gospel: Have you seen and heard enough to respond in faith? The answer that this provocation, or dare, or passionate utterance calls forth from us is what I have above referred to as testimony. And testimony, gathered across various levels and written in the connective "cursive" of human thought, becomes constructive theology. Theology itself, in this sense, is an analogy: the speaking of God that we can, with care and community, come to repeat in a limited, imperfect, human idiom.[14]

This latter idiom begins in encounter, and the encounter is never separate from, or even temporally prior to, the responses that we give as we come to see what or who it is that we encounter. The point here is that even if there is no secure line where human language ends and divine speech begins, this does not rule out the possibility of God's speech as a kind of passionate utterance that motivates ours, nor of ours as a periperformative response that is anarchically faithful to the provocation of God.

Witnesses to the Spirit

Returning to the line from the Creed, we can call "Pneuma," or Spirit, that character of divine speech that evokes passion within the world. In Paul's letters, the term recapitulates the Old Testament accounts of the provocative energy of the Lord who, for instance, appears to Moses as a friend, and whose language motivates called-for events like the Exodus and uncalled-for acts like the smashing of the tablets and the beating of the rock.[15] To encounter God in the tent of meeting, or as Paul does in the appearance of the risen Christ, is to have a demand placed upon oneself, as Rilke noted in the poem "The Archaic Torso of Apollo": "There is no place in it which does not see you. You must change your life."[16] The god "speaks," and the words encounter us as a deep inspiration (in-spirited-ness) to respond in an adequate way.

When the New Testament speaks of the Spirit as the personal presence of God, it often works with the language of testimony or witness. Jesus in John's Gospel refers to the one who testifies on his behalf (chaps. 14–15), and in Romans the Spirit bears witness within us that we are God's adopted children (Rom 8:16). The Johannine writings expand their account of Spirit's witness as an abiding of comfort and teaching "within you" (for example, 1 John 4:4). Paul works out various accounts of the habits of the Christian, which he takes to be "fruit" revealing a tree nourished by the Spirit (Gal 5:22-23). The acts of love, the life of patience and kindness, in this sense, become themselves testimony to the provocative work of the Spirit.

In fact, when the apostle notes a lack of such fruit, the response is never first to say, "Start being more patient and forgiving." Instead, as I noted in the preface, Paul suggests that perhaps the churches to whom he writes have not yet heard the gospel. They have, of course, "heard" the story of the resurrection, and so Paul is suggesting that they have missed a key moment in their reception of this story. In my idiom: they have not yet been provoked to countercultural Christian virtues by an encounter with the crucified and risen Christ. The Corinthians suggest by their words and actions that they have perhaps encountered only the spirit of politicized baptisms: Christ's Spirit appears not to be in them. If it were, they would surprise themselves and one another with the fruit they bore.

Returning to the problem with which I began, how it is that a human speech can bear an excess that mediates divine speech, we might consider this question of *surprise*. One way to check in on whether we have in fact encountered something that exceeds our own conceptual structures is to note whether we have been surprised by what we heard. After all, in any conversation, a listening that "always knew in advance the movement of my phrases without ever being taken by surprise," would fail to be a listening at all.[17] The seventy disciples whom Jesus sends out come back "with joy," apparently taken aback by the way the power within them domesticates even the demons (Luke 10:17). Similarly, Maximus the Confessor compares the Christian ascetic to one who is transplanting trees in a garden, and happens upon buried treasure. "For when the Lord will have given us who did not expect it the wise contemplations of his own wisdom without labor, it will be granted us suddenly to find a spiritual treasure."[18] The discovery of treasure is a surprise, and comes independently of the work of transplanting the trees.

Still, this image of surprise seems to take us back to the "*Inception* problem," and so to the very attempt I have been challenging, the attempt to split apart human receptivity and God's speaking-agency. What is the content of the treasure that I find buried, such that it can demonstrate to me its divine origin? The treasure contains "wise contemplations," Maximus says, that are given to us. But where do my unwise contemplations end, and the Spirit's wise ones begin? Is this really discovered "without labor"? Can God surprise me without my own interference?

Perhaps not. Paul offers another listing of the habits of the Christian life in Romans 5, and concludes with the explanation that this way of living is possible "because God's love has been poured into our hearts through the Holy Spirit that has been given to us" (5:5). Theologians of the Middle Ages debated this text, since it seems to suggest that human virtue has been replaced by the Spirit of God, who has in turn lodged herself in human hearts. How does virtue increase, if God's Spirit simply *is* our virtue?[19]

The desire for theological clarity in what is admittedly a rather circuitous grammatical construction ("poured . . . through . . . that has been given . . ."), reveals once again that we are dreaming of precision in our description of encounter. We would like a clarification of the boundaries of divine speech and divine act, which, if we could trace it with sufficient heaviness, would remove all suspicion surrounding the integrity of our theological language. Perhaps true hope and true character are not human at all, and when we see them in ourselves or one another we will be assured that God has replaced the human operational mechanism with God's own Spirit.

But we never have such clarity. What we have, instead, are burning hearts motivating us to act. Or, shifting the metaphor, we are left with "fruits": carefully nurtured habits of joy, peace, and kindness, which challenge us to accept the framework of a world made of passionate divine speech. Thomas Aquinas reads Romans 5 and suggests that our words of love and acts of patience are neither ours alone nor God's alone, but our active participation in the Spirit's holy activity, a "likeness" to the Spirit issuing forth in human joy.[20] He thus suggests that the human response nests within the divine action, not in a competition between actors. The grace of God's Spirit always perfects the spirit of the creature, it never overwhelms it or destroys it or replaces it.[21] If we can use Sedgwick to interpret Thomas here, we can hear him saying that the love of God is a provocation to an endless set of responses that cluster around it.

Maximus' image is in fact nicely complex in a way that anticipates Thomas' rendering of Paul's pneumatology: the ascetic cultivates the virtues (the *habitus*), which in his parable is signified by the transplanting of trees. She does so in an attempt to move human desires away from soil that misshapes us with dishonesty and self-deception, and to place them instead in the soil that births habits of honesty and self-knowledge. This, indeed, involves much labor. When she notices that it is actually happening, though—say in the heat of an argument when she bypasses the insult or twisted truth and speaks a charitable word of self-disclosing honesty—she will experience this as a kind of treasure that she did not generate, since it just happened to be in the spot where she was "digging." She did not bury the treasure, and yet she would never have found it if she had not been transplanting the tree.

The Holy Spirit is the character of surprise that greets us when our desire for God's holiness converges with excessive habits of virtuous fruit-bearing. It is the divine agency that "underwrites," in Ben Quash's helpful image, our energies, actions, and decisions.[22]

Maximus' image also points us toward the eschatological horizon of our encounter with God. My labors to cultivate God's honesty and wisdom in my life will never be adequate to the God that encounters me, and in this sense, again drawing on the notion above that the unreceived gift is not yet given, we see that the life that has not yet fully reflected back the image of its creator has not yet fully encountered its creator. Perhaps this too has something to do with the way that the apostle repeats his story differently at each telling, or with the way the evangelists' versions of Jesus' story diverge from one another: our provoked response is God's revelation of Godself to us, as it meets us and transforms our lives toward faithfulness, truthfulness, and forgiveness.

We see something of this, also, when Jesus offers Simon a provocation: "Do you love me?" What would be an adequate response, noting the harrowing account of his recent cowardice and betrayal? The question is designed for a periperformance more than it is for a simple affirmative. Indeed, Simon's life from this moment forward, from the preaching at Pentecost to the gathering of the church to his own suffering and execution, will be one long response to Jesus' question.[23] And only at the eschaton will his answer, side by side with all ours, be complete.

Thus the epistemological test of God's presence with us collides with the testimony of Christian life-testimonies: "If we live like this, has revelation occurred?"[24] The answer can only, finally, come in the form of a gathering of periperformative witnessings.

The Measure of the Spirit

What, though, is the "this" that we must live like? How does the disciple of Christ discern what a life shaped as a faithful response to God's pneumato-logical provocation might look like?

In Haruki Murakami's novel *Killing Commendatore*, the narrator must enter a kind of alternative dimension in order to find a young woman, the daughter of his neighbor, who has disappeared. A guide in this alternate dimension has told him he must find a river, and a ferryman to cross it, but he finds himself constantly questioning his steps as he walks on endlessly. Almost unbelievably, he does in fact come to the river, and, thirsty from his long journey, drinks from it. He then chooses randomly to walk to his left, and before long finds the man with the boat. Having crossed the river, he turns to the boatman, who is beginning his return trip to the opposite shore, and admits, "I don't know which path to take. Or which direction to go."

"Such things are inconsequential here," he hears the man's voice reply. "You have drunk from the river, have you not? Now each of your actions will generate an equivalent response, in accordance with the principle of connectivity. Such is the place you have come to."[25]

Something like this principle of connectivity is at work, I believe, in the faith of the risen Jesus. There may be a "voice" behind us, as Isaiah puts it, whether we turn to the right or the left, showing us the way to walk (Isa 30:21). This will be our own voice, our own testimony, gathered with the testimony of many others and structured by discursive reason. But for all that, it will also be—can also be—the voice of God. Such is the principle of connectivity, or the deep analogical structure of creation, "the generative interconnectedness of all things"[26] in Christian theology.

"By this you know the Spirit of God: every spirit that confesses that Jesus Christ has come in the flesh is from God, and every spirit that does not confess Jesus is not from God" (1 John 4:2-3). Ignacio Ellacuría expands on this verse in saying that a life "filled with the Spirit" has as its norm "the historical life of Jesus, even though it is not exhausted by what that life was."[27] In other words, the new performances will be shaped by the life, liberating teachings, humble death, and excessive resurrection of Jesus, even as they embody this pattern in new contexts. This is perhaps why Paul suggests that in his body he is "completing what is lacking in Christ's afflictions" (Col 1:24), since what is lacking is nothing other than new repetitions of these afflictions and of this life.[28]

The endless "completions" of Christ's life, the inexhaustible provocations to an inspired life that "cluster around" the stranger at Emmaus, are daunting. For this reason there will always be something lacking in language about seeking out God's will or God's plan, as if we might encounter such a thing the way we receive a degree audit from a university registrar. To encounter God as a passionate utterance is to move, to act, and to discover in the midst of things how it is that God is acting too, "underwriting" my actions: a Holy Spirit testifying with my spirit.

Cleopas and his companion leave Emmaus with a world of wild possibilities clustering around their encounter with risen Christ. He will be their measure, moving forward, as they complete with their own bodies what they have encountered in his. Where will it take them? What does one do, having encountered the incarnate God? The next steps are, if not "inconsequential," at least unscripted. The place these disciples have come to is God's creation, a landscape filled with God's passionate utterances, or spirit-filled words. And the guidance, the calling they hear from this encounter, is toward an improvisational life of "love, joy, peace, patience, kindness, goodness, faithfulness, gentleness, and self-control"—that free life against which there is "no law."

3

TRINITY

Divine Integrity

God is Spirit: God is the active agent who summons a desire within creatures, a desire manifesting in an animus, a spirit, a movement toward our Creator as well as toward creation. We move toward one another, toward places we call home and places we have never been, toward new ideas, toward stories we want to hear and we want to hear again. And all the while, God's Spirit testifies with ours (Rom 8:16) that all this desire within us is, at its deepest level, a desire to rest in the presence of our Creator.

Still, it takes a seven-mile walk for these two disciples to "feel their hearts burn" with this divine agency, and another seven before they can put this testimony into words and explain "how he was made known to them in the breaking of the bread." If we return to what they know, or think they know, at the outset, the evidence seems conclusive: their companion, "a prophet mighty in deed and word before God and all the people," whom they had hoped "was the one to redeem Israel," had been handed over by the priests of Judea and crucified by Romans (Luke 24:19-21). He was a prophet "before God," who turns out not to have been the one to redeem Israel. They seem caught between those moments when they were sure God was acting through Jesus, and the reality now in which those hopes have been torn apart.

The challenge, perhaps the greatest of all challenges for a people who believe in the unity of God, is to continue to find hope that God is one and acts in a unified way in spite of apparent evidence to the contrary. "Essence is revealed in action" is the Aristotelian way of putting it,[1] and to experience what seems to be the inconstant care, shifting will, and changing activity of God is to have one's faith in the identity of the divine essence challenged. "Has God forgotten to be gracious? Has he in anger shut up his compassion?

And I say, 'It is my grief that the right hand of the Most High has changed'" (Ps 77:9-10). The psalmist's grief is also the grief of our travelers.

The philosophical principle is painfully simple: to act in contradiction to oneself is to be split, to be two beings. A goose who lays an alligator egg would no longer be simply a goose. A person who makes contradictory promises lacks integrity, which is to say that person is not unified within him or herself, both essentially and actually manifesting as (at least) two distinct "people." Likewise, a God who forgets to be gracious, who breaks promises, who changes God's mind, is not recognizable as the one, eternally faithful, constant God of Israel. Hear O Israel: your God is many.

In this sense, Israel's Shema, which they recite to their children and talk about at home and as they travel, when they lie down and when they rise, is in an affirmation of unity despite everything, a prayer of stubborn resistance to the apparent infidelity of God: "YHWH alone." It is a prayer of faith, which is not, however, to say that it is a prayer of blind affirmation in the face of all observable evidence. Faith, rather, is the resistance itself; it is a return to the evidence so that we can ask it to tell us a new story. Faith is the attempt to gather new testimonies, and, together with them, to "seek understanding" where there was none before.

The poet, after grieving the duplicity of God in Psalm 77, begins an eighty-one verse recollection of these testimonials through the lives of Jacob, Joseph, Moses, Aaron, and David. "I will call to mind the deeds of the LORD; I will remember your wonders of old, I will meditate on all your work, and muse on your mighty deeds . . ." (77:11-12). These gathered witnesses present a different scenario than the one that opens the Psalm, in which my experience of God's absence suggests that God has changed from compassionate to indifferent. Recalling Joseph's redemption, the Exodus from enslavement when "the waters saw" God and "were afraid" (v. 16), the days after when "he split rocks open in the wilderness and gave them drink abundantly as from the deep," (78:15), the psalmist suggests that perhaps the evidence points to something else, hidden at first glance: toward a faithfulness that endures through loss and absence, toward a higher exegesis that he had not yet, at the beginning, known. Like Celie in Alice Walker's novel, he allows this gathered testimony to make new connections and critique his original theological claim. The psalmist returns, we might say, to the Shema, and now wonders how God could still be one, despite what seems evidence of a lack of integrity. In the end, across these eighty-one verses, the psalmist encounters and attempts to address the one, changeless God he has not yet known.

This is the task at Emmaus as well. God was with the prophet, God seemed to be redeeming Israel through the presence of the prophet. The prophet was crucified, and so it has now become their grief that the right hand of the Most High has changed. Now, though, the stranger on the road offers them a higher exegesis that challenges their reading of the entire canon. In this new reading, a Roman crucifixion could be evidence for, rather than evidence against, the unity and integrity of the gracious God of Israel.

In order to put language to this interpretation, however, they would need a new understanding of divine unity. They would need a new way of talking about the one God of Israel.

Opera Ad Extra

The unity of God is an affirmation of faith in the consistency of God's acts. "The unity existing in the action prevents a plural enumeration," is the way that Gregory of Nyssa puts it,[2] developing the psalmist's recitation with the aid of Aristotle. If in fact we can find evidence of a single agent at work in the deeds of God, then we cannot reasonably divide the characters or eras of divine revelation—say, "YHWH alone" of Israel, Jesus the incarnate one, and the Spirit of Pentecost—into three distinct beings. Gregory urges, further, that we not go seeking this unity in an infinite essence, saying, for instance, that God self-manifests in three "modes" while somewhere in the dark infinite of God's being these three are one. This would place divine unity beyond human understanding, or we could say beyond human testimony.[3] Instead, he insists that the one reveals itself, just as much as the three, in the works of God that we can see, hear about, and write hymns about. The sentence "God is one" has no meaning for us unless we can name and discern a unity in the actions that human testimony attributes to the God of Israel.

In this case, the question to ask as we leave Emmaus, which is to say as we come to terms with this new exegesis that calls us away from the comfort and familiarity of our convictional homes, is this: if Jesus is the prophet before God; if he is the one who was to redeem Israel; if he is, further, the one handed over for crucifixion, the one whose sufferings are strangely revealed in all the Law and the Prophets; and who, finally, meets us on the road and comes to be known to us in the burning of our hearts and the breaking of the bread, then who is the God of Israel?

I said above that what the Emmaus travelers experience is something like a passionate utterance that calls forth a periperformative response. It summons, that is, something free and inventive and unscripted, but also consonant with the series of events which provoked it. To invoke, again, the traditional theological language: the risen one is "Word," what God has spoken into creation from the beginning, and the passion that "rests on" this utterance is the Spirit. Cleopas and his companion leap at the stranger's new exegetical word with burning hearts, ready to let this Spirit press them toward a new encounter with God. What they are in fact discovering here is that the revelation of divine unity, coordinated as it is to the lives of those who are "foolish and slow of heart," takes time. That is to say, it takes place in time, just as it does for the psalmist as he calls to mind the deeds of God in ancient days, and as it does for Celie as she slowly gathers her life experiences and the witness of her friends into a vision of God. The testimony of the Spirit that all these things are the work of the one God comes mediated through our spirits, and so is a "slow burn" of our hearts toward a reaffirmation and a re-praying of the Shema.

This temporal manifestation is a primary theme in John's Gospel. The Logos who is in the beginning, beyond human witness, "became flesh and lived among us" (1:14) in a way that invited human witness: it became possible both to recognize and not recognize him as God's Word. In this way the unseen Logos was "made known" (1:18), or spoken, we might say, in a discernible voice that those around him could hear. The Baptizer "testified to him" (1:15), and we eventually learn that all such testimony comes about because the "Spirit of truth" bears witness in people's hearts to the true identity of the incarnate Logos (15:26). The great challenge is in the lag time: it takes time to read "the signs" (2:23) and come to a conclusion about his identity.

Part of the challenge, perhaps, is that we likely begin with the assumption that anything unfolding through time and on earth must be in opposition to the identity of God who is eternal and celestial. The great controversy over where Jesus is from in John is based in the misconception that if he is *from* human parents in the town of Nazareth he cannot be *from* God: "I have come down from heaven" (6:38) in a way that is beyond knowing, and yet at the same time "You know me, and you know where I am from" (7:28). Likewise, it stretches Jesus' audience (the Judeans, Pharisees, disciples, and ultimately "you" who read what John has written [20:30]) to imagine that the God who "finished" the work of creation might also be "still working" in the actions of Jesus (5:17). They and we assume a flattened understanding of time and work, so that what was done by God at the beginning of time remains over and done with through time. In this case "the blind, the lame, the paralyzed" are somehow finished creations of God who must live with the lot they have drawn, and perhaps try to interpret their sufferings as part of the "very good" creation that God rested from.

Jesus, though, says otherwise: The healing of the lame man on the Sabbath is also a continuing of the man's creation on the "sixth day" of creation, because "My father is still working, and I also am working" (5:17). Time itself is a kind of participation in, or slowing down of, the seven days of creation, so that the work of making the man's legs can be both over for God and still happening through the healing command of Jesus. All of this is only an unpacking of what we read in the Gospel's first verses: he is the Word spoken in eternity that is also, and surprisingly noncontrastively, the Word that continues to be spoken in time.[4]

John subtly shows us that to read these signs, and thus testify to the possibility that Jesus is doing the work of the Father, is to find ourselves caught up in the noncontrastive work as well. The dialogue with Nicodemus anticipates the confusion about where he is from, but here Jesus makes it a question of where *we* are from. To see God's kingdom, Jesus tells him, is to be "born from above." Nicodemus' confusion is the same as that of the "people of Jerusalem" later: "Can one enter a second time into the mother's womb and be born?" (3:3-4). To be "born of the Spirit" here is not exactly a different meaning of the phrase "being born," as if Jesus were simply saying that he means "born" as a metaphor for the life our mothers give us. By connecting the image with his own sending (3:16-17), he is saying that only the Spirit can provide the testimony that will allow us to see this rabbi with human parents as also the one born in God's eternity; by extension, this same testimony will also allow us to see ourselves as both children born of mothers and children born of God. The two seeings, in fact, coincide: to see Jesus as the one with divine healing power, for the man at the pool, is also to see himself as one "made well" by God.

This, in turn, allows Jesus to connect his own work—the delay of a temporal Sabbath—with the work of his disciples: now it is just "I" who work, but "we must work the works of him who sent me" (9:4). To receive the Spirit is here to find oneself continuing to do the work of the six days, and to "finish" what is finished and very good within creation. "The Holy Spirit opens up the creative path for history" by letting us hear in the testimony to the Logos "what there is that is not fixed in advance . . . not finished in Jesus' redemptive and saving mission."[5] Again, we might originally see only the contrast, so that if there is work of healing and reconciling to do, it is ours and not the Creator's, since the Creator's is finished. Or perhaps it is ours and not Christ's, since his work too, he tells us from the cross, "is finished" (John 19:30). But the stubborn exegesis of the Spirit, like the psalmist returning to the Shema, "opens up the creative path" for our historical inclusion, and so leads us to seek an understanding of a God who is beyond such contrasts.

The classical Latin formulation of this divine sharing of agency insists that *opera ad extra indivisa sunt*, or works done by God in creation cannot be divided according to Persons of the Trinity.[6] The agency of God in creating world, in coming to dwell in that world, and in pouring itself into our hearts (Rom 5:5) so as to provoke our own periperformative actions, is one. Paul's Epistles are almost frenetic in their experimentation with new ways of identifying divine unity in light of his own encounter with the risen Christ. God is now "the one who raised [Christ] from the dead" (Gal 1:1), Jesus is "the risen Lord," and the Spirit is God's presence through which this rising happens in him and again in us (Rom 8:11).[7] He opens up the Shema without denying its affirmation: "Yahweh our Elohim, YHWH alone" becomes "The Elohim and Father of our YHWH Jesus Christ."[8] Paul further suggests that the Spirit of Jesus the YHWH makes him the "firstfruits" of a resurrection for all of creation.

Paul is here offering a variation on the themes we saw in John. Faith in the resurrection of Christ is faith with a triune shape: God does the raising, our Lord rises, and the Spirit at work in his resurrection is at work in us.

Gregory of Nyssa, once again, helps us see how these three "characters" are all united in a single creative, redemptive, perfecting work: what is true of the resurrection is in fact true of every act of God in creation, since "every operation which extends from God to the Creation . . . has its origin from the Father, and proceeds through the Son, and is perfected in the Holy Spirit."[9] We catch the Emmaus disciples in the dual moment of "proceeding" and "perfecting": returning to the Law and the Prophets, they begin to wonder if perhaps "what has taken place in these days" and what is waiting for them in Jerusalem in the days to come is, after all, occurring as a consistent act of Israel's God. They are thus moving out into a newly discerned reality (in the Spirit) in which the death of a prophet (the Son) is a faithful iteration of the originating work of creation (by the Father).

Personae Ad Intra

Essences are made known in action, but this is not to say that any being is *only* what it does. The goose will never lay an alligator egg, but the goose is not simply a dispenser of goose eggs. To say what she is, one would have to account, at the least, for her biological classifications, her long genealogical tree of adaptations, and her full expression of characteristics. Similarly, the God of Israel will never act in ways that are ultimately contradictory, but these actions indicate a unity that transcends what God does in creation. The epistemological affirmation of God's oneness is supported by and participates in an ontological oneness: God is a unity of action *ad extra* (in relation to the world) because God is a unity of essence *ad intra* (in relation to Godself), not the other way around.

In one of his many rich dialogues with God in the *Confessions*, Augustine asks how it makes sense to suggest, as the Bible suggests, that the eternal God says "let there be" seven times, on different days of creation. Does God really have to wait until Friday morning to call the fish and the birds into existence? Moreover, *can* an eternal being "wait" until Friday? The answer Augustine imagines God giving is this: "Listen, human creature: what my scripture says, I myself say, but whereas scripture says it in terms of time, my Word is untouched by time, because he subsists with me eternally, equal to myself."[10] What God says on the Monday of creation is nothing other than what God says eternally, now simply spoken in a temporal mode. God as Logos is in an eternal saying, and the time-filled narrative of Genesis "says" Logos "in terms of time." The seven days of creation are God's time-taking way of saying "Logos." So, too, is Scripture as a whole, and again, in a very basic sense, so is creation itself, as the church fathers often add.

Similarly, the reception of the Spirit that we have been noting in the Emmaus story is a creaturely way of participating in a kind of energetic lurch within the eternal God. Augustine sometimes refers to this lurch as "gift." "The Spirit, to make myself clear, is everlastingly gift, but donation," or temporally given gift, "only from a point of time." The Holy Spirit can come to Cleopas as the surprising gift of joy that dispels despair because that is who the Spirit is in all eternity: something like a surprising gift of joy within the divine being. The Holy Spirit proceeds in God's essence as a gift, and "so proceeds" in God "as to be giveable" in time.[11] Athanasius, as usual, has a rather barbed way of putting the same point: "Is it not blasphemy for you to say that the Spirit is a creature, in whom the Father through the Word, perfects and renews all things?"[12] If the Spirit of God, which is visible in the perfecting and renewing love and acts of justice and forgiveness in the world, is "finishing" the work of Christ, which is itself "finishing" the work of the Father, the relations that exist on earth must themselves be something like "true analogies" for relations that exist in God's being.

There is, then, Word and Gift, or Son and Spirit, in God, along with an origin of both, one whose relation to the others invites us to identify that one variously as Speaker, Giver, Father, or Sender. Augustine in particular helps us see not only what it is that Christians affirm about God, but why: why go to the trouble of returning to the affirmation of the one God and saying that God is not only one but also, noncontrastively, three? The reason for this renewed exegesis is that we want to say that God is not only eternally faithful to or consistent with the unity we perceive in God's actions in time, but that God is also eternally faithful to or consistent with the three characters or personalities that we experience in these actions.[13] God speaks in the world because God is a speaker and word; this word stirs up responses because God is a Gift of joy. This is most especially visible in the experience of meeting the risen Christ. When Paul, again, says, "the Spirit of the one who raised Christ from the dead is alive in" us, this suggests one of two alternatives: *either* God is a unity that is altogether unlike the joyful lurch toward the Father of the risen Son, *or* this temporal event of Easter is patterned on—faithful to, consistent with—an irreducible relationality in God. Thomas Aquinas might ask us to consider which of these two options we consider to be more "fitting." Which gives a fuller account of the testimonies of faith?[14]

In this sense we have no grounds for calling God an eternal or "immanent" Trinity except for what we experience through the gathered testimony to a God who dwells with us and is poured into our hearts as a temporal or "economic" Trinity. And this is how Christians name the experience of meeting the risen Christ. As Russian theologian Sergius Bulgakov puts it, using somewhat technical language: "The supra-eternal interrelation in the immanent Trinity becomes accessible for us in the economic Trinity, that is, it becomes accessible christologically."[15] In simpler terms: we allow ourselves to speak of a God who is eternally and essentially three in one because we have encountered in and through Jesus Christ a God who seems to be three without ceasing to be one. Either God is not what God appears, in Christ, to be, or God is an eternal Trinity.

One way to imagine what I am describing here is to consider the first part of the parable of the prodigal as a pattern, or an analogy that holds across a certain division, for the interrelations of the Godhead.

> Then Jesus said, "There was a man who had two sons. The younger of them said to his father, 'Father, give me the share of the property that will belong to me.' So he divided his property between them. A few days later the younger son gathered all he had and traveled to a distant country, and there he squandered his property in dissolute living. When he had spent everything, a severe famine took place throughout

that country, and he began to be in need. So he went and hired himself out to one of the citizens of that country, who sent him to his fields to feed the pigs. He would gladly have filled himself with the pods that the pigs were eating; and no one gave him anything. But when he came to himself he said, 'How many of my father's hired hands have bread enough and to spare, but here I am dying of hunger! I will get up and go to my father, and I will say to him, "Father, I have sinned against heaven and before you; I am no longer worthy to be called your son; treat me like one of your hired hands."' So he set off and went to his father. But while he was still far off, his father saw him and was filled with compassion; he ran and put his arms around him and kissed him. Then the son said to him, 'Father, I have sinned against heaven and before you; I am no longer worthy to be called your son.' But the father said to his slaves, 'Quickly, bring out a robe—the best one—and put it on him; put a ring on his finger and sandals on his feet. And get the fatted calf and kill it, and let us eat and celebrate; for this son of mine was dead and is alive again; he was lost and is found!' And they began to celebrate. (Luke 15:11-24)

The narrative has a similar shape to the Emmaus story: there is estrangement, a recognition that brings joy. There is also the added question of dual recognition: not only will the estranged son know himself as son, but the father will also know the son as son, and therefore himself as father. I am suggesting that we read this not only as a story of our distance from and return to God, but as an analog for a distance and return within God.

At first glance, the relationship of the parable is between two characters alone. In these two moments of recognition that culminate in an act of celebration, however, there is a hint of what Augustine calls a third "whatever it is" in the relationship.[16] The first moment of recognition begins when the son "came to himself" and recalls his father's provision for him. "I will arise and go to my father." There is a new presence with him here that was not with him while he was squandering his inheritance or taking a job on the pig farm. It is in a sense the presence of his father, despite the fact that his father is far away and absent from him. It is also in a sense "himself," as the English idiom puts it, since he is only now recalling who he is. But it is himself manifested in a new way. The parable opens with the son affirming his difference from the father; but there is a different difference at work now, a noncompetitive difference, suggesting to the son that difference does not negate relationship. He comes to himself by seeing, as it were, *I am not my father, but I am not not my father: I am my father's son.*

The second moment of manifestation lies in one sense with the father, but in a deeper sense with both. "But while he was still far off, his father saw him and was filled with compassion; he ran and put his arms around him and kissed him" (Luke 15:20). The father could have followed the son into the far country, presumably, or even tracked him down once there and brought him home. What he is waiting for, though, is the son's return, which itself will be an event manifesting to the father than the son has "come to himself" and received the gift of the father's irrevocable fatherhood. The manifestation of that relationship is itself manifested to the father. *My son knows who he is,* we can imagine him saying the moment he sees him returning from afar. Further, because the son had squandered his inheritance, he assumes he will no longer be treated as a son, hoping only to live in the servant's quarters. So, in a deeper sense, the encounter on the road is not only a manifestation to the father of the son's return, it is a manifestation to both father and son that their difference is what allows them to embrace: to be together in a loving relationship. Here again, there is a new difference: the father waited to see not just his son, which could have happened whenever he wished, but his son plus the gift of his son's returning. He waited to see his son plus the gift of his own fatherly "claim" on the son. Likewise the son waited, though dared not hope, to see not only his father, but his father plus the surprising gift of his father's recognition of him as son.

The two moments of recognition become a single event when they embrace in the road, and especially when the father throws a feast to celebrate the son's return. It is as if their hearts are "overflowing with a goodly theme," in the language of Psalm 45, and the celebration is the expression of this excess. The "third something" in the parable then is the witness to the love, or perhaps the love witnessing to itself.[17] The father loves this son, the son loves the father, and they both love their love (to use an Augustinian idiom) for one another so much that they not only feel its claim on them but also want to celebrate it.

In order to read this parable as an analogy for the Trinity *ad intra* (and a parable is, after all, an analogy of a certain kind), we must imagine the pattern of relationships, abstracted from roads, pigsties, far countries, famines, and the passage of days and weeks and months. We read it, to borrow a phrase from David Bentley Hart, across an "analogical interval."[18] We can encounter God in countless ways in time because God is in God's very essence an eternal encounter. The Trinity is like the father's embrace of the son in the middle of the road, because this could not have happened without the third something, the presence in the parable of the relationship itself, the celebrated fatherhood of the father *for* the son, the sonship of the son *for* the father. This third presence is, in the parable, not a person, but still is a presence no less dramatic than the first. The "first difference" in the family, you might say, is the son's going off into the far country, and marks the duality of relationship; the "second difference" begins in the arising and going to the father, and shows that true relation requires a third, the "different difference" that does not preclude a celebration of loving union.[19]

Indeed, it may not be too much to say that any relationship, insofar as it involves real difference, must have not only an affirmation of difference but also the surprise of a different difference, or a third "something" that mediates between the two. This is the insight that leads Augustine to say that "you do see a trinity if you see charity."[20] If I love my sister, I not only love her, but I love loving her, I love the love that holds us together so much that I want to celebrate it. Further, I celebrate it not just by naming or exhibiting things about myself or about her, but by recalling with her experiences and jokes and memories that we have in common.

If, finally, we abstract the relations even from the human characters in the parable, we get something like the essential rhythm to the doctrine of the Trinity: a giving of love, a receiving of love, and the witness to that love without which neither the giving nor the receiving would be what they are.[21] Moving beyond anthropomorphic characters into patterns takes us beyond gendered names as well, which is why Ephrem of Syria assumed that there was something obviously orthodox about giving the Father a womb and giving the Son breasts.[22] If we can go on speaking of the pattern of relationality in the transcendent God within human language, that language will have to bear the marks of its own limits.

The hypostases, or Persons, are distinct points of interrelationship; yet because they are related only across this essential sharing, the two differences make them one essence: the First Person gives the fullness of the divine essence to the Second, and the Third is the essence turned celebratory as a manifesting, a divine testimony, of their union. In this way, the doctrine of the Trinity redefines unity, beyond being a description of uniqueness, as a term that describes an intensity of relationship. The three hypostases are "more one" together than anything in the world is on its own. They are one in act, both in the world and among themselves, because love is the activity of unity across relationality.

Participants in Divine Anarchy

Across this analogical interval, then, we could say something initially surprising: God is something like a passionate utterance and a periperformative response. The word "God," for Christians, means the eternal being who is like a father saying "you are my Beloved Son," and like a son who receives that love as though a dove were descending on his head, and who responds by making his entire life a loving, unscripted, surprising, celebratory response of love: "I will get up and go to my father."

I said above that there is a hint of anarchy in our "inspirited" responses to encountering the risen Christ, in that there is no predicting or in some cases even governing of what might constitute an appropriate response. The leper in Mark 1 testifies to his encounter with Jesus by disobeying his command, and this does not seem to be anything but an authentic way of responding. The great Methodist preacher Jarena Lee, when challenged about the authenticity of her calling, wrote,

> If then, to preach the gospel, by the gift of heaven, comes by inspiration solely, is God straitened; must he take the man exclusively? May he not, did he not, and can he not inspire a female to preach the simple story of the birth, life, death, and resurrection of our Lord, and accompany it too, with power to the sinner's heart. As for me, I am fully persuaded that the Lord called me to labour according to what I have received, in his vineyard. If he has not, how could he consistently bear testimony in favour of my poor labours, in awakening and converting sinners?[23]

The witness of the Spirit places Lee at odds with her ecclesiastical leadership, calling for a return to the texts, as in Psalm 77 and Luke 24, to discern what this new witness implies for the common theological language. What does it mean for what we know about God, what we thought we knew about faithfulness to God, if God's Spirit can give rise to testimonies not only in her own voice, but in the voices of those who hear her preach and feel that lurch within them? The encounter with God is not just the hearing of a Word, that is; it is also the responding of a Spirit with our spirits, a way of making new testimony from what we have received. A response that at times even takes shape as a faithful disobedience.

Although I have called this response "anarchic," this is perhaps not quite the right term, in that our encounter has as its *arche* the encounter, at an analogical remove, within God. As Kathryn Tanner puts it, when the Son meets us and the Spirit moves within and among us, "the persons of the

Trinity just keep doing what they are always doing, but now with humanity along for the ride."[24] If there is an anarchy, it is not primarily in us but in God.[25] By finding ourselves addressed by the loving God, and moved to love God in return, we find ourselves involved in a conversation that precedes us, a conversation echoing with the passionate utterance that is the eternal God. In this encounter, as we attend to the way our hearts lurch Godward at the presence of the risen Christ, we find ourselves along for the ride, becoming "participants of the divine nature" (2 Pet 1:4).

4

CREATION

Life out of Nothing

God is the parable of the prodigal son transposed into eternity. A Father gives his substance (*ousia*) to a Son; the Son "comes to himself" when the Spirit manifests as the recollection of unity with his Father; the Spirit manifests again as the Father's own celebratory joy at his Son's return. The Father looks on the Son as one who, as we might put it on our side of the analogical interval, "was dead and is alive again." So also our encounter with the one who was dead and is alive again, with all the implied complexities and reliances on testimony and critique that allow us to name such an encounter, begins a process of re-imaging the character of God. The encounter with Christ is a revelation of the Trinity.

Along with revealing God, the encounter also reveals the deep secret at the heart of creation.

It was not long after those first encounters that the early Christians began observing this connection. Saint Paul identifies God as the one "who gives life to the dead and calls into existence the things that do not exist" (Rom 4:17). To the Corinthians he goes even further, extrapolating from the Easter gospel the character of a God who "chose the foolish things of the cosmos in order that he might shame the wise," and "the weak things of the cosmos in order that he might shame the mighty." God is like that, he suggests: a God who makes a humiliating death the beginning of a calling to abundant life is a God who needs, literally, *nothing* in order to give the gift of life. This is what God is doing in the creation of all things: "And God chose the lowborn things of the cosmos and the things treated as nothing, the things that have no being, in order that they might nullify the things that do have being" (1 Cor 1:27-28).[1]

In verses such as these the apostle makes the Easter encounter into an analogy, or perhaps an icon, of the act of God from the beginning of all creation.[2] In light of his experience of Christ, joined together with the witness of others and mediated through the interpretation of Israel's Scriptures and teachings, Paul is prepared to call the creation of the cosmos a calling of life out of a grave-like nothingness. God has never "done" anything besides what God does at the tomb of Jesus.

Little Words

According to a central teaching of the medieval church, grace perfects nature, rather than destroying it or replacing it with something else.[3] Said differently, the surprising acts of God open up new dimensions in the world that God makes. They do not override the agencies of creatures with the divine will any more than, in the parable, the father's desire controls the son's return. This is a development of Paul's insight about the connection of the cross and resurrection to the creation of the world. It may seem that the reanimated appearance of the one Cleopas and his friends had hoped "was the one to redeem Israel" (Luke 24:21) is a complete and utter break with the history of the world, the moment in which nature is suspended and the unprecedented miracle of the ages occurs. But Paul suggests that this is not the case. In raising Jesus from the dead, God is not breaking in and overriding nature, but manifesting the truth of creation that has been from the beginning. What is that truth?

The Greek Fathers take up this question by arguing that creation has the character of "wordiness." Each thing called into being is a miniature logos, a little word made in the image of the Logos itself, the Word.[4] This analogical relationship in turn links God's work in creating (through the Logos) to God's work in redeeming (through the same Logos). "The first fact that you must grasp," Athanasius tells his readers, "is this: *the renewal of creation has been wrought by the Self-same Word Who made it in the beginning*. There is thus no inconsistency between creation and salvation for the One Father has employed the same agent for both works, effecting the salvation of the world through the same Word Who made it in the beginning."[5] Once we have learned to follow St. John in calling the second person of the Trinity the Logos through whom all things came into being, we see that creation and salvation are sewn from the same cloth, or spoken in the same voice. The same dynamic that we see at work in the meeting of the Logos with creatures, the "crying out" even of stones with the passion invoked by his presence, is at work in creation from the beginning itself. God is in the world in the form of the same deep and ontologically basic passionate utterance that manifests itself in the Emmaus encounter. The procession of Word and Spirit within God is the deep and often hidden truth of all things.

Every object or thing, animate or inanimate, in the world is saying something. "Looking from the side of the Creator," says Jewish theologian Peter Ochs, "one might regard any thing in the world as God's reified speaking: a living dog is God's having spoken 'dog.'" If this is true, though, we also get a glimpse of the fathomless mystery of any created thing that we encounter: "Looking from the side of the creature, one might regard any thing in the world as a hidden face of its Creator: this dog is not just this dog, but God's voice still speaking 'dog.'"[6] Philosopher William Desmond makes a similar point: a thing presents itself to us as an "inward otherness,"[7] a particular manifestation of the infinite power of being. Where we see a dog or a marriage or an orchid or even a broken bit of a rocky overhang, he suggests we see an emergent divine work:

> Suppose we think of a thing as a poiesis, a work of creation. But a creation is double—both a whole unto itself, and also an openness of being that resists complete containment within the boundaries of any framed whole. Thus seen, a thing is a gracefully formed flourish of the creative power of being.[8]

What emerges in each of the world's creatures, once we see them as little speakings of God, is a testimony. The dog and the broken bit of rock have something to say. They point to something.[9] They make present the character of one who is absent, or perhaps not bodily present, as when one testifies on behalf of another.

Here again, we must look to the eternal for clues to the origin and shape of the temporal. John Scotus Eriugena calls us to begin contemplating creation by imagining the way in which the Father "brings forth" the Son:

> Before this visible world proceeded through generation into the genera and species and all the sensible individuals, God the Father, before the secular ages, brought forth His Word, in Whom and through Whom He created in their full perfection the primordial causes of all natures, which, under the administration of Divine Providence, in a wonderful harmony, in their natural course bring to perfection . . . this visible world from the start at which it begins to be to the finish at which it ceases to be.[10]

In this powerful image the endless pathways of creation, with the unpredictability of cause and effect, the surprising diversification of genera and species and individual, are expressions of the Word, the eternally begotten Son. The Logos is, in this popular image from the traditions of creation theology, the eternal Idea of the First Person, and all the ideas of creation live within this Idea. St. Paul says something similar in Colossians:

> He is the image of the invisible God, the firstborn of all creation; for in him all things in heaven and on earth were created, things visible and invisible, whether thrones or dominions or rulers or powers—all things have been created through him and for him. He himself is before all things, and in him all things hold together. (1:15-17)

The Son then is the Idea in whom all the ideas of creation eternally dwell, and through whom they (we) come to expression in the course of time.

It may seem as if this construction makes the Son passive in the divine act of creating, as if he is the blueprint the Father reads just prior to beginning construction. The problem with this image, as Augustine reminds us,[11] is that it makes one person the sole agent, with intellect and will, and subordinates the other as only passively involved.

Here, following Eriugena, we can say that the Father looks to the Son and sees the possibility of the eternal Logos manifested in time as little logoi. In the one Logos the Father sees dragonflies hovering around sunflowers, Leviathan dancing with the sea creatures, the spinning of galaxies, and *Hamlet*. And while the Father is the origin of the Son as the one who eternally calls the Son into being, in this gaze the Son calls back to the Father, summons forth a response from him. We might even say that the Son compels the Father to respond, in the same way that the beauty of Apollo's Torso or a harrowingly beautiful performance of *Hamlet* does to us. This is not the ordering of an autocrat or the necessity of fate, but the demand of beauty. We are in the grip of the beautiful, and here the Father is in the grip of the Son, his only begotten Idea. The Father creates while gazing on the Son who actively presents his infinite beauty to the Father: "It is as if the Creator had spoken: 'Let it be made,' and because God, who is eternity itself, could not be made, that was made which could be made, which would be as much like God as possible."[12]

Little Spirits

This image of the surprising "revelation" of beauty that even the Father receives, returns us to our pneumatological theme.[13] God's speech is a meeting of utterance and passion, of Word and the resting of the Spirit on the

Word. Christ's baptism is in this way a window, an audible and animated vision of the immanent Trinity, with John as human witness. "And just as he was coming up out of the water, he saw the heavens torn apart and the Spirit descending like a dove on him. And a voice came from heaven, 'You are my Son, the Beloved; with you I am well pleased'" (Mark 1:10-11).

The Spirit comes to rest on the Son, and it is in this coming to rest that the Father knows him as Son, and also that the Son knows the Father as Father. This is not to say that the Father did not know who Jesus was until after the baptism, but rather that the baptism is a material performance of an eternal event. Without the Spirit the Father does not recognize the Son, but the Father is never without the Spirit. Said differently, the Spirit animates the Unbegotten God with love for God's only begotten Idea, manifesting its richness, beauty, and infinite depths.

And so this is also the case with the interactions of logoi in creation. Divine speech is also an address, and not just an address, but a language that moves and animates the world. The dog's utterance, too, is passionate. "Deep calls to deep," in the imagery of the psalm, in the rushing of a waterfall toward the river bed (Ps 42), as if the presence of this language demands something from the creatures who hear it—creatures who are themselves poetic emergences of God's language. To see a thing as God's poiesis, or "gracefully formed flourish of creative power," to see the leaf or the broken bit of rock as the emergent call of the Creator, is to find a demand made upon oneself: it is like finding oneself dared or provoked by the world around us. Again, we are standing before the torso of Apollo with the poet, and realizing that the beauty will not leave us as we were.

Thus the little logoi are animated by spirits: little pneumata perhaps. Recalling the discussion of Romans 5:5 from the second chapter, we can call the passion of the presence of the orchid or the animal in front of me, as it makes its way within me and calls forth a surprising and perhaps periperformative utterance from me, the participatory manifestation of the same Spirit that calls for passion between Father and Son. The Spirit is the presence of God as God "fills all things with his power," as Saint Basil puts it, and so the presence of these motivations indicates something of the excessive emergence that is each "uttered" thing: "The Spirit is given to each one who receives him as if He were the possession of that person alone . . . Everything that partakes of His grace is filled with joy according to its capacity—the capacity of its nature, not of his power." This latter indication is Basil's way of reminding us that the orchid is still a formed and limited thing: the "joy" of its new growth and flowering is the passion of its poetry, an analog for the

God in whom there is no form and no limit of joy. Its bursting forth is its periperformance of that divine joy, what I have above called the anarchy of its sharing in the God with no origin. There is no end to the ways the perfect orchid can respond to the Spirit of the infinite God moving within it.[14]

Creation is the "bodying forth," to borrow a Shakespearian phrase, of this eternal event, so that the same Spirit that descends eternally on the Idea descends on the ideas in time, even as the creation of time. When God hears Leviathan breach, or sees the beginnings of a friendship, or smells the coming spring or the rich decay of autumn, God sees the Spirit coming to rest on each, and says, "this is my beloved Idea." Created things, in turn, hear themselves called into being like Christ hears himself identified as "Beloved" by his Father, both in the baptismal waters and in all eternity. Creation, we might say, stands in the place of the Son, and so finds itself in the Son's relation to the Father, receiving its entire *ousia* from his originating invitation, and experiencing the doubly manifesting presence of the Spirit who both shows God who we are and reveals to us whose we are.[15]

The Spirit is God's eternal gift, since God is an eternal sharing. When this God creates, the Spirit continues in character, now with "humanity along for the ride." The Spirit is a radical act of sharing the being of God with the non-being that is not God. God calls the nothingness as though it were, and it is. The very "fact" of this sharing of being is evidence of the work of the Spirit: the Spirit is at work where the Father sees and proclaims the belovedness of his Idea, and so also where, in the actuality of the Eternal Idea, the Father sees the potency of the many ideas. The doctrine of creation out of nothing holds only that there is no primordial stuff, no raw material from which creation issues: there is only this act of sharing his eternal "belovedness," an act so radical that it creates the beloved.[16]

And all of this revelation works itself out of the encounter with the risen Christ. Paul's claim in Romans that "creation groans together and labors together in birth pangs," waiting for its liberation through "the revelation of the sons of God," is his observation that the resurrection changes everything.[17] The decay and anxiety that fills the cosmos is waiting to be re-logified, re-pneumatized. Humanity, as Paul says here, has a key role to play in this redemption, and I will return to this theme in a later chapter.

Analogical Reasoning

The icon-space that the encounter with the risen Christ opens up for us, then, gives us a new context for asking what the world is, and what it means to see the world in relationship with God. This latter question, though, requires a degree of nuance.

Much theological skepticism hinges on that puzzling question: how could God and the world be related to one another? Faith in Scripture and in the prayers of the people seem to demand this relationship, and yet we immediately feel the inadequacy of its framing. "The world" is our name for everything, visible and invisible, near and distant, present and not; God is apparently something else. Yet how can we imagine "something else" except as another "kind of thing" that exists? It is difficult enough to conceive relationships between beings of the world who do not belong to the same planes of existence. Think here of the etymology of the word "alien," which simply indicates that a person or thing in question is not among the regulative set of persons or things: this one is "other." What we tend to do is imagine a greater kind, and make both patterns instances of this kind, the one belonging to the world we know, the other belonging to some other world. We do not know what alien life might look like, but we imagine a planet like ours, with patterns like ours, and then we begin adding or subtracting. There is, though, no "kind" expansive enough to contain both God and creation. This relationship is less like human to Time Lord (say) than it is like humans to adverbs. There is no category that would allow one to speak to, pray to, or even appear within the same universe as, this other.

Perhaps, though, we are beginning in the wrong place. To ask about how this thing relates to that thing, thing 1 to thing 2, is to force our logic to do the very thing it cannot do: that is, create a category of "things," and make God a version of ourselves, just bigger and better. We already have reason, though, to think of God not as a thing, but as a dynamic interaction of Persons. Theologically, then, the primary relationship is not that of God to creation at all, but of God to God.

In order to begin to imagine creation, then, we must continue to think not simply comparatively, but analogically. The created world, the heavens and the earth, are not first of all a partner in relationship with God, but a mirror of God's own Trinitarian relationship to Godself.[18] Creation lives in relation to itself as God lives in relation to God, if creation is a reflection of God.[19]

The language of analogy itself has limits. This way of stating things might be taken to suggest that the only connection of God to creation is one of ratio or proportion, which could go on being true even if God and creation were entirely oblivious to one another's existence (wolf is to pack as student is to class). This would not fit well with the previous chapter, in which I argued that the Holy Spirit is the gift that circulates in the eternal Trinity *and also* the gift that is given to creatures in time. Or that the Second Person is the Word uttered in eternity *and also* the Word that speaks into existence the things of creation of things. Or that the First Person is the one who gives being to the Godhead *and also* the one who sends the Word and Spirit into creation. These formulations require that the divine Persons them-selves remain the connective tissue of God to creation. In this respect, using technical vocabulary, we could say that the processions of the Triune God generously give themselves as missions: the movement of Son and Spirit from and to the Father, the movement that renders God eternally relational, becomes the gracious opening for the creation of a world. This donation, in turn, invites a further dimension of analogy, which is the mutual generosity exchanged between creatures. The "ratio," or proportional aspect of analogy, exists within this sharing of Persons.[20]

This further dimension of analogy, then, nests in the missions of the Son and Spirit within creation, and becomes for us a place to see the image of the relational God: if in fact it is the case that created things are God's pas-sionate utterance, modeled on Trinitarian speech, then the place to look for God's presence in the world is in the pattern itself, rather than in the direct intervention of the uncreated God. When the psalmist speaks of the rhythms of the created order, Christians read him as saying that the same relating-through-love that holds God together holds the world together as well, across the analogical interval.

> The heavens declare the glory of God,
>   and the firmament shows his handiwork.
> One day tells its tale to another, *
>   and one night imparts knowledge to another.
> Although they have no words or language, *
>   and their voices are not heard,
> Their sound has gone out into all lands,
>   and their message to the ends of the world.
>   (Ps 19:1-4, from *Book of Common Prayer*, www.bcponline.org)

Here the way that the heavens declare God's glory is by becoming a language in which one creature calls to another. One day calls to the next, inviting it to dawn; one night invites the next to display what it "knows" about the heav-enly depths and bodies. The dawning of the second day and the falling of the second night are not simply regulative advances of time, but responses. The heavens, part of the original pair of God's creatures ("In the beginning God created the heavens and the earth"), repeats for a new order the language which first gave it being, when God called its sun and moon and stars into being and they, in answer, "were." The sun here especially shows this language to be one of celebratory love, as the psalmist continues:

> In the deep has he set a pavilion for the sun;
>> it comes forth like a bridegroom out of his chamber;
>> it rejoices like a champion to run its course. (v. 5, *Book of Common Prayer*)

The touching of day and night is like the touching of a bride and groom, and the brilliance of sunlight is the racing forth of the groom, his invitation to the heavens and the earth to witness and celebrate the intimacy of dawn and dusk. The loss that we feel at the death of a friend also holds this pattern: how can I be who I am without you? This yearning is, I am suggesting, what the Trinitarian "passionate utterance" looks like on our side of the analogy.

For the psalm, creation is not simply filled with, but here made of this language. Day *is* a calling for the next day, in the first image, and a summoning of its beloved night in the second. In the Wisdom writings of the Old Testament, this language spreads not just through the heavens, but from one end of the earth to the other.[21] The churning of milk calls forth butter (Prov 30:33), the working of the ant is an invitation to other creatures to "be wise" (Prov 6:6). Well-rooted trees (Ps 1) and cliff-dwelling badgers (Prov 30:26) are parables of the interdependence and mutuality of friendship. The presence of a poor child is a calling for blessing (Ps 10:18), and a neighbor an invitation to kindness (Sir 9:14). These "language bids" are not metaphors or descriptions or "ways of taking" these creatures, but names of their essences. "There is no speech nor language" in creation beyond these voices of creation, issuing invitations within and among the beings within it.

This vision of creation as analogical expressions of wisdom-in-relation is also the force behind the many injunctions against foolish conversations. To use language for one's own selfish end is to manipulate the fabric of creation itself, perhaps analogically repeating aspects of creation that, beautiful in themselves, are not fitting models for our imitation. So "the conversation of the godly is always wise, but the fool changes like the moon" (Sir 27:11-12).

There is a courtesy at the very heart of creation, one which we will see in a following chapter is far too easy to violate. The existence of one being (a neighbor, a sunflower, the winter) is not first of all a threat to another, but a word of hospitality, a making way for the other. Just as the first and most basic word uttered throughout the heaven and earth is "Let there be," so each being within creation exists as an invitation to others to exist: creation is a chorus of letting be.

Providence, Angels, and Miracles

The pattern of an impassioned exchange across difference, then, allows us to say something about how God relates to God, and through an analogical imagination allows us also to reframe the interrelations of creation. What help does this give us in naming the ways in which God relates to that world God loves into being?

The lines from John Scotus Eriugena, above, characterize the harmony of divine and human movement in the world as divine providence, a theological term that speaks to the way that God cares for, or provides for, God's creation. And while it may seem as if the active provision of God must encounter us as a clear and present agency, this is again to violate the analogical distinction. The question must first be "how does the Father provide and care for the eternal Son," which then leads us to the way of answering "how does God provide and care for God's temporal children?" The Father, according to the poetry of John of the Cross, wishes to create a new lover for his Son, not in competition with his own love for the Son, but as an excessive flowing outward of the infinite bond between them. This creature will

> eat at our table,
> the same bread that I eat,
> that she may know the good
> I have in such a Son;
> and rejoice with me
> in your grace and fullness.[22]

There is no limit to the bountiful being and love of God. Like the father in the parable, here God the Father decides to throw a feast so he can share "the good I have in such a Son" with a created world. Creation is thus an excessive provision for the being of what is not God, bursting from God's own eternal love.

Providence, then, is God's act of creation extended through time. We might see providence especially as the thematic affirmation of God's courtesy toward creation.[23] God is not a unilateral "big agency," but rather a sharing of bounty, corresponding to an invitation to speak, live, and come to be at God's table. Rather than an extrinsic agent at work "on" on the world, God always appears both as a non-creature who encounters the world and a passion within the world. Divine care is a cooperative agency of Logos and Pneuma, moving the world to act in ways that respond to God's invitation to be.

Ephesians especially reminds us that it is not just earthly powers that are given space and extended the invitation to harmonize with God's call. "The wisdom of God in its rich variety" encounters not only dogs, orchids, and humans, but is also "made known to the rulers and authorities in the heavenly places" as well (3:10). The angels who are active within creation throughout the Bible as carriers of the divine message often provide grace within time and history. They are, that is, a heavenly sharing of God's own providential agency. "Greetings, favored one! The Lord is with you" (Luke 1:28). God does not will to provide alone, but creates beings to share in God's joy as well as in God's acts of provision.

Heavenly beings are given a share in God's agency in pathways and dimensions that remain beyond the knowledge of humans prior to the perfection of our knowledge in the vision of God; this, though, is the same pattern that holds on earth, where God's providential care is evident in the way God shares real agency with beings. Notice, for example the way Gabriel's mediation of YHWH's greeting is repeated differently through the blessing of Mary's cousin Elizabeth a few verses later when, "filled with the Holy Spirit," she calls out, "Blessed are you among women, and blessed is the fruit of your womb" (1:41-42). The angelic mediation of grace does not negate the call for the earthly blessing, but rather offers God's attention mediated through a more transcendent source. Similarly, when I care for my children, my dog acts along with me to calm their anxieties (or perhaps my own), the lavender oil my daughter is burning mediates another layer to this care, and heavenly beings at various remove also turn their attention toward our home. And all of this is God's providence, the care of a God who creates the heavens and the earth by "letting be."

We might think of miracles also as a kind of providence, the manifestation in creation of divine surprise. I would consider it wrong—by now I hope it is obvious—to define a miracle as an act of a transcendent God tearing apart the laws of the natural world in order to override creaturely agency and do something. Just as the rules of courtesy insist that I cannot talk over you or act as if you are not present, the "rules of providence" insist that God's activity will appear in what God invites to come into being from the world in which we live. Even in dealing in miracles, grace perfects, rather than destroying or negating, created nature.

A sudden healing, the appearance of an unexpected friend at the moment one most needs her, an inexplicable rescue . . . all of these may be miracles, but we misclassify them if we call them such in light of the inexplicability itself. Indeed, no earthly event is nearly strange enough to allow us to characterize it as the direct action of the eternal God. The very fact that a sudden disappearance of cancer registers to us as a bodily event connotes a mediation of multiple agencies and levels of causation through time and space, through bodies (where healing happens) and cognition (how embodied souls understand it as healing). Nutrition, the flow of information within the body, the curiosity of a doctor or nurse, the flowers brought by a friend, the change in weather, and the attention of those heavenly causes we call angels: all these various "secondary" causes interact and intersect, mediating God's activity to us in a miraculously noncompetitive way.

Sylvia Plath's early poem "Black Rook in Rainy Weather" speaks to this insight.[24] "I do not expect a miracle," she says, "although, I admit, I desire,/ Occasionally, some backtalk/ From the mute sky . . ." What she has learned, though, is that while the mute sky may not speak, the objects around her may still surprise her with the way they call to her, as if "hallowing an interval/ Otherwise inconsequent/ By bestowing largesse, honor,/ One might say love." Though she remains skeptical, she is now alert: "I now walk/ Wary," she says. "Ignorant"

> of whatever angel may choose to flare
> Suddenly at my elbow. I only know that a rook
> Ordering its black feathers can so shine
> As to seize my senses, haul
> My eyelids up, and grant
>
> A brief respite from fear
> Of total neutrality.
> . . .
> Miracles occur,
> If you care to call those spasmodic
> Tricks of radiance miracles. The wait's begun again,
> The long wait for the angel,
> For that rare, random descent.

A miracle is a sign, in St. John's idiom, and the true sign is in the change that takes place within: "believing," that is, is the periperformance of the miracle, since without the human response to the sign it would be just a strange occurrence—just a shiny rook with no descending angel above it. The miracle is that the infinite distance between the eternal God and the limited creatures of the heavens and the earth, the unfathomable interval, can be rendered analogical, or "hallowed" by divine courtesy. For Plath, the "respite from fear of total neutrality"—a moment's rest from the fear of a lack of care or provision, from the mute heavens—is what the "spasmodic trick" of the bird's feathers brings. And the work within her, the "passion" invoked by the rook's utterance, is the transformation from this posture of fear into the wary patience, ready for the "long wait" for the next surprising messenger from within the made cosmos. "Miracle" is the name for a revelation of the inspired Logos of God ringing out within the creator order.

Little Trinities

The story of creation is the story of God sharing this language outside God-self. There is no "purpose" to God's act of creating, insofar as this term indicates that its coming into being accomplishes something that God lacks without it. The word *God*, spoken with a Christian dialect, means "perfect exchange of gifts." If God desires to bring another into this exchange, it cannot be because there is something missing. God is a fullness of loving companionship from all eternity. Rather, the logic of creation is a working out of this logic of love. "Perfect love casts out fear" (1 John 4:18): in God there is no fear of competition, so the inclusion of another is an opening of the gift exchange to a new and excessive sharing. In the above poetic image, God expands the divine table for more seats. If this were an imperfect feast, one in which there is barely enough to go around, the act of inviting others to share God's bread would be a threat. As it is, God's love feast is boundless, so there is always more to share. Creating a nondivine world is how God's love acts beyond need or necessity, and yet still does what "comes naturally." As Eugene Rogers puts it, "creation is neither *necessary* for God nor *arbitrary* for God: it is however *characteristic* of God."[25] It is the characteristic act of a God who celebrates relationship, love, and the exchange of gifts. To invoke Thomas Aquinas' language again: it is fitting that such a God would create a world and invite that world to God's feast.

On occasion theologians will avoid talk of God as sole creator of a world out of nothing, since this seems to suggest that God is a ruler of absolute power who imposes his full will on what he makes with no limits.[26] But if, as I have argued, the relation of God to creation is not one of tyrannical power but instead one of mirroring companionship, it would seem that when God "calleth those things which be not as though they were" (Rom 4:17), as the Authorized (KJ) Version has it, this call must be something other than the cold command of an overlord. If God is truly transcendent, "beyond compare," then God is literally beyond comparison with any worldly agency—including a dictator with absolute authority. God is not just different from us, but "differently different."[27] The comparative tense of adjectives is inappropriate here: greater, bigger, smarter, more powerful; but so also is the superlative, which is simply a comparing with a greater array of competitors: God is not the greatest, biggest, smartest, most powerful actor in the world. God is not *in* the world at all, in the way that sunflowers and dragonflies are. God is, rather, the eternal circulation of gifts in which all creaturely circulation has a share.

God relates to the world, John of the Cross says, by a loving invitation to come to the feast. "Let there be," as I have suggested, is already a kind of courtesy, a power transposed into the optative: not simply "God demanded light, and there was light," but God invited the light into being. God "let" there be light. The great mystery at the heart of creation is that God calls to it in the same voice that the Father eternally calls to the Son, who eternally comes forth from his being. Creation "is not" until this call, and God's call constitutes its being: God calls to what is not as though it were. And at this call, this unprecedented "as though," creation bursts into being.

The "letting be" is what is most basic to the courteous interactions, providential miracles even, among God's creatures. If God is primarily related to God, then we image God in relation to one another. Our relation to one another *is* our relation to God, in that this is where we are most like a God who is eternally relational.

All created things are, in this sense, not just little logoi, or even little pneumata, but little trinities, as Augustine suspected: all created things are participatory manifestations of what happens when a word goes out from its source and is lit up from within by a passionate spirit. The Spirit is at work when creation manifests us to God as "beloved," but then also at work when creation manifests us to one another in the same way. "The Holy Spirit is not only called the Spirit of the Father and the Son who gave him, but also our Spirit who received him."[28] Fondness, affection, loyalty, desire: when these and other expressions of feeling manifest themselves within the world, they are manifestations of the Spirit repeating the eternal pattern in time. The Spirit is "our" Spirit when it appears among us. It would be unfitting for a Trinitarian God to create a world of isolated units; we are most godlike in discovering and being discovered by one another as beloved. And this, in obvious ways, extends beyond human interaction to the needs, interdependencies, and system ecologies of the cosmos. "Creation can be seen as the taking-form ad extra of the Trinitarian life itself . . . an act of communication and self-giving by the divine life proper," so that at its deepest, most essential being, "each thing, within its own limits, is a limited way of being God."[29] The dragonfly refuses to *be* without its beloved sunflower, the moons Io and Europa refuse to be without their beloved Jupiter: all creation finds itself within the descending and resting, manifesting power of the Spirit.

The created world is, at its heart, in its deepest and often most hidden essence, nothing but a moving, contingent, constantly surprising image of the Triune God. This is what we learn of the cosmos when we encounter the risen Christ, and it has particular implications for how we understand the place of human beings within creation. It is to this question we now turn.

5

HUMAN BEINGS

Awakening to Desire

What do Cleopas and his companion—some ancient iconography suggests his wife—learn from the stranger on the road and in their home about being human persons in the midst of God's creation?

Their first bit of evidence on this question is simply that something happens to them in his presence. Encountering him, they actually stop in the middle of their journey, overcome with grief: "They stood still, looking sad" (v. 17). They note a sense of betrayal: it was after all "our chief priests and leaders" who "handed him over to be condemned to death and crucified him" (20). Then they tell of ruined hopes: "But we had hoped that he was the one to redeem Israel" (21). After this comes confusion: "some women of our group astounded us" (22) with stories of an empty tomb and missing body, news which clearly does not encounter them just yet as "good."

The mood shifts on the long exegetical walk. Where they had recently been too sad to walk, they now "urged him strongly" to stay at their home. Then comes the recognition scene, an ancient example of Aristotle's plot-shifting *anagnorises*, dramatic events that gather up the story we have just heard and transform it in a critical moment of epiphany. Having seen anew the one whom they walked with in prior days, the disciples now can redescribe their slow progress out of sadness as the burning of their hearts. Finally, these two who found the journey too long to continue now hurry off "that same hour" to join and bring testimony to the companions from whom they had recently sought isolation. With hearts overflowing, their tongues are "like the pen of a ready scribe" (Ps 45:1).

When the apostle tells us that "it is the very Spirit bearing witness with our spirit that we are children of God," he is suggesting that something awakens within us, something that he calls "our spirit" rushes to greet and celebrate the encounter with the risen Jesus. Even more: the testimony of this rushing forward is that I am not just meeting a stranger outside of me, but I am at some very basic level meeting myself—my encounter with God's child allows me to bear witness that I myself am God's child. (Could this be what was happening in the gestation of Jesus' cousin John? "The Forerunner's spirit, illuminated by the Holy Spirit, knew the Savior even in his mother's womb."[1]) It is as though the encounter puts my experience as a human being within a new context, and I have a new sense of where I come from, what I am called to, and what meaning can emerge from what happens to me and around me in the meantime. God is, Augustine tells us, more intimate to us than we are to ourselves.[2] This intimacy opens a new world before us: "and if children, then heirs," the apostle continues, "heirs of God and joint heirs with Christ—if, in fact, we suffer with him so that we may also be glorified with him" (Rom 8:16-17). The encounter with Jesus, that is to say, both awakens and renames the deepest longings of human beings.[3] We feel our hearts burn within us, even if we do not yet have the language to describe the experience.

Strange, and perhaps hyperbolic, to call this encounter an awakening of their deepest longings. After all, these two are otherwise unknown characters in the gospel drama, and it seems likely that they are included here primarily to show the diaspora in Luke that will take center stage in Acts: the last events in the life of Christ, after he turns his head to Jerusalem, evoke passionate hope within villages surrounding the capital, even beyond the "core" companions of Jesus. Passionate Judeans, but not exactly Galilean fisherman and who have left home and family to place all hope in Jesus. Whatever it is they find in their dinner table guest, is it really their deepest desire?

In a certain sense, the passage suggests it is not. Or at least not at first: by opening up new interpretations of the familiar Torah and Prophets, Jesus shows them that they were not in fact hoping as fully as they might. They were hoping for a redemption that could be defeated by death, whereas he presents them with a redemption that had always, in a hidden sense, been one for which suffering and death were the appropriate path. In this way their hope is taken from them and handed back to them as something like a hope beyond hoping, a fullness of past memory, future expectation, and present experience that they were only beginning to glimpse.

Let us take this critical discovery of a desire that is both mine and strange to me as the fundamental human experience in the Christian story. It will require some more space—the remainder of the book, in fact—to work out this idea. Who is the one who hands us "back" this desire (chapter 7)? Why am I a stranger to myself (chapter 8?) What is the experience of re-encountering myself through this strangeness (chapter 9)? How do we reimagine life in light of this encounter (chapter 10)? What is the ultimate hope of this reimagined life (chapter 11)? This chapter will address the question that opens this inquiry: if it is human persons who come to discover themselves in the presence of this stranger, what does it mean to be human?

The Great Hope

There is, as the author of Ephesians puts it, "one hope" for all humans, because there is one Spirit who rests on the one body of all creation (4:3-4). Karl Barth calls this "the great hope," a framing of the human person as such that is given prior to and beyond created and experienced particularity. This hope "has come down, as it were, from above, from God into the world of men loved by God," so that we can say that this hope is identical to God's sixth day invitation to "let be" the human beings. This hope is "incorporated or implanted into their status and being and non-being, so that objectively they cannot be without it, objectively they have their goal and future in Jesus Christ and therefore in the service of God."[4]

The classical tradition of Eastern and Western theology—to which Barth himself had a rather complex relationship—identifies this unifying hope as the invitation extended to all creatures, and to humans in a unique way, to share in the divine being, or, as 2 Peter 1:4 puts it, to "become participants of the divine nature." Drawing on the creation story in which humans are made according to the "image and likeness" of God, Maximus the Confessor identifies the first term, image, with the nature which we are given as abounding gift, while the later, likeness, is a habit of life that we are called to. We are, that is, made in God's image and called to God's likeness. A person pursuing the habits of divine likeness celebrates the original imaging gift of her creation—such a person "places himself wholly in God alone, forming and configuring God alone throughout his entire being." This is the single great hope of all humans made in God's image, for "what could be more desirable to those who are worthy of it than divinization?"[5]

For this great hope, the gaps, or what Barth calls our "non-being," is key. "Creatures exist first in potential,"[6] and so we have the hope of sharing in their creator's life and being as a promise of what is not yet realized for us. This is, we might say, the "only" difference between the being of the Creator and the being of creation: while God eternally *is*, with an existence identical to God's essence, creation exists both from (as image) and toward (as likeness) an evasive essence. The language of the previous chapters can help us here: God is an eternal Logos lovingly spoken by the Source of all, and God is equally and from all eternity the Pneuma that comes from this Source, rests on this Logos, and reveals the one to the other. "This is my Beloved Son . . ." "My Father has sent me . . ." By analogy, all created things are little words, modeled in time on the eternal Word. Creation is simply "the one Logos as many logoi."[7] As such, we are also little pneumata, spirits testifying to this resting of God's Spirit, and this Spirit reveals to us in time what the Spirit reveals to the Son in eternity: "And because you are children, God has sent the Spirit of his Son into our hearts, crying, 'Abba! Father!'" (Gal 4:6).

"In the creaturely world, the divine world is clothed in becoming; it is not, but becomes."[8] We are something like God's triune being "slowed down" to the pace of temporality. If the Triune God is the parable of the prodigal told in the fullness of eternity, we are the same parable back down at the earthly tempo, where one can wander off into a far country, come to oneself in a pigsty, and return home in hope that the Father in heaven is still *our* Father. All this, and yet we can still exist as an analogy for God, a model of the Godhead seen through a glass darkly.

The limits on our size, our powers, our inability to be present in multiple places, times, or realities all "at once" . . . all this means that our being is framed by lack, or Barth's "non-being." And yet it is this lack itself that forms us as beings called to hope: just as God came to visit Adam and Eve for garden walks "in the cool of the evening," humans are those creatures who can encounter God anew again and again, and thus become a bit more godlike—grow into the likeness—with each passing day. Our very limitations, the "nothingness" that we carry around with us at every point of our lives, is the remarkable gift of an invitation to become more than the image that initiates our journey: we can become like God. Not eternal and uncreated beings, but timely creatures who model the divine being through love, faithfulness, truth-telling, and the joy of living at home in God's world.

This is, finally, the ontological hope of every human, expressed or not, a conclusion which follows from a doctrine of creation. "You have made us for yourself," Augustine prayed. If we are made on the model of the eternal celebration of joy-filled love that we call the Triune God, then the *de profundis* of our being will be this great hope, the desire to rest in God, or to come to the feast, to recall John of the Cross.

Small Hopes

At the same time, though, these very limits mean that even in the act of hoping a human being remains, as Auden put it, "a creature/ Who comes in a median size."[9] We do not first of all experience hearts burning for the Logos in which all things hold together; our hearts burn for more proximate and immediate things, nearer experiences, and closer companions in the world around us. A child hopes for a particular birthday cake that she had once, or a friend once had, or that she invented in her mind while rummaging through the pantry; a man hopes that his sick friend will get well; a woman hopes that a project to which she and her colleagues have given years of attention will succeed. I hope for what I hope because of the places in which I have existed, the people who have existed around me, the past that I can remember, the future I can imagine, and the present in which I feel so many absences.

These are the energies of life that Barth calls "small hopes,"[10] which is not to say they are insignificant. In fact, they are what lives are made of, and something like a fingerprint of each person. This is to say that we discover who we are as we come to know, through these contingent and unpredictable pathways, what it is we long for. Our existential pathway is not given to us, like a map for a journey: we have the discerning, discovering, and creating of purpose as the project of a lifetime. We are the creatures, as Heidegger put it, for whom existence is a "thrown project,"[11] and the longings we feel give shape to that task before us. We find ourselves thrown into being as a context we did not choose, and then feel the challenge—often anxiety-producing challenge—of moving toward the evasive hopes that also tell what sort of beings we are.

We discover ourselves, also, in what we lose. We feel our inability to fully achieve the task. We note irreconcilable loss in each new creation. Humans are not the only creatures who grieve lost loves, who feel a deep connection to and aching for a lost home, or confused at the unfamiliar. We are simply the creatures who write stories and songs and poems about such things.[12]

The Emmaus companions are troubled by a particular loss, the loss of a friend and of a hope. They come into the gospel story as two characters we only know through the way that Jesus' death affects them, and then through the way that the epiphany of his resurrection changes the way they experience themselves as hoping humans. If the stranger tells them that they have missed something, he does not tell them that their small hopes are inappropriate.

Significant here is the almost obsessive attention to place. "Two of them were going to a village called Emmaus," which, the author wants us to know, is "about seven miles from Jerusalem." The city comes up again—presumably they are just leaving it, since they refer to their traveling companion as "the only stranger in Jerusalem" who has not heard about the crucifixion of the prophet. Then they come near their village, the stranger goes a bit down the road, and they call him back to come to their home. Finally, we read of the return to Jerusalem.

All of this suggests that there is something irreducible in the places they live and travel that connects to the hope they express. This is a hope that comes mediated through the memory and present reality of sharing a home in a small town near Jerusalem, under Roman occupation; mediated also through the days and years of walking to their local synagogue to hear the Torah and the Prophets read and interpreted. Willie James Jennings points out the way that the question of where the Israelites are is always, in the biblical story, central to their emergent identity: their task before God is "to gather the fragments of identity to learn from them who we might become in that place."[13] This centrality of place is what makes Psalm 137 such a harrowing expression of alienation:

> By the waters of Babylon we sat down and wept,
>   when we remembered you, O Zion.
> As for our harps, we hung them up
>   on the trees in the midst of that land.
> For those who led us away captive asked us for a song,
> and our oppressors called for mirth:
>   "Sing us one of the songs of Zion."
> How shall we sing the LORD's song
>   upon an alien soil? (*Book of Common Prayer*)

Babylonian rivers are not—not yet, anyway, for the poet—a place from which Israel can "gather the fragments of identity to learn" who they are. The songs of Zion are unsingable there.

The modern world, Jennings goes on to note throughout his book, was built on the denial of place, especially in the economic drives that brought expansion, the conquering and colonizing of lands, and the conversion of human communities on one continent into units of labor on others. To live without connection to a place is to live without these intimacies, split off from the objects and persons of one's affection, and without an ear for the language of particular created things around us, to return to the imagery of Psalm 19. To kidnap and extract a person from her home in chains is to place the intimacies and contingencies of her future under my control, and form her around a loss with no real hope for return.

I will add here that extraction and enslavement take away also the possibility of leaving home in the sense that I spoke about it in the opening chapter. To leave a place of small hopes and kindnesses so one can set off on a journey of discovery is to cherish a memory, to hope for a homecoming and all the returns of lost things and lost loves this involves. To leave home in this way is to encounter a new world while remaining someone "from somewhere." This allows the encounters of new languages, new social customs, and new religious ideas to challenge the familiarity of my own experience. To leave home is, as Ulysses and his dog discovered, to come home again both changed and recognizable. On the other hand, to be forced away from a homeland makes the crossing of new rivers and mountains and seas not a journey of discovery but a nightmare of self-alienation. It is to feel the threat of a life without the small hopes that have become our existential thumbprints.

The novels of Marilynne Robinson center on the shapes of human lives that emerge out of long memories that are born from particular places, and give rise to powerful hopes and painful losses. In *Housekeeping*, the inhabitants of the town of Fingerbone tell themselves and their children, over and over, the story of the tragedy at the lake that everyone feels even in the changes of the weather. It is the hope, as much as the loss, that shows them who they are. They are the people of Fingerbone, who live with the memory of what they have lost and with a hope that all that is lost will come home to them.

> There is so little to remember of anyone—an anecdote, a conversation at table. But every memory is turned over and over again, every word, however chance, written in the heart in the hope that memory will fulfill itself, and become flesh, and that the wanderers will find a way home, and the perished, whose lack we always feel, will step through the door finally and stroke our hair with dreaming, habitual fondness, not having meant to keep us waiting long.[14]

Finding our way home is, at least metaphorically if not literally, at the heart of human experience. To be at home is to dwell at peace among the things and the people that life has given me affection for. "Housekeeping," as Robinson puts it in an essay, is "a regime of small kindnesses, which, taken together, make the world salubrious, savory, and warm."[15] We emerge as the persons we are as we care *for* the people and the things that we care *about*—we dust off an heirloom, we brew coffee for a sister, we bake bread for strangers who will gather around the dinner table, we recenter a cherished photograph, we play or put on a song that takes us back to a happy or sad day, we invite a friend to retell a story that always makes the family laugh.

Community, on this model, is something like an expansion of this realm of affection, an "imaginative love for people we do not know or who we know only slightly."[16] I know that woman's face because I have passed by her on the sidewalk several times before today. I know that dog's bark, the lean of that fencepost. And while it is not my responsibility to keep house here, to dust and feed and straighten and arrange, I notice the affection I have for this familiar place, and I begin to imagine the small ways I can care for it.

I am suggesting here that a theological anthropology is one that attends to intimacy, the intimacies of small or "person-sized" hopes, loves, and losses.[17] We discover what it is to be human as we name the affections, losses, and hopes that give shape to our lives.

Let us say then that the freedom to keep house—to cherish small hopes and make things warm and savory—along with the freedom to leave home and return, are fundamental to human flourishing. It is to have a place in the world where, even as I and the world change, I could gather around myself all the people, the memories, the material things that matter to me, and be at peace.

Humanness and Loss

Of course, no sooner have I said it this way than I notice, as Robinson's novels refuse to allow me to forget, that our desires are never so fulfilled, and so that my identity emerges as much in the absences that my longings reveal as in the presences. Perhaps this provides a hint as to how it is that enslaved humans have endured extraction from place and bondage in the home of another and continued to live in hope.[18] Or how it is that survivors have lived on in hope for those who have been taken from them.[19]

I will say more in a later chapter about how we creatures can turn menacing and violent faces to one another. For the moment, I want to note the ways that something like grief seems to be characteristic of life even in its kinder expressions. The movement of the depths of the river toward the deeper depths over the falls is a "deep calling to deep," a kind of recognition of lack and promise of fulfillment. The thirst of a deer is a longing for water. Biological life demonstrates a longing down to the very level of genetic interactions. The codings of living bodies change when they explore random phenotypic expressions in the gaps between the bodies they inherit and the possibilities still unexplored. There is an ontological marking of absences here, as a longing for life, for family, for neighborhood, surges outward in the adaptations of things to their environment, and even in the adaptations of environments to mirror the organisms within.[20] Humans are one of many beautifully intricate stories of such longings, as we stood on two legs, grew larger brains, migrated, mated, and continued to adapt, in genetically coded minutiae like stature and skin color, to the lands we came, variously, to inhabit. Deep within and beneath the conscious small hopes of various *homo sapiens*, we have emerged as a species out of the simple and wild desire for the life that we lack.

Framed as our lives are within patterns of life that we share across species, we should not be surprised at the way that these small hopes become something like the signature of a particular human person. In a brief account early in *Housekeeping*, the narrator describes her grandmother's pendant, given to her by her husband before the tragedy at the lake took him away. The pendant is painted inside with seahorses, and the woman protects it as a treasure not so much as a token of his absence but simply because she loves the painting of the strange water creatures. She eventually stops wearing it because the chain is not sufficiently long to allow her to turn it and look at the painting inside. "It was the seahorses themselves that she wanted to see as soon as she took her eyes away, and that she wanted to see even when she was looking at them. The wanting never subsided until something—a quarrel, a visit—took her attention away."[21]

Not only the presence or absence then: whatever it is we humans are, we seem to emerge at our fullest when our desire for presence is so intense as to be insatiable. Grandmother is the one—the only one—who loves those painted seahorses in this way; more, she *becomes*, in an important sense, this unquenchable desire for these painted creatures. A human person is what we call a being who blooms into life as a particular set of hopes and loves that, though small, are unique trailheads into an infinite desire that she carries with her through her life.

In and Beyond

There is one hope, yet every particular emergence of hope is radically unique. How do these two levels coexist? Am I the ontological hope for rest in God, or am I the sum of all my existential hopes that form my identity? Am I hoping to receive that Spirit of adoption that allows me to greet God as a parent, or I am hoping to finally hold those seahorses in my hand?

Or, to return the question above, is it truly myself, in harmony with all that I love, have lost, and long for, that I discover when I meet the stranger on the road? I wish to suggest that it is, and this is because our essence as ideas in God's mind—little logoi—is revealed both in and beyond our particular existence.

James Cone writes in *The Spirituals and the Blues* that in the songs of the American slaves, heaven was the historical freedom from oppression, and "also hope in the future of God, an expectation that the contradictions of slavery were not ultimate." Hope in heaven is a hope born of resurrection, and so always excessive of what human action and organization can accomplish. This is what he calls the "transcendental future" invoked in the slaves' music, and what I have called the analogical interval between the earthly and the heavenly activity of God. "I've heard of a city called heaven," as one song puts it, and "I've started to make it my home": started, here and now, a work that only God can complete. So when they sang about crossing the Jordan while looking out on the Ohio River toward the North, they were invoking an eschatology according to which heavenly hope provides an invitation to embodied action, even illegal action: their periperformative response to the hope for freedom in them is just as disobedient and faithful as—and infinitely riskier than—the leper's in Mark. Equally important, however, is the excess of the analogy. The singers of those songs did not *just* mean the Ohio River, according to Cone. Their hope was in an ultimate crossing that would take place on the banks of a Jordan even more real than the one Moses looked out over, and so ever that much more real than the banks of the Ohio.[22]

The point here is that the great hope remains the great hope, framing and structuring all human existence, even as the contingencies of life and circumstance alter the way in which this great hope is lived out in small hopes. The great hope is—or can be—the analogical font of all the small hopes that come after, just as essence is revealed in each moment of existence as that which is both within and beyond it, to invoke the Catholic philosophical language of Erich Przywara.[23] To be human is to be a creature of God formed with a natural hope for a home, a belonging, that exceeds our natural capacities. As I hope for the lives, the presences, the freedoms that collect around my home and my community in this particular time and place, I discover that these hopes themselves give shape and materiality to a hope beyond them that will always elude my attempts to name and achieve it.

Does this evasiveness not, though, bring us back to the notion of the indwelling of the Spirit and Word as both utterance and passion with me? I am spoken by God into being; as I come to experience the Logos revealed to me in the love of a sister or spouse, the promise of freedom, the return home, the evasive paintings on a pendant—all the little logoi that are God's creation around me—I find my heart burning within me, pressing me toward unscripted, anarchic, yet "reasonable" and appropriate responses. We respond with the surprising periperformances of the hope that is in us. The slave will chance the current, the child will carve a gravestone for the beloved pet, the migrant will risk arrest . . . the leper will shout, the foreign woman will talk back to her daughter's potential healer when he refuses her request, and all because in the revelation of what we are not, of what we lack, we find an analogy of the love for which we were made.

Noticing the ways that hope works within us allows us to register the peculiar kind of freedom that constitutes the human person. "For freedom Christ has set us free" (Gal 5:1) is the rather bent way Saint Paul puts it, as if the freedom is not simply free to be whatever it wants, but only free to remain free. To feel the Spirit testify within us, responding to the beauty of the Logos that we have just encountered, is to find ourselves called to respond in a wildly free way, a response that is at one and the same time fitting to the call and also utterly novel. No one ever before or ever after responded to the passionate utterance of Christ the way those disciples did, because no one ever lived the convergence of hope and grief and confusion that they lived. They were free to respond freely, so long as they did not deny the burning in their hearts, ignore that passion of the utterance, and refuse to be free. In other words, so long as they did "not submit again to a yoke of slavery." And so it is with each person, each community of persons, who lives within God's world.

Perhaps one way of putting this is that the transcendent, differently different Triune God is not the sort of being who plans the lives of creatures. A God who makes us free for freedom itself is a God who can only be spoken of as one with a plan for a life in a very distant, analogical way. A purpose, certainly:[24] the Spirit-filled Logos is the eternal purpose of God, and through personal and communal habits of love, truth, and faithfulness this purpose becomes the pathway of creation too. But this path will always be marked by freedom—the unscripted possibility of a periperformance of burning hearts. The love and faithfulness themselves are the plan, as Maximus might have put it, and the entire question of "what God wants" at any moment transforms into a new question: *how does this moment invite an unplanned event of faithfulness to God's eternal beauty?*

Life concresces, to borrow a term from philosopher Alfred North Whitehead: the world comes together and offers itself to each moment in an utterly novel way.[25] To be a free person in the midst of such a world is not to follow a divine plan, but neither is it to write my own story on a sheet of blank notebook paper; rather, it is to receive the world as a gift of itself, and also at the same time as an invitation to me: an invitation to discover myself in and through the movement from invitation into action that each moment presents to me. The theological possibility held out by such concrescence is that each existential shaping of freedom-for-freedom's-sake can also be a new manifestation of the Logos within me, as the Spirit moves me, and thus reveals the Father who calls to me out of love. There is no limit to the

possible lives that could come to reveal this analogy, and no moment of concrescence that could ever be anything other than such an invitation—this,
at least, is the suggestion of Paul's theology of the cross, where even failure,
humiliation, and foolishness show the Logos of heaven and the true character of God.[26]

The essence of human creatures is revealed in and beyond the infinite
moments of existence that discover it. Our essence as these temporal analogies of divine Pneuma-filled Logos, that is to say, will reveal itself through
a thousand tiny concrescences, as we stand before the river, hold the frightened child's hand, or weep over those evasive seahorses.

6

THE GOD-HUMAN

Saying Who He Is

The central question of the Gospels is, very simply, "Who is Jesus?" No sooner is it asked, though, by a governor in his courts or followers in a boat or Pharisees outside the Temple or even Jesus himself, than we begin to suspect that we have not quite understood the question.

Cleopas and his companion, whose "eyes were kept from recognizing him," make two initial attempts to identify him. First, in asking "Are you the only stranger in Jerusalem who does not know the things that have taken place there in these days?" (Luke 24:18), they name him as "uninformed foreigner." The plot unfolds in a similar way to Plato's *Sophist*, where the ignorance of the stranger becomes the catalyst to new discovery. The irony of their question also coordinates with Plato's use of "knowing ignorance," since the answer will be yes, in a certain sense: yes, he is in fact the one who does not "know" what they know. They will, in turn, slowly unlearn the things they know about what has taken place in Jerusalem over the next several hours. Jesus is, in this sense, the one stranger who does not "know" what happened in Jerusalem with the same faulty epistemology by which others know.

Immediately after telling the unknown Jesus who he is, they tell him who the Jesus they knew was, or at least who they were hoping they knew him to be. "A prophet mighty in deed and word before God and all the people" whom they "had hoped . . . was the one to redeem Israel" (vv. 19, 21). It has now been three days since Jewish and Roman leaders collaborated to put him to death, thus showing, first, that he was not as mighty in deed as they thought, and, second, that he was apparently never Israel's redeemer. Mixed in with the disappointment, "besides all this," is sheer confusion: a missing body and reports of angels with a message about him being alive.

As we are aware, though, where this vignette from Luke's Gospel ends, is it too much to suggest that their confusion and disappointment is an indispensable part of the question? Even of the "right" answer? "He is not what they thought him to be, and thus they must 'learn' him afresh, as from the beginning."[1] To answer the Jesus question—even to ask the question well, or to hear it asked—is not simply to find the correct words. It is to go beyond curiosity (is this not Joseph's son? [John 6:42]), and to speak out of the depths of one's humanity: to say what it is we hope for, and to risk pinning all those hopes on our encounter with him. Indeed, it is to continue "staying" with these hopes even when we see them dashed, when we wind up standing still in the road, looking sad. Answering the christological question requires a *metanoia*, a conversion of the one asking it toward a new horizon of hope.[2]

When Jesus asks his disciples the question about his identity, he does not say "Who Am I?"—such a question would prod them toward a conceptual vocabulary that could hardly address the radical event of a God-Man standing by the Mediterranean Sea—but "who do crowds say," and then "who do you say that I am?" (Luke 9:18, 20). He asks what the witnesses say. Even the "correct" testimony, given by Peter, turns out to be profoundly mistaken in the very next scene, when Peter sees Jesus' identity unveiled on the mountain and responds nonsensically, "not knowing what he said" (v. 33). This is perhaps a question we can only answer with our own confused humanity.

In this sense, the Gospels suggest that Jesus' identity can be authentically spoken of only by placing it into a narrative that invites the reader along. To know him is to testify to the encounter, the meeting place between our desire and his provision. John is only the most explicit about this invitation. "These [things] are written so that you may come to believe" (John 20:30). But the synoptics as well are written not simply as preservations of a biography, but as testimonials to the transformation made possible by an encounter with this life. "I too decided, after investigating everything carefully from the very first, to write an orderly account for you, most excellent Theophilus, so that you may know the truth" (Luke 1:3-4). To describe a truth that is a simple matter of positive identification requires some piece of persuasive evidence, argued as well as possible; to tell a truth of the one in whom all Israel and the nations may place their deepest hope involves an invitation to a journey from grief and vulnerability through to joy.

The True Human

The Gospels describe this journey from sorrow to hopeful joy in some surprising ways. When Jesus in Mark's Gospel explains to his disciples why he speaks in parables, he quotes Isaiah: so that they will "not understand" (4:12). We see him always drawing back from immediate identification, and in this way challenging the desire that his listeners assume they bring to encounters with him. Jesus' reluctance to give a direct answer to their queries implies that his interlocuters are missing something. In voicing their curiosity about the origin of his power and acts, the crowds have only scratched the surface of the deep anthropological desire that is our truest inheritance from the Logos through whom we are made.

The Syrophoenician woman is a noteworthy exception to the responses characteristic of Jesus' interlocutors in Mark. When Jesus responds to her plea for help with a confusing and insulting parable, she enters the parable with him, and shifts the imagery so that she stands under the flow of healing gifts that come from him. "Even the dogs under the table eat the children's crumbs" (7:28). Not being among the covenant people is no impediment to receiving grace from Israel's prophet, she insists. The foreign woman over-accepts his evasive parable, and his response is an acknowledgment of the depths of the desire that expresses itself in her creative reframing of his own grace. "For saying that you may go—the demon has left your daughter" (v. 29). The woman "remakes" Jesus as the one able to meet her need, and he celebrates her Christology! This, apparently, is the response to his parables that he has been waiting for: creative agency expressed in a way that crafts a meeting of human need and Christic hope. Like the leper's proclamation, we see here an encounter in which refusal to "listen" to Jesus becomes a periperformance of faith.

I call her an exception not because expressions of faith are rare in the Gospels—they are not—but rather in light of the celerity of her response. She immediately matches her hope to the healing gift of the one before her, and refuses to leave until Jesus acknowledges the match as well. In most cases the transformative match takes longer to perceive. At the Gospel's end, robed men at the tomb tell Mary, Mary, and Salome to pass along to Peter and the others the news that Jesus "is going ahead of you to Galilee" (16:7). The disciples have failed Jesus, and have now returned to their lives with ruined hopes. Jesus does not intercede to stop them from returning to their families and boats and remaking what is left of their lives; rather, he tells them that wherever it is they are going, he is going there "ahead of them." Like Cleopas, Peter and the others will return home, no doubt recalling memories of their first sightings of Jesus, and the excitement that called them away at the beginning of it all. A new question, though, will hover over their return: will you have the courage to face yourselves there? To name the needs and desires and hopes that have been lost? To name the ways that you failed? As they go, the robed men tell the women, they will not go alone. He will go ahead of them, and be there as they re-encounter him by reencountering their own journeys with him.[3] The original text of Mark, in fact, has no other resurrection scene, as if suggesting that the risen Christ is only visible as a meeting of true human desire with ultimate human hope. They are not yet prepared to make the Syrophoenician match after the tragedy at the trial and crucifixion.

This Syrophoenician match reveals a *poiesis* embedded in all authentic Christology. "This language is poetic, which is to say, it is a creator of a new mode of existence, signifying a redeemed subjectivity."[4] The true naming of his identity involves matching, a kind of rhyming of our own being with his. *Poiesis*: we "make" the Jesus who responds to our great hope, and when we make his gift and our great hope rhyme, we have answered the question. He is, she says, the crumbs that spill off the table to feed the dogs. And she is correct: "For saying that you may go—the demon has left your daughter" (Mark 7:29).

Dante's great three-part poem from the thirteenth century dramatizes this slow encounter with Christ as a gradual journey toward oneself. The poem opens with the poet waking in a dark wood, desperate to find his way out again. In fact, he sees the pathway out, but a leopard springs up and blocks his path from all angles. "And, everywhere I looked, the beast was there."[5] As Virgil approaches and makes himself known, Dante calls out, "'Save me from her, I beg you, famous sage,/ She makes me tremble, the blood throbs in my veins.'" Virgil's response is not what Dante was hoping to hear: "'But you must journey down another road,'/ He answered, when he saw me lost in tears,/ 'If ever you hope to leave this wilderness.'"[6]

The road, of course, will take him through hell, and then to purgatory, and finally up into the mystical reaches of Paradise. Dante the pilgrim changes along the way, as he wrestles with his own pride among the damned, and then with his own wavering spirit as he climbs around among those who are still seeking repentance. All the while, as the beauty of Paradise seems ever farther away, he begins to note a yearning growing within him. The lack of courage he shows at the beginning—"Why am I to go? Who allows me to? I am not Aeneas, I am not Paul. . . . and if I should undertake the journey, I fear it might turn out an act of folly"[7]—transforms into a deep desire to keep moving. His final vision of the humanity of God, to which I will return below, is of a piece with the long journey he undertakes. The pilgrim must first learn what it is to be human before he can come to rest in the presence of his God. That is what had him lost in the woods, and that is why Virgil insists that the leopard blocked any path but "down," into the terrifying depths of his own humanity.[8]

Not that we are ever adequate to the vision itself. Peter on Mount Tabor, as we saw, experiences the terror of a beauty beyond his comprehension, as do Mary, Mary, and Salome after hearing from the robed men. The Gospel writers want us to know the truth, but they always want us to know that we can only know this truth by first asking ourselves what it is we think we know, what it is we want to know, and who we think we, as knowers, are. The truth of Jesus' identity remains, throughout, an excessive truth. This sort of knowing and matching and rhyming will take time. It will come mediated through experience, through loss, through little resurrections along the way. We will know how to say who he is only in the way that we learn any deep human truth: by becoming vulnerable to the truth that will require our very selves.

The end of this journey, both for Dante and for the New Testament, is to see the face of Christ—to "know fully, even as I have been fully known" (1 Cor 13:12). Just as when grief surges through the pilgrim when he hears that he cannot take the path straight out of the woods, or later when his saintly guide Beatrice refuses to smile at him because her beauty will—at this point on his journey—blind him, the Christian pilgrimage is one of losing and regaining hope, of having one's deepest desires and longings transformed, so that the face we see will be the true face of Christ that we long for, not an idol of our own creation. This change is what 1 Peter calls "a new birth into a living hope through the resurrection of Jesus Christ from the dead" (1:3). The central question of Christian theology, then, "Who do you say that he is?" is only answerable with a pattern of life, a pilgrimage through oneself that risks grief and loss, that involves losing one's life, as Matthew's Gospel puts it (10:39). In this sense, the question "Who is Jesus?" translates as *what is the true, hidden, living hope that you find within you, as you uncover the most terrifying aspects of your own humanity?*

This connection of Jesus' identity to the array of human fears and hopes helps explain why Saint Augustine relies so heavily on the Psalms in his Christology. Israel's poems and hymns give expression to joy ("I was glad when they said to me . . ." [122]), to rage ("O daughter Babylon, you devastator!" [137]), to jealousy ("Such are the wicked; always at ease, they increase in riches" [73]), despair ("Darkness is my only companion" [88, *Book of Common Prayer*]), and nearly every imaginable human emotive impulse. When Augustine says, "We must apply it all to Christ,"[9] he is not saying that the ancient Jewish poet somehow channeled the not-yet-embodied words of Jesus as a future forecast. Rather, he is allowing the anthropological courage of ancient Israel to shape his own understanding of Jesus, or perhaps to guide him in understanding his own humanity so that he may have an answer to the question of Christ's identity.[10]

So, for instance, in his reading of Psalm 9:12-13, where the poor cry out for mercy, Augustine says that alongside the voice of the poet we can hear the voice of Christ, the one "that is, who first was made poor for our sakes, although he was rich." If Christ speaks through human suffering, though, all humans also speak through Christ's exaltation:

> But in him it is not only the manhood he assumed that is exalted, not he alone who is the Head of the Church, but every one of us who are numbered among his members. And so in him humankind is lifted up away from all wayward desires, desires which are the gates of death because the route to death goes through them.[11]

If Jesus is the one crying out for mercy in the Psalm, that is, he is crying out in such a way as to let all humans find themselves in his cry, and to let all our cries, our desires, find themselves reshaped in his. The invitation, then, the christological question, becomes whether or not we can make this cry with him. If not, it must be that we are not yet desiring, not yet hoping, for what it is that we encounter when we meet him. In this case we are living, like Cleopas, with hopes that are less than the human hopes that God made us for.

Augustine's insight into the cry of mercy as the voice of Christ speaking for all, what he calls the *totus christus* or whole body of Christ,[12] takes us back to the development earlier of the Spirit as the presence of passion within us that moves us to respond to the speaking of the Logos. We might rephrase Paul's assurance that "no one can say 'Jesus is Lord' except by the Holy Spirit" (1 Cor 12:3): no one can hear the psalmist's cry as the voice of Christ, giving voice and so giving hope by speaking the human desire from an unsurpassable depth, unless the words ignite a passion within her to hear this as her own voice as well. To call Jesus Lord is not an epistemological evaluation in light of observed evidence; it is rather an acknowledgment of a burning in one's heart to find in his life—his humility, friendships, his laying down of his life and his return to those he loved—the ultimate and most profound expression of the living hope within me.

Following Augustine's insight, and recalling as well what I said earlier about the necessarily communal/historical character of testimony, it is further appropriate to acknowledge the eschatological character of this ascription of catholic hope to Christ. Said otherwise, the totality of hope found in

Christ can only be a meaningful pronouncement of the Christian faith when all the human hopeful, and all the created expressions of the Logos, have encountered Christ as the possibility of hope. "The fulfillment of human destiny has been revealed in Jesus through his resurrection from the dead. Jesus did not experience this event for himself alone, but for all men; Jesus' resurrection allowed the destiny of all men to a life in nearness to God, as Jesus had proclaimed it, to appear in him."[13] I will return to this theme below. Here I simply wish to note that 1 Peter's claim of finding in the resurrection a living hope will be a partially abstract claim until this hope is "lived" by each particular creature. This claim, or Paul's in Colossians that all things hold together in Christ, or John's that all things are made through Logos and so find their being and harmony in this risen Logos incarnate, has the character of what classical logic calls an inductive, rather than a deductive, argument. We do not, in a certain sense, "know" that all broken and aching and loving and lonely creatures find their hope in him. We have the testimony of saints, across every thinkable division of human identity (gender, sexuality, ethnicity, class, education, location in space and time), who have found in him their hope. We have scriptural narratives of winds and waves finding peace in his words. We continue to baptize children and adults into this hope, to tell stories of re-creation of devastated lands and species as little resurrections,[14] and so to find matches between the testimony of our spirits with the testimonies of hope in the Bible. Thus we induct the claim that can only be verified at the end of the age: nothing exists outside of the living hope found in the resurrected Christ.[15]

In order to hear Christ speaking in this integral, catholic, human voice, there is no avoiding the integrity of his humanity. All that is implied by what I have said about God's human creation above is true for him: he is a limited expression of Logos, a little logos who is a faithful analogy to the eternal Logos, with a hopefulness that expresses itself in loving connection to those around him, the weeping for a lost friend, the compassion for the sick, anger at abuse, the temptations to despair or to grasp for control that come from being a naturally limited creature with a desire that finds its fulfillment only in a supernatural fullness. He cannot be present to all the sufferers of a single small town in Israel, let alone to all the sufferers of the world. This very limit, as the Anglican Lancelot Andrewes points out, becomes the impetus in the Gospel of John for the sending of the Spirit. The disciples "were to be sent abroad into all coasts," and so "his corporal presence would have stood them in small stead." They needed a Comforter because at best "He could have been resident in but one place, to have comforted some of them."[16] The human Jesus has all the gifts, and all the limits, that characterize the human form; this, we are surprised to learn, is no more an impediment to his offering of hope to all creation than is the election of Abraham an impediment to the blessing of all nations.

The Savior

Readers familiar to the rhythms of Chalcedonian Christology will at this point be expecting the dialectical obverse of the paradox: "yet he was also divine." And there is, to be sure, conceptual ground to cover that can never fully transcend paradox. The trouble, though, of layering the experience of his humanity with a contrasting claim of his divinity is that we thereby limit our experience of this contrast to a kind of sheer paradox, as if they were oppositely charged poles held together only by a faith in the integrity of Christic magnetism. The word "God" does not mean "the biggest thing around," and so Christ's divinity, whatever it means, cannot signify another nature alongside and comparable with his humanity.

Throughout this text we have begun from experience, from the experience of encountering the risen Christ as that encounter comes mediated to us through our growing trust in gathered testimony nested within the testimony of Scripture. The paradoxical claim—two natures without confusion, with transmutation, without division, without contrast—is not the initial experience; hope is. We begin in the agnostic position of the man whose eyesight is restored, who answers the christological question, "I do not know whether he is a sinner. One thing I do know, that though I was blind, now I see" (John 9:25).

In an important meditation from the late classical era, Maximus the Confessor is seeking to understand the identity of Christ as it comes to us in one of the most difficult passages of the Gospels, the Gethsemane prayer, when Jesus prays "not my will but yours be done." In Maximus's time, the question about Christ's identity had come to a controverted focus on the question of will: when Jesus of Nazareth acted, did he will these actions with a human will or with a divine will? The conundrum reveals the difficulty of the balance. Surely a divine will "operating" a human body would render Jesus only partially human; but a human will without the divine would be a human as out of touch with God as any other, and thus not a faithful account of the one who claimed that his work—action, operation—was his Father's work. Maximus also notices, though, the inadequacy of the immediate appeal to paradox: one could simply say "he has both wills," but this simply pushes the problem deeper down, and raises the question of his integrity. Surely an account that included a discernible duality of wills would fail to do justice to the unity of character exhibited by this man in the Gospel. What, then, are we to say?

Maximus finds his opening for a new christological space in the way that he frames the question. "Whom do you understand as the subject," or the one doing the praying here? Is it "the man who is just like us?" Or is the voice here "the eternal divinity of the Only-Begotten?" It is neither, Maximus says—at least neither at the prayer's beginning. It is the human voice, clearly, since it is as human that Christ says everything we and his companions hear him say, but it is "not the man just like us but the man we consider as Savior."[17] Christ is fully human, and yet, Maximus is saying, there is something unique about his humanity. He is the one who can be human without this humanity putting him at odds with, or in competition with, God. In praying as a human savior, Jesus demonstrates something new and surprising about the human will, something that seems to have been ruled out from the way that Adam and Even recrafted the human will: it can come to expression in a way that "absolutely precludes opposition and instead demonstrates harmony" between the human and the divine.[18] This harmony is what saves us, the opening of a possibility that all humans, even all creation, might find ourselves in the prayer "Not what I will but what you will." The harmony, we might say, is the analogical interval between God and creatures coming into its own.

Again, jumping straight to the paradoxical "but he was also God" claim will not quite do here. The will acting in Jesus' prayer is not identical to the divine will, since obviously it negates itself in favor of the divine. But it negates itself only as a new discovery of itself, since even to pray this is to will it. There is a kind of understood elliptical beginning here: *I will* "not what I will but what you will." Jesus is, we might say, losing himself in order to find himself, and to find himself in God. This is what Paul and Irenaeus call his recapitulation of the human form: he remakes the human as the one capable of a non-opposition to God.[19] He is the second Adam, the human who performs humanity as a noncompetitive agent in relation to the acting God. Thus what the human Christ wills repeats in nonidentical fashion what the divine Logos wills from all eternity: the loving companionship of the like-minded Father.

In this way the one like us but "more" than us (as harmony is "more" than discord) is the one in which we can find our hope. The one, moreover, in which we can hope for the recapitulation of all created things. Jesus' excessive humanity is the rearticulation of all creation, and so it is our salvation.

The Deifying God

The Christian's account of Christ could stop at this. This savior would gather all the hope of creation and refashion it as God made it and intended it, providing a model for existential agency in which all could live and move and find our being. This Christ would stand as the embodiment of the Wisdom of God that "reaches mightily from one end of the earth to the other" (Wis 8:1). He would be the first born among all created things, the one made in the beginning of God's ways and works (Prov 8:22-31).

In order to see why this is insufficient, we must note a certain pressure on the doctrine of Christ's person, a pressure to go beyond this already dizzyingly expansive account of Mary's son and say something that catapults him into a mystery that stretches theological language nearly to the breaking point. The Council of Nicaea, inventing and adapting a novel vocabulary for this most basic of Christian questions, proclaims him to be *homoousian to patri*: "of the same substance as the Father."

If salvation were all that I have said and nothing more, a refashioning of the calling and journey back to creaturehood of all that is, the Nicene account of Jesus as divine would be entirely unnecessary. But the biblical account of salvation exceeds this definition. Christian salvation itself is the pressure on the doctrine to go beyond the "first among creatures" Christology and make the bold and outlandish claim that this particular human is also God.

The excessive pressure I am speaking of originates in the startling and excessive acts of intimacy that characterize God's redemptive work among the tribes of Israel. "Israel's story opens to all people . . . the drama of peoples in the presence of the living God."[20]

There is a pattern to notice here, and one that challenges any prima facie notion of what the word "God" means. When humans fall into sin and violence, God enters into dialogue with them. When violence threatens to overwhelm the whole of creation, God befriends one family so intensely as to make this friendship itself the site of a world saving act. God then chooses one aging couple to birth a family that God will connect Godself to through all ages, and through this marriage-like covenant God will see that all the world is blessed (Gen 12:1-3). When later generations act unfaithfully within this covenant, God tells a prophet to bring a prostitute into his home, marry her, sleep with her, and then feel the pain of watching her go out to work each night. Then he will know what it is to be the God who "loves the people of Israel, though they turn to other gods" (Hos 3:1).

This is a God who follows God's beloved creation, who does not hover aloft from the chaos and contingencies of creation, becomes vulnerable to the actions and shifting desires of his people.[21] Jesus is God's agency cut according to this same pattern: "you have found favor with God," Gabriel tells a poor unwed mother-to-be (Luke 1:30-31). "I have called you friends," (John 15:15) Jesus tells a collection of fishermen, tax collectors, and prostitutes. His restoration of Simon Peter after the latter's abandonment of him and infidelity to the promises he had so recently made is not a proclamation of absolution, but a vulnerable and harrowing plea for love, as difficult to bear as the confrontations between Hosea and Gomer: "Simon son of John, do you love me?" (John 21:16).

Origen of Alexandria works with the image of the Beloved Disciple reclining on Jesus' breast to suggest something about the divine intimacy we enjoy in Jesus' company: "But if we incline on the bosom of the Word made flesh and are able to follow Him when He ascends the lofty mountain, we shall say, 'We saw his glory.'"[22] To lean as this disciple leaned, or to go with Peter and others up Mount Tabor, is to lean in on divine glory, to lean in on the human whose very presence changes us, so that we are, like Moses, covered in the shine of the divine nature.

The point here to keep in mind is that the declaration of Christ's divinity is not so much a foundational doctrine of Christian theology as it is a conclusion drawn from the way Christians give an account of their encounter with Christ.[23] Early Christians took The Wisdom of Solomon, referenced above, to be a key source for Christology, and they interpreted the female personification of Wisdom as a figure of Christ. One of these passages imagines wisdom as a resident within the souls of men and women: "in every generation she passes into holy souls and makes them friends of God" (7:27). These Christian exegetes found this to be a fitting description of their experience as Jesus' disciples, since a relationship to him gave them the experience of friendship with God. Like the gift language we saw Augustine using for the Holy Spirit, Wisdom configures the connection of God to creation as one of a circulating gift passed along to us: "But I perceived that I would not possess wisdom unless God gave her to me—and it was a mark of insight to know whose gift she was . . ." (Wis 8:21). As in the writer's experience of wisdom, so in the disciple's experience of Christ: in her/him, I experience myself as one in love with the one whom God loves, desired by the one whom God desires, and thus I receive the gift of love and friendship with God as well.

If I am "called friend" by Christ, and experience in this friendship the gift of divine friendship, then I am prepared to say that in Christ, God loves me not simply as the creature I am, but as if I were God.[24] To find myself moved by the Spirit who moves in the risen Christ is to find myself not simply enjoying God's graces from a position near the divine being, but to be "hidden with Christ in God" (Col 3:3). In this way the encounter moves us along our vocational trajectory, from God-imaging toward godlikeness.

Returning to Maximus' interpretation of the garden prayer, we find the real mystery is that the one who prays this aching petition for mercy is, after all, none other than the God of Israel, having followed us across the analogical interval between eternity and time so that the Logos could pray the divine prayer in a human, saving way: "not my will, but yours be done." The technical language that the later ecumenical councils adapted for the purpose of interpreting "God with us" as Jesus' proper name is "Hypostatic Union." Jesus is the Second Person of the Trinity, who lives a full and undiluted human life in unified harmony with his own eternal existence. When he feels sorrow, when he grows tired, when he asks for Simon's love, this is the action of the one eternal Son, behaving in time in a way surprisingly consistent with the act of God in all eternity.[25]

This union is inevitably one that will change our understandings of the very words "God" and "human." So the apostle tells us that being "in the form of God" is not, surprisingly, incompatible with being in "the form of a slave" (Phil 2:6-7).[26] Origen, in fact, affirms that it is exactly the act of self-emptying that shows Jesus to be godlike.[27] At the same time the human form does not "stay put" either, since now to be truly human is to be godlike, harmonizing with the divine will as if we were God's eternal friend. Again, the "only" stable distinction between God and every other being is that God's existence is identical with God's essence from all eternity, while creation's existence is a distinct gift added to little analogies of divine essence. And the nearer we draw to Christ, the more ambiguous this analogical frontier becomes. So Gregory of Nyssa, imagining himself to be standing with the apostles in Acts as Jesus ascends, says that "all those characteristics here seen to be associated with what is mortal have been transformed into the characteristics of the Godhead," so that "no distinction between them can be perceived; for whatever one can see of the Son is divinity, wisdom, power, holiness, and impassibility."[28] Recalling his life of companionship with Peter and Salome and the rest, his followers see only the acts of God done humanly, only the acts of a human done divinely. This is what it means to call Jesus Christ the God-human.

Thus one does not turn to Jesus to see what two natures lived in a single being look like; one turns to Jesus because the Spirit bears witness in us that in this man a human is life is lived in such a way that "whatever one can see" in him "is divinity, power, holiness, and impassibility." And if that Spirit is alive in us, as Paul notes, Jesus' remarkable deification will be ours as well.

The Love That Moves

In this way, the affirmation that Jesus' presence is deifying, or brings divine likeness to creatures, is also an affirmation that God's agency in the world is one, and Jesus on earth "work the works" of the one who sent him (John 9:4). He is the one who is eternally intimate with—the Beloved Son of—the Father. The surprising message of all of Scripture as Christians read it is that God's eternal simplicity in being and acts is not incompatible with a vulnerable temporal agency, mediated through the strange words and deeds of prophets and the wet tears and hot anger and healing touch of a Galilean rabbi.

When the pilgrim Dante finally comes through the mediation of the saints and the Virgin to the vision of God, his final wish is to know what it is like to look on the Second Person of the Trinity. As he fixes his eye on the Son, though, he sees a kind of "human-colored circle."

> The vision before him
> seemed in itself and in its own self-color
> to be depicted with man's very image.
> My eyes were totally absorbed in It.[29]

As he contemplates this vision of a human-colored Logos, he wonders how it is that "our image fuses" with the eternal Person, if in fact that Person is not two beings but only one. If he is looking at a human face, like his own, how can he be looking at the face of God? He finds, in the closing lines of the entire poem, that the description of the vision is too much for his pen, but he can only describe the sensation: it is as though his very desire to see the humanity of God at one with the Logos is itself caught up in the vision, and what he sees is his own will and desire "turned, Like a balanced wheel rotated evenly,/ By the Love that moves the sun and the other stars."[30]

What Dante discovers is that the very question of who Jesus is can only ever come back on us, and ask us what we think it is to be human, and how it is we live and plan to live this humanity; and again what it is we think it is to be God, and where exactly we think the lines of demarcation are. We have only ever spoken well of the ancient rabbi Jesus when we have found our own desires moving toward him, and so moving toward God, so that, with all the surprise and wonder of the Bethlehem shepherds, we can say, "surely God is with us."

7

SIN

Failing to Imagine

Cleopas and his companion leave Jerusalem and begin the long Emmaus walk in grief, having lost hope in the redemption of Israel by their God. "Our chief priests and leaders handed him over to be condemned to death and crucified him. But we had hoped that he was the one to redeem Israel" (Luke 24:20-21). Or perhaps they have lost hope in their fallen companion as the means of that redemption. Either way the good news of their creation that his life and death call them back to, that they are created as little pneuma-filled logoi and called into being by the Father of all things, is lost to them.

Noting our tendency to move away from the source of our being, Augustine writes, "If our will moves away from you, who are, toward anything which less truly is, that movement is transgression and sin."[1] Sometimes this wayward movement takes the form of "sheer despair" in that we lack "the courage to reach up to" God. On other occasions it takes the form of "pride in our own worth," which keeps us from seeing ourselves as those in need of communication with God.[2] Often the two motives are mixed.

Indeed, in many (most?) instances there is a measure of ignorance that seasons our errancy.[3] There is an expansiveness to Augustine's definition—a willed movement away from the God who *is* and "toward anything which less truly is"—that we may miss, if we assume that the operation of the will makes sin a matter of deliberate movement away from God.

Suppose I have a friend who has a gift to give me. I might will myself "away from" that friend and that gift for me for a variety of reasons. I may, indeed, know that she is there and is waiting to share her gift with me, and I may choose to avoid her in order to hurt her; more likely, though, I will move away from her for some other reason. Perhaps I do not know that she is back in town, or that she has a gift for me. Or perhaps I have forgotten how to find her. Maybe I know where she is, and that she has a gift, but I do not feel worthy of the gift, or her friendship. In all these cases, my will "moves away from" her, toward something else, though to understand how or why this happens would involve a deeper analysis of what I know, what I think I know, and what I do not know about our relationship.

For this reason, though we are perhaps accustomed to associating sin with moral failures and the guilt that accompanies them, here we should notice a blindness and a deafness—"their eyes were kept from recognizing him," they are unable to take in "all that the prophets have declared"—that characterizes the movement of their wills away from Jesus.[4] Cleopas and his partner are moving away, both literally and theologically, from the incarnate Logos, in that they are no longer looking for redemption in him. By Augustine's definition this is sin, but it is certainly not the sort of sin that involves deliberation or moral culpability. Moving away from the Logos, like moving away from a gift-bearing friend, is something a creature might do for a complex variety of reasons. Common to all of them is not a knowing transgression or guilt but something else, something deeper, that has us sharing and repeating patterns that are harmful to us and to each other. In our movements we are not quite, somehow, the creatures we are made and called to be.

This "something deeper" is the place where will and knowledge intersect with the overall vision of one's place in the world, an intersection we could identify as imagination. The hopelessness that the Emmaus companions are experiencing stems from an inability to imagine themselves called toward the act of redemption that they have just witnessed in Jerusalem.

Sin is first of all a failure of the imagination. We do not or cannot or will not imagine ourselves as the created recipients of Word and Spirit, as Trinitarian analogies whose very appearance in being implies that we are loved by God as if we were the Logos itself. This failure to imagine might be one that shows up first in our actions—my refusal to tell the truth, for instance, reveals a failure to meet the world truthfully, though I may not be fully aware of this failure until I begin to analyze my lie. We may fail to imagine ourselves rightly because something we think we know (who Jesus is, what God's redemption ought to look like) is interfering with our ability to live within a new and different reality. It may be for more nefarious reasons. Whatever the case, the failure seems ubiquitous, as the Christian story is of a Logos who "came to those things that were his own, and they who were his own did not accept him" (John 1:11, Hart translation).

Original Sin

This failure of the imagination is first of all one that comes to us as a structural and oppressive power. It is asking a great deal of creatures like us, composed of being and limit, creatures "who come in a median size," to live with the constant imagination of ourselves as God's beloved analogies. This is especially true if the most obvious thing about the world is the limit itself, and not the analogical interval that holds it in place.

Here we must tread carefully. Human limitation itself is not sin, but merely "a deficient presence of the divine"[5] that is appropriate to the creatures God made us to be: creatures made in God's image and called, through time and the long and slow process of friendship formation, to be like God. Distraction, fatigue, shifts of mood: such complexities are part of a "dynamic openness"[6] that characterizes us as the creatures we are, and makes the Godward journey possible.

Human limit is not sin, and so we can see sin as invasive to a creation that precedes it. Indeed, this conclusion is theologically unavoidable. If we began by saying that the lack of charity and hope that seems to characterize the world of humans and nonhumans alike were the ultimate truth of things, then charity itself would become unnatural, the futile attempt of a handful of optimistic beings to make the cosmos into something it is not. The Christian doctrine of sin is, in the first place, a hopeful doctrine in that it refuses this conclusion, and affirms that the world is not what it seems: it is good, and the power of charity is in fact on the side of creation, nature even, not opposed to it.

The first thing, then, is to give an account of the eclipse of our true nature as "partakers of the divine nature," the eclipse which reverses things and makes the presence of hope and charity appear to be an intrusion into the world order. The Bible explicates the distance between the "very good" world of God's making and the world of our experience by means of a rebellion narrative—a rebellion that is at one and the same time everyone's story and no one's story. The Adam, as Saint Paul puts it, is a figural type (Rom 5:14) in whom all humans perform the story of willing something besides a periperformative response to God's invitation to be. This is not a figure that we are free to refute: all are under its power (3:9), even those who do not, like the Genesis archetypes, willingly talk themselves out of obeying their Creator (5:14). Indeed, Christian readings of the Bible's apocalyptic literature find that the archetypal rebellion transcends humans, as the heavens too are filled with warfare. "The great dragon was thrown down, that ancient serpent, who is called the Devil and Satan, the deceiver of the whole world—he was thrown down to the earth, and his angels were thrown down with him" (Rev 12:9). If angels who are created to praise God and tend to the causality of the earth rebel, then their rebellion will certainly cast a shadow over the "very good"-ness of the earth as well.[7] The earth is deceived by the heavens; our failure to understand ourselves as called into being by God's compassionate invitation is tangled up in a rebellion of the cosmos that goes far beyond human will.

For Paul especially, sin is a power that has overtaken the humans of the world as well as "creation itself" (8:21).[8] And this is true prior to any question of what we know. We awaken, you might say, in a commonwealth that has been in rebellion so long that its citizens have forgotten that they are, in fact, in rebellion. In the figural analysis of Saint Augustine, we are the inhabitants of the city Cain built. It is now Abel's home, the City of God, which is unstable and nomadic in the world. Cain's city is the dwelling of "a nature vitiated by sin," a vitiation stemming from his violent act after Abel's sacrifice is accepted. East of Eden, we come into the world as if there never were a garden, as if survival were a competition of limited goods, as if violence against other creatures were a fitting response to our own fears.[9] This vitiated natural origin becomes a kind of new—and false—origin of creation, separate from and counter to our origin in the divine invitation. Thus is created life structured within what Augustine names "original" sin.

Surely, though, it is a step too far to call these citizens of Cain's city, as the author of Ephesians puts it, a people "having no hope and without God in the world" (2:12)? Do not even a heaven and an earth that have departed from God's invitation remain within a creation whose hope is "with God," in some sense? Said differently, would it not be more appropriate to identify the problem of sin as epistemological rather than ontological, as a failure in the order of knowing that does not reach the level of being? After all, Cleopas *has* a hope: the hopefulness of the world exists, and his hopelessness stems from a lack of consciousness of what this hope *is*.

In fact, the very question of "remaining within creation" is what is at stake here. Athanasius sorts through the twisted logic of universally captivating sin by noting that if we are made from nothing, and drawn toward being by God's grace alone, then any "missing" of that invitation can only be a return to the nothing from which we came: "It followed naturally that when men were bereft of the knowledge of God and were turned back to what was not (for what is evil is not, but what is good is) they should, since they derive their being from God who is, be everlastingly bereft even of being . . .

In other words, that they should be disintegrated and abide in death and corruption."[10] The power of sin is the inescapability of this de-creation:[11] to move from "the God who is" is to move away from being itself.

Called into being by the loving invitation of God, we come to be in the midst of a universal pattern of conversion toward nothingness. Athanasius is working here with Paul's connection of sin to death: our hopelessness before the figural hold that sin has on us is most like our hopelessness to escape from the hold that death has over life. Indeed, this is hardly for him a metaphor: "turning back to what is not" is a fitting description for both dying and for sinning.[12]

There is a further way in which to be without hope is to be "without God in the world." Hebrew Bible scholar Jacob Milgrom has pointed out how the key to the damage that sin does in the Pentateuch is not in the first place in the impurity that affects a person or even a community, but rather the threat of the contamination of the place where Israel worships.[13] "You shall keep my sabbaths and reverence my sanctuary: I am YHWH" (Lev 26:2; YHWH is used here instead of "the LORD"). The entire logic, in fact, of mitzvah regarding separation, including everything from the farming practices to the kosher laws to the sending out of the goat into the wilderness, is that of ritual performance of the separation of sins from the place of worship: "Thus you shall keep the people of Israel separate from their uncleanness, so that they do not die in their uncleanness by defiling my tabernacle that is in their midst" (15:31). There is a crisis playing out in these passages from Leviticus. A holy God can only be in the company of a creation that is "holy as I am holy." Said differently, the good God can only recognize Godself in a creation that is very good, and this goodness is precisely what is "vitiated by sin." I will return in the following chapter to the question of worship in a sinful world. Here I simply wish to point to the crisis as a whole. Sin plays out in what Karl Barth calls the "impossibility possibility"[14] of a creation that does not know and desire the company of its Creator, and has the damning consequence of a Creator who ceases to recognize that creation as God's own.

Theologians tend to be consistent—frustratingly consistent, perhaps—in refusing to give a "reason" for this cosmic, archetypal, and ontologically devastating rebellion. This seems to me to be appropriate, given what Athanasius says about creation as God's Logos refracted into temporality. There is only a "logic" to goodness, to holiness, to the analogical interval, whereas the figural rebellion of all things simply lacks sense. We might imagine God, as the divine parent, demanding that Cain "give one good reason" why he killed his brother, and obviously the only correct answer is that there is none.

Sin has its own twisted logic, but not a sound logic. Cain "reasons" from his experience in the family prayers that if he simply annihilates the competition he will receive the blessing he missed out on. Any explanation of his act that gave it logos therefore would turn it into a fitting event, a little word that belongs in creation. Sin is rather, in itself, the perversion of the divine logic of the heavens and earth.

Evil

We saw above that Athanasius refers to evil as "what is not." This is not simply to say that the lack of being is the same as evil, since as I have noted the goodness of creation is itself mediated through these very limits. Connected to the twisted logic of sin, it becomes possible to "turn to what is not," to treat these limits as if they were not the "edges" of creaturely analogs for divine fullness, but rather something in themselves. When this happens, the turning itself becomes a "fatal, destructive force in creation."[15]

The limitations are not evil, but the battle against them gives rise to this destructive force. Mary Shelley's *Frankenstein* unfolds a battle against human limitation through the ambition of a doctor who seeks to create life. The story has a surprise for us, though, when the doctor's repulsion of the "monster" he has created unwittingly subverts itself. The creature learns to read and finds a copy of Milton's *Paradise Lost*, which in turn leads him to the contemplation of his own creation. "I sickened as I read . . . God, in pity, made man beautiful and alluring, after his own image; but my form is a filthy type of yours, more horrid even from the very resemblance."[16] The creature who, he tells Victor, "ought to be thy Adam"[17] is instead coldly rejected, and the reader begins to question which is the true monster: the half-made creature or the compassionless creator?

In fact, Victor seems at least partially aware of his own descent into monstrosity, when he admits that he is "seized by remorse and the sense of guilt, which hurried me away to a hell of intense tortures such as no language can describe."[18] Returning to the Genesis story, we might say that Victor was made to be godlike in a human way, and seeks instead to be godlike in a divine way. He is bound by the figures of Adam and Eve here, who attempt to become godlike not through the daily walks in the garden with their Creator, but through the immediacy of an inhuman intervention—a supernatural apple, a chemical composition. The desire to be godlike is not the source of evil, nor are the natural limitations of our bodies and minds. Rather, our turning against these limits as if they were enemies to be overcome twists our own action toward monstrous outcomes.

Shelley references in her subtitle the Prometheus myth, the account of the titan who steals fire from the gods of Olympus, and there is a generative ambiguity to the reference. Is Victor Prometheus, as we usually assume, transgressing on the life-giving hearth that only rightly belongs to the gods? Alternatively, if Victor's creature has brought up the very question as to what sort of god his creator is, another possibility presents itself: Victor is the ungenerous divinity who, so different from Adam's creator, refuses to make a gift of fire to his creation.[19] Or, again, perhaps the two readings come together in that Victor has made himself into a "modern Prometheus" by his very assumption that his own creator is an ungenerous divinity analogous to himself, and one from whom fire must be stolen. He has imprisoned himself in a hell of his own making. Dr. Frankenstein has made a creator in his own image, and in doing so confined himself to a hell analogous to the one his own creature dwells within.

The evil that takes over the stories here—Adam and Eve's story, Victor's story—is, again, of a turn toward "nothing," since there is no "created thing" that, in its own essence, is evil. "Everything that exists is good, then; and so evil, the source of which I was seeking, cannot be a substance, because if it were, it would be good."[20] Augustine's conclusion on the metaphysics of evil does not preclude the terrifying energy of this nothingness, though, any more than Cain's invention of a god with insufficient resources for blessing precludes the horrors of his fratricide or of the ethics that follow it within the city he founds.[21] Creation, as I noted in an earlier chapter, is a temporal actualization of essences discerned in the eternal mind of God. Evil then is something like an actualization of non-essences, "actualized nothing,"[22] the spinning into false reality of all that God does *not* discern in the Logos. Cain and Victor discern a god who is not real, and they act accordingly. If we know what a thing is because of what it does, evil presents us with the terrifying intrusion of an activity within creation with no essence behind it, which then places creation under its power.[23] Like Othello's suspicion of falsehood in Desdemona, such insubstantiality can unleash an actuality of violence and tragedy that leave us stunned with horror.

Social Sins

Sin is a failure on the part of creation to receive itself as God's beloved. The twisted logic of this failure is so devastating as to render the situation irreparable—creation has sought to unmake itself, and this can only result in a generalized and ontologically binding power within creation that sets itself up as a counter origin. Sin gives birth to death, and death structures life in a way that gives birth to more sin. Being without substance makes it no less vicious; evil attacks being something like the way an ulcer attacks the lining of the stomach. Evil is the name we give the vicious false reality of actions that tear through the world from out of these gaping ontological ulcers.

But sin, as the New and Old Testaments present it, is not only a power that enslaves. It is also a responsiveness or nonresponsiveness on the part of creatures, with an element of deliberation, or intention, involved.[24] To live without hope and without God in the world, for the apostle, is to fail to imagine life in the Spirit, and so act in ways that reveal this failure (Gal 5:16-21). Called to generosity, I can, like Cain, choose envy. In doing so I am not only under the power of sin: I am actively sinning.

As Ellacuría explains, "All created things are a limited way of being God, and the human being in particular is a small God." Humans are thus characterized by what he calls an active openness, a dynamism toward godlikeness. The limit and openness work in tandem, as I have suggested, allowing creatures to grow and change in healthy, holy ways. "When this dynamism remains limited merely because at a certain level of creaturehood no more of the self-divine is offered, it is not yet sin but only a deficient presence of the divine . . ." Our movements toward and in tandem with God are not just limited, though, by natural deficiencies. They can also be limited by a "deliberate negation in the historical process—whether personal or social—that by absolutizing the limit embeds and even explicitly negates the dynamism of the Trinitarian life (although it cannot destroy it)." In such cases "we have a case of sin in its formal sense."[25] By formal Ellacuría means here sin in its theological shape, regardless of the particular act: sin as deliberate counter-offensives within history against the invitation from the Triune God to receive the witness of the Spirit and take on the adopted likeness of the Son.

Calling sin deliberate can, but does not necessarily, imply a positive choice to "negate the dynamism of the Trinity." Sin is a habit, and habits have a way of taking over our willed agency. Ellacuría's category of social sin is helpful here. Frederick Douglass, in an account of his escape from slavery in nineteenth-century Maryland, tells of his own conversion to Christianity as a teenager in the midst of the Second Great Awakening, and how he makes use of his clandestine literacy to hold "Sabbath School" classes for young slave children. He then tells of his excitement when his master too attends a tent revival and "got religion,"[26] and his hope that Master Thomas would either free his slaves or at least treat them more humanely than he had before. Thomas becomes a great pillar of the revivalist fervor and of the local Methodist Church. Douglass' excitement ends, however, when Thomas interrupts a meeting of Douglass' Sabbath School with a group of slave holders armed with clubs. In the midst of a reading about "the Gospel of the Son of God," the masters drive them out and threaten to do worse if they carry on studying the Bible. Douglass's analysis, for once, is taciturn: "The reader will not be surprised when I say that the breaking up of my Sabbath school by these class leaders and professedly holy men did not serve to strengthen my religious convictions."[27]

This episode in American Christianity, made famous by the future fame of the author, is iconic of a broad pattern of social injustice within the churches of the South, injustices repeated in different ways (as Douglass was always quick to note) in the North. If we recall Augustine's definition above, sin as "a will that moves away from you who are," that is, God, "toward anything which less truly is," or Ellacuría's as explicit negation of "the dynamism of the Trinitarian life," we will find that there is plenty of negation here to go around. Master Thomas certainly lacks the imagination to see Frederick and the others as more than units of labor, and therefore as fitting recipients of "the Gospel of the Son of God." But the sin goes beyond a personal deliberate choice, since the Methodists and revivalists among whom Thomas had his conversation failed—and perhaps feared—to make connections between the Bible they preached and the barbaric economy they relied on. Douglass himself, quite reasonably, never truly trusts Christians again, but in this case he experiences his own movement away from "the dynamism of the Trinitarian life," finding community among activists who take a wide berth around religious language. Thomas, we could say, participates deliberately in a social failure of theological imagination; Douglass is an unwilling participant whose theological imagination never recovers from its wounds.

I could cite many other examples of social sin, patterns of life that we unknowingly, half-knowingly, or woundedly follow because we are unable to imagine the triune shape of our historical existence. In the twenty-first century many citizens around the world are turning to nationalism and away from immigrants and refugees out of a fear of a scarcity of resources. The good of economic security seems to be necessarily pitted against the good of hospitality, and our failure to imagine both together leads us into a social pattern of life that undercuts the passionate utterance of the Trinity. Western nations, similarly, are stuck in a rhetorical failure around abortion, where the vulnerability of a pregnant woman seems to be locked in a competitive struggle against the vulnerability of an unborn child, and our inability to imagine a creative space in which neither vulnerability needs sacrificing implies that all must choose sides. In this and other ways, we find ourselves locked in social habits that limit our ability to name ourselves as periperformances of the divine being.

Personal Sins

Ellacuría suggests that along with social sins there are also personal sins, and here we come to deliberate actions performed by willing human agents, those actions that Augustine classifies as shaped by despair and/or pride. Even here, though, we would do well to maintain connections to the social. The personal habits that we fall into are often at least partially socially formed; consider for instance the way that an abusive parent might be responding to her or his own formation within an abusive economic or social environment. Douglass tells, in a subsequent writing, of his former master's slow contrition for his role in Douglass' life, and even of a reconciliation as Thomas lies on his deathbed.[28] Thus the slave master's participation in a *social* failure of theological imagination became the site of his confession of *personal* sin to one of those he had sinned against. A failure of the theological imagination does not have to be private in order to become the subject of a personal responsibility-taking.

Douglass' story thus provides us with a good example of sin as both a social and a personal disease, and helps us see also how the guilt the Bible associates with sin is less about a debilitating feeling than about a naming and taking of responsibility even for a sin that exceeds our own deliberation. In the Bible a sinner is far from the worst thing one can be. To call oneself a sinner, or as the prophet puts it "a man of unclean lips" (Isa 6:5), is not an act of self-pity or degradation, but rather a confession. The Gospels describe Jesus as constantly sharing the company and table of sinners, and so confounding those who have spent their lives resisting not so much sinful habits as public identification as a sinner. "All who saw it began to grumble and said, 'He has gone to be the guest of one who is a sinner'" (Luke 19:7). Sin is personal not because a person sins alone, but because a person "gets" to identify as a sinner, and so as a companion of Jesus.

The Gospels associate sinfulness with various kinds of human depravity that make up the very focus of his presence in Palestine. Jesus comes to share tables and exchange words of companionship with the poor, the blind, the sick, the captives, the tax collectors and prostitutes—all forms of life, as Augustine might have put it, that could in various ways move one's will away from a participation in the divine nature. A world made out of God's passionate utterance has lost itself in an economy centered on the collection of taxes, the prostitution of bodies, and the alienation of the sick. The way to miss out on his companionship is, Jesus emphatically states, to proclaim one's health or one's righteousness, and thereby to refuse to be the sinner that God comes to earth to save (Luke 5:31-32).

Of course, being a confessing sinner is something different from being one who, as Paul puts it, goes on sinning (Rom 6:1). Personal sins are those acts of conscious creatures that lean toward the impatient distrust of Adam and Eve, and the fear of Cain that there will not be enough blessing to go around if he does not eliminate his rival. These acts, in other words, respond to the rewritten origin of Cain's city rather than our true origin in God's garden. Particular namings of sins, like the ones that Paul calls "obvious" in Galatians 5, are not primarily lists of behavior that offend or disgust or anger us, or even behaviors that cause harm, but first of all the discernment of those actions that treat ourselves and the creatures with whom we share the world as if God did not create us in the divine image and call us to God's likeness. Augustine, for instance, calls lying a sliding toward nonbeing, thus emphasizing the way that our actions can align with the nonsensical trajectory of de-creation. "By withdrawing from what is, they slide away toward what is not."[29] To name sins is to keep this theological framework close at hand, so that we remind ourselves and one another that we were not made for citizenship in Cain's city, but for trust in God's abundant blessing.

Again, though, the irony runs deep here. To commit a sin is not to be a sinner, in the New Testament idiom, but rather to deny, at least momentarily, that there is anything wrong with human life the way we have inherited it. It is to act in a way that reimagines a world that does not come to be out of God's passionate utterance. A landlady overcharges her tenants because she can, and because her gain and the welfare of her tenants are a competition that she must win: the one who has met the God who puts a mark on Cain and eats with tax collectors is prepared to call this a sin, but the one who persists in these acts carries on as if there is no resurrection, no grace beyond a competitive life framed by death and loss, and thus no sin. This is to live as one "having no hope and without God in the world."

Awakening to sin means opening one's eyes to the way that what seems to be basic and true about the world—life ends in death, kindness and generosity and faithfulness must submit finally to competition for limited resources—is in fact a false origin.[30] It is, also, to awaken to the way that I myself—personally—have been complicit with a general failure—ontological, social—to imagine the world as it most truly is, as a response to God's loving invitation to be. This is why the truth of creation must first break through the false origin if it is to make it all the way to our ears; the appearance of the Logos and witness-bearing Spirit must come to us as an encounter with one risen from the hopelessness of the grave.

8

SACRIFICE

Strange and Necessary

At first, it was just a death. A violent execution, a tragic loss, but nothing like a sacrifice.

At the center of the radical reframing of reality that occurs in Luke 24 are the words of the stranger that first startle the disciples out of their grief by reframing the execution they have just witnessed. Having just watched the violent death of the one they "had hoped . . . was the one to redeem Israel," they then hear this death described as the secret heart of their ancient faith.

> "Oh, how foolish you are, and how slow of heart to believe all that the prophets have declared! Was it not necessary that the Messiah should suffer these things and then enter into his glory?" Then, beginning with Moses and all the prophets, he interpreted to them the things about himself in all the scriptures. (Luke 24:25-27)

There is a deep connection, as yet not explicated in this text, between the sufferings of Jesus as God's anointed one and God's work of salvation, here described as culminating in the entrance into glory. The challenge of this connection is difficult to overstate: what place can a violent death have in the midst of a religious understanding of reality centered on a loving God's care for the world? Reviewing what I have said above: if God is a Trinity of eternal Persons who creates a world out of an excess of love, who calls the world good and goes on seeking fellowship with the beings of the world through the rebellion of the heavens and the earth, who sends the Spirit to move the hearts of all created things toward our creator, who comes as the creating Word to encounter and recreate God's own creation, what theological sense can we make of the violent death of Jesus on the cross?

The term "necessary" in the passage is one of the places where we may, at this point in our theological journey, find ourselves lost. Is anything necessary for God? Is Jesus here suggesting that there is no other way that God could have handled the multilayered problem of sin, than with the obscure violence of the cross?

We can think of necessity, though, in different ways, and here I suggest that Jesus is using the term less in a metaphysical sense—where it contrasts with "contingency"—than in an aesthetic sense, where its contrasts might be words like "inappropriate" or "unfitting." Thomas Aquinas, referring to these words from the Emmaus story, tells us that that there is a fittingness to the death of Jesus on the cross, in that here God acts in a way that is consistent—though to be sure unexpectedly so—with the divine activity throughout God's covenantal relation with Israel and, through and beyond Israel, in God's dealing with all creation. In this sense the necessity of the cross is something like the necessity of a particular ending to a novel: no one compelled the author to end the book the way that she did, but the ending itself is so appropriate as to compel the response, *yes, of course it had to turn out that way in the end.*[1] God's "determination regarding the Passion of Christ, foretold in the Scriptures and prefigured in the observances of the Old Testament, had to be fulfilled."[2]

In this chapter I will explore this aesthetic necessity and attempt to give an account of the strange death of Christ as the fitting means of creation's saving. We might imagine our Emmaus friends, talking things over on the long walk back to Jerusalem, and rehearsing for themselves the exegesis that Jesus offered on the same path hours before. Though the shock of the cross and the heartbreak of their loss has not left them, there is perhaps a moment when they nod and say *yes, of course it had to turn out that way in the end.*

Sacrifice in Israel

To talk of salvation is to assume the need for what gamers call a saving throw, and we now have seen this need take place in the triple contagion of what the Bible calls sin: ontologically binding, socially and personally habit-forming. The problem of sin is not first of all that a moral flaw makes us unacceptable to God, but instead that our movement away from God is not something that a freedom-granting God is willing to override. In the imagery of Genesis, God comes looking for us to pass the evening in the Garden, and we are hiding. In the imagery of Leviticus, God invites us for a Sabbath day's worship in the tabernacle, and we make the space inhospitable to a holy God.

At this point in the Bible's narrative of human origins, anything that follows must be seen as grace, or God's surprising response to our desire to be out of God's company. Logically, the story could simply end (leaving no one to write it down or read it later!): God created a world for loving exchange, God's companions in heaven and on earth tried to be something other than what they were created for, and so they ceased to be at all. That God keeps looking and keeps speaking to creatures who are actively attempting to unmake themselves reveals something about the stubborn love of the God of the Bible.

"You came down to earth to save Adam, and not finding him on earth, Lord, You descended into Hades to seek him," says the Lamentations on Great Saturday from the Orthodox liturgy.[3] Hades is the Hebrew name for "place of the dead," and we already have a hint of this in the opening of Genesis 4, immediately following the exile from the Garden. Cain and Abel bring offerings to God, fruit tilled in their toil from the ground, and the fatty portions of a ram or sheep from the flocks. Before we even get to Cain's violent act, we should note the remarkable grace implied by the new cult of a post-Edenic world. The curse of toil and the mortality brought on by the distance of humans from the tree of life have now become something surprising: toil and death have become ways of praying to the God of the garden. Both are offerings to bring toward a newly restored, if deeply tragic, companionship with the Creator. It is as if the God of Scripture looks on the tragedy of a violent and rebellious creation, and decides that there is no way around sin and death, only through it. So Israel's God goes searching for the Adam, the Mother, among the creatures spiraling toward nothingness.

Genesis as a whole is the account of the God who follows the archetypal human out of Eden, who marks us for saving, and who begins to restore the goodness and holiness of God's originating idea. The pivotal moment comes in chapter 12, where the calling, separating, and blessing of creation refocuses, after the invasion of sin and death, into the calling, electing, and blessing of a people:

> Now the LORD said to Abram: "Go from your country and your kindred and your father's house to the land that I will show you. I will make of you a great nation, and I will bless you, and make your name great, so that you will be a blessing. I will bless those who bless you, and the one who curses you I will curse; and in you all the families of the earth shall be blessed." (12:1-3)

Soon the marking of Cain for protection in the land of Nod will develop anal-
ogously into the marking out a land and its people for covenantal blessing with
God: "And I will give to you, and to your offspring after you, the land where
you are now an alien . . . As for you . . . Every male among you shall be circum-
cised" (17:8-10). If the mark on Cain is the sign that God will not abandon
God's violent creation to its own demise, the mark of circumcision becomes a
ritual representation of this involvement of God in blessing-through-threat-of-
violence. The path of God outside Eden reaches to a terrifying height in the
calling of Abraham to slay his own son. Here the rebellious fratricide of Cain
crescendos into a commanded filicide, and the knife that threatens castration
hangs over his living and breathing offspring.[4] The substitution of a ram for
the son amounts to a revising of the sin of Cain, but, significantly, not a substitution that acts from a distance. The God of goodness and blessing has chosen
to become involved with, implicated in, the violent economy of Cain's city,
where the shedding of blood has become a way of life.

The deep irony, then, is that the curses and death, even the knives of violence, have now become a means of renewed fellowship with God. Joseph's
words to the brothers that cast him into slavery could serve as the thematic
response of God to violence, betrayal, sin, and death throughout Scripture:
though it all is bent on causing the greatest harm, "God intended it for good"
(Gen 50:20). So the sacrificial exchanges that the scribes write into their
prehistory in Genesis 4 thickens into a cult in the rest of Torah. If Eden is
a story of loss, Leviticus describes the various kinds of losses—the giving
away, shedding of blood, burning, consuming—that God transforms into
pathways of reconciliation. For Israel, the killing of an animal can become
a celebration of God's provision of a substitute sacrifice. Not that the goat is
sent out, or the ram or heifer is put to death, instead of the people, but rather
that the substitution becomes a new place for the people's involvement. They
are to God as this animal, the rites suggest, and their death can be as this
one, exiled and yet remaining in the assembly, placed on an altar and made
into smoke, yet smoke that drifts toward the heavens.[5]

The logic of Israel's sacrificial system is thus not that of an angry God in need
of appeasing or a greedy God prone to temptation by kitchen aromas. Rather,
sacrifice shows a God beyond need, who can nonetheless invite creatures to
involve themselves in their own overcoming of sin.[6] The logic of sacrifice in
this way responds to the logic of sin. Sin is the refusal of holy friendship with
the holy God, whether through pride, despair, blindness, or simply impatient
experimentation (could I manage my own holiness, become godlike, without

waiting and depending on God?). Further, if God has invited creation into being—"let there be . . ."—with this vocational call to holy godlikeness, then the refusal will erode the entire fabric, as we have seen. Worship, the name for the unthinkable communion of the infinite God and the finite creature, is impossible if the creature walks away. Israel's God does not force the creature to return, nor does God turn away; instead, God follows the beloved one out of the garden, and creates a sanctuary in the wilderness.

Sacrifice then is, as Irenaeus might have put it, already a recapitulation, or revised retelling, "of that disobedience which had occurred in connection with a tree."[7] If death is the logical result of the story of a creation that clings to its own means rather than to the God who gives us being, sacrifice is the holy-making way that God inhabits this end, and that God calls Israel to inhabit it too. The family who depends on agriculture will offer the best portion of it to a God who is beyond dependence or market exchange; the mad clinging to life that drives families and nations to violence will enter into a life of blessing with God by ending their own claim to immortality through a representative slaying of one of God's blessed creatures. A nomadic people terrified of not having food, water, and shelter to survive will spend an entire day, sundown to sundown, ritually reminding themselves that that they are not slaves forced to make bricks without straw, but a people called to become like the God whose work is finished, and very good.[8] In all of these recapitulations, a sanctuary threatened by the sinfulness of human worshipers will be ritually and sacrificially renewed as a place of holiness, not by divine declaration, but by the participation of these humans themselves in an economy that transcends the economy of Cain, one based in gifts of abundance rather than thefts of scarcity.[9]

There are freewill offerings, burnt offerings, offerings for purification and the atonement for sins. A regular morning offering takes shape as a kind of daily atonement (Exod 29:38-46), keeping Israel within the covenant until the annual Yom Kippur sacrifices. There is the offering commanded as a ritual remembrance of the exodus from Egypt, when the slaying of a lamb marks out the elect people as those willing to offer up their lives to the God whose holiness, surprisingly, does not stay insulated from the violence and wickedness of enslavement and torture. All of this eventually creates, both in the temple and in textual commentaries that sit at the center of Israel's cultic life, a thick culture of recognition: recognizing the different form of life called for now, by the Creating God, in a world governed by sin and death.[10]

The Universal Sacrifice

What is Israel to do, though, when the sins are against, rather than within, this cultic sacrificial system? If the altar for offerings is made profane, or the priests and people simply neglect the cult as a whole? If they refuse Sabbath, stop showing up for festivals? When the prophets challenge Israel's sacrificial system, such as when Jeremiah says that Israel may as well eat all the sacrifices they offer on the altar for all the good it will do them (7:21), it is not the case, as it was thought by an older generation of Protestant scholarship, that this shows an evolution of Israel's theology beyond the sacrificial cult—as if the ("Catholic") cult of priests was always intended to blossom into the hortatory ("Protestant") religion of the prophets.[11] Jeremiah is pointing rather to the risk in the entire system: if God's elect people repeat the impatient grasping of Adam and Eve, the fratricidal rage of Cain, the sins of those who live as though without God in the world, if they continue to observe the cult while they "oppress the alien, the orphan, and the widow, or shed innocent blood" or pursue destructive covenants with idols (7:6), this can only mean that "truth has perished" (7:28). The covenantal expressions of the temple are hollow and valueless.[12] Worse even, their claims to announce God's peace "when there is no peace," and to rely on God's wisdom while lying and cheating the vulnerable among them, makes God's wisdom itself into a lie (8:8-11).

This is a radical train of thought, but we can see rather easily how the prophet gets there: God has followed a sinful creation into exile and bound Godself irrevocably to Abraham's descendants as the surprising means by which all of creation will be saved from the end which has overtaken us. God has refused the path of uncreating, or (which amounts to the same thing) of intervening in such a way as to take over both ends of the covenant while ignoring the flaws and limits of Israel's response. Grace perfects, it does not destroy, replace, or override. If the Temple cult tells lies, then the God of this Temple tells lies. In that case there is no saving a world in ontological exile.

And so the prophet goes to extreme measures to warn the worshipers: "When people fall, do they not get up again?" (8:4). If God's elect people will return to the countercultural acts of offering themselves to God the sacrificial cult will once again do its work, and the nations will, as Isaiah puts it, stream to the light of this God. If not, they are not just sinning, they are refusing the system in which sins are named, truth is revealed, and lives are transformed into holy analogs of the holy God.

The crisis that Jeremiah names is the crisis of the world's salvation that God has tied to the faithfulness of Israel. His notion of a "law within them," written on Israel's hearts (31:31-34), initiates a response to this crisis with the hypothesis of a new covenantal connection. Other writings from the second temple period take up this idea as a transcendent sacrifice, a kind of cultic act beyond the confines of the temple and altar, though resonating deeply with the temple cult. So Isaiah imagines a servant of God whose very life might be a "an offering for sin" (53:10), one who could be like the lamb of Leviticus's sin offering, but could atone even for the sin of refusing true worship: YHWH "has laid on him the iniquity of us all'" (53:6). Later Eleazar, the martyr whose refusal to revoke Torah inspires the last great revolt of the Maccabees, asks God to make his own death a sacrifice for the whole of Judah. "Make my blood their purification, and take my life in exchange for theirs" (4 Macc 6:29).[13] In both cases, we have an alarming analog of the temple cult, mediated as it is through the death of a human being. This is a kind of meta-rite performed or imagined outside the temple, atoning potentially even for the meta-sin Jeremiah names, that of profaning the place where YHWH is named and from which YHWH's salvation proceeds.

In Maccabees, the tale of torture and execution of seven brothers takes shape as an echo to this radical purification rite: it is as if the tyrant king has "learned nothing from Eleazar" (4 Macc 9:5). The death of the martyr for all becomes a work provoking periperformative responses of loyalty, new habits of faithfulness, among the assembly. This connection allows us to begin to see the way that a theology of sacrifice coordinates to the problem of sin, a problem which the Bible names as dual: it is a power that controls, and it is a habit that deforms. Sacrifice, in turn, is a path of worship that both liberates and transforms. YHWH provides a cultic response that can make of sin and death something which the sinning and dying alone cannot make it, namely, an offering to God. The people who receive this gift can then "die into" this cult, by making a habit of Sabbath, of leaving some of the harvest at the edges of their fields, of bringing their grain and their rams and their birds, and eventually, at the extreme edges of Israel's cult, the habit of living out a participation in an undefined sacrificial offering that atones for those sins which make worship itself a sinful and death-dealing encounter. The people can live this way, and thus make the gift of the sacrifice a pattern for a new way of life.

All of these layers of Israel's cult become resources in asking the very basic question that the Emmaus disciples, and all the early witnesses to the crucifixion, ask. How was it "necessary that the Messiah should suffer these things"? How does the loss of hope presented in the execution of Jesus coordinate to a saving act of God?

The various responses throughout the New Testament take up the prescriptions for sacrifice, acts in which violence, death, and loss of blood is a pathway to forgiveness and holiness, and reimagine Christ's death through this layered imagery. So Paul says the cross is a kind of *kippur*, referencing the day when Aaron purified the sins from the holy place by shedding the blood of the bull and sending the goat out into the wilderness. The Epistle to the Hebrews adds to this the language of covenant sacrifices, the "day after day" offerings made by priests, which in Christ's death is made once for all (7:27). When John the Baptist calls Christ "the lamb of God who takes away the sin of the world" (John 1:29), he could be read as taking the imagery a step further: the lamb is the daily sin offering, but also the blood of the Passover lamb which takes away the social and political sin of Israel's enslavement.

All of this typology also passes through the universal sacrifice imagery of the late prophetic and intertestamental eras, where the radical idea of a human becoming a sin sacrifice is already reshaping Israel's imagination. Jesus can be to his cousin John the cultic lamb because the imagined servant in Isaiah was the lamb, and because Eleazer Maccabeus took on the sins of the people. Hebrews' argument about the once and for all nature of his atoning death relies on this apocalyptic imagery as well: now it becomes important that Jesus is both priest and sacrifice in a heavenly temple of which the one in Jerusalem is a "sketch," or we might say the earthly analog (Heb 9:23). Jesus' death "outside the city gate" (13:12) aligns him with Jeremiah's naming of the meta-sin of not keeping covenant with the temple and city, in this way making Jesus into a new Moses who brings a new covenant, one which does not abolish but fulfills the promise to Abraham.

Paul picks up on this imagery of universal sacrifice as well, especially as he considers the saving effects of this sacrifice as they stretch beyond Israel. Now even those not under the law can become participants in covenant through it (Rom 9-11). In this way the "suffering servant" of Isaiah moves the saving work of God beyond the threat of human division, and indeed beyond any threat imaginable. If Israel's covenantal relation to God is made good once and for all, preparing the way for their own salvation as well as for the healing of the nations, beyond the power of sin and death to corrupt it, then "neither death, nor life, nor angels, nor rulers, nor things present, nor things to come, nor powers, nor height, nor depth, nor anything else in all creation, will be able to separate us from the love of God in Christ Jesus our Lord" (Rom 8:38-39).

Sin is the counter movement within creation that invades God's beloved pneuma-filled logoi, an ontologically binding power that locks God's world into an unbreakable cycle of suffering and death. When Cleopas sees the risen Christ, he has seen the end of this power: the universal offering who becomes "sin" itself, the goat sent out into the godforsaken wilderness, the iconic expression of the movement away from God, who turns this movement itself back to God. Even in the grave, which is the universal "wage" of the world's false occupation in sin, the Logos can hear the Father say, "This is my Beloved." In light of this revelation, Paul can say that the resurrection is the announcement to the world that "in Christ God was reconciling the world to himself" (2 Cor 5:19).[14]

The Cross as the Habit of Salvation

If sin is both a power and a habit, then our account of salvation in Christ must address both aspects if it is to be truly healing. Said differently, salvation is not saving if it remains only something God does for us; it saves only as we become involved, participating in the work, "working out" (Phil 2:12) in our shared lives the recapitulation of sin and death into new and healing habits.

Shusako Endo's *Silence* offers one of the most challenging images of this participatory involvement.[15] The story follows Rodriguez, a Jesuit missionary, to Samurai-controlled territory in seventeenth-century Japan. Throughout his travels he is motivated by a heroic desire to avoid sin, and in particular the sin of apostasy that seems an omnipresent temptation for priests and laity alike. He is also, though, increasingly disturbed by an awareness of God's silence in the face of Christian suffering, "the feeling that while men raise their voices in anguish God remains with folded arms, silent."[16] This, to put it mildly, places a strain on his Christology. His entire vocation, he says, has been motivated by the image of Christ's face, beautiful in its suffering; in Japan, he finds that suffering is meaningless and ugly, and that God never appears to beatify it.

What Rodriguez must eventually come to see is that his image of Christ is in a sense *too* beautiful in its sufferings, in that he has imagined Christ as the partner of the one who suffers by avoiding sin, rather than as the one who becomes sin in all its hideousness and hopelessness. And only in this way does he begin to love, rather than despise, the weak and broken man who has hounded him through the entire mission. Although he had been longing throughout his formation and mission for an encounter with his savior, he only finally meets Christ in a call that issues from an icon placed before him in the mud. He hears the voice inviting him to give up his hate for the apostates, his willed efforts to avoid their company, and "become" the sinner Christ came to save: "Trample! Trample!" he hears the voice calling to him from the icon. "It is to be trampled on by you that I am here!"[17]

If the book ended here, it would leave us with an unsettling image of a humiliated Christ who invites habits of faithlessness from his followers. Though the ending is far from "settling" in this regard, the story does not conclude with this image. Instead, it returns to the framing question of the story, which is what it is that we expect when we listen for the voice of God. Reflecting on the event of his own apostasy years later, the defrocked Rodriguez realizes that God was, in fact, never silent, since his own life came to take the shape of Word, thus of God's response to suffering with a cruciform love: "Even now I am the last priest in this land. But our Lord was not silent. Even if he has been silent, my life until this day would have spoken of him."[18]

Rodriguez's great discovery, that God is not quite silent insofar as God moves as a divine speaking within us, recalls the burning hearts of Emmaus after Jesus' disappearance, or again the flames over the heads of the apostles after the ascension (Acts 2). He was not "saved," which is to say he did not find himself affirming a healing taking place within and around him, until this experience. The death and ascension of Christ, we might say, manifests God's desire to save us through the witness of the Spirit, not just through the sacrifice of the Son. Salvation is something God does within us, when the kenotic Spirit moves us to respond passionately to the kenotic Christ, the one who showed the true and surprising form of divinity by emptying himself and taking on the nature of a servant.[19] The lives of those formed by this kenosis "speaks" the incarnate language of God.

Sharing in God's saving mission forms the basis for Saint Paul's affirmation of what Michael Gorman calls "co-crucifixion":[20] "I have been crucified with Christ; and it is no longer I who live, but it is Christ who lives in me. And the life I now live in the flesh I live by faith in the Son of God, who loved me and gave himself for me" (Gal 2:19-20). Salvation, a gift from God, also—and "only"—occurs through the slow work of justification, or becoming humans who in visible ways participate in God's justice and righteousness. Becoming humans, that is, who practice the human analog of divine just-making. In some cases this involves intentionally taking on the habits of suffering with the suffering Christ; in others, as Ellacuría helps us remember, this involves bearing witness to the ways that those who suffer are already living as a "crucified people."[21]

God calls us justified; this is not simply a performative utterance, one which makes true what it states in the very act of stating it, but in fact a periperformative utterance, since the making-just takes shape not only in the uttering by God but in the calling forth of our surprising responses.[22] The point, after all, is not the forensic dynamic in which the all-powerful God has made something true in spite of our attempts to make it false, but rather that the all-powerful God has led with justice as a kind of quiet power: the gospel of the crucified and risen Son calls to the spirit within us, so that we desire the transformation that God also desires for us.[23] Salvation, which from both the Latin and Greek contains the metaphor of healing in its etymology, is work done within us by the God who has only ever chosen to be with us. When Paul meets the risen Jesus, and, gathering the witness of Leviticus, takes him to be the ultimate sacrifice in which the great day of atonement itself nests, his response is a passionate utterance called forth by the excessive generosity of this act: it is as if I have been crucified with Christ, and risen to greet strangers on the road just as he once greeted me.[24]

In one remarkable string of connections, Saint Paul lays out the intersecting analogy of God's saving work that takes shape only in our participation.

> And he died for all, so that those who live might live no longer for themselves, but for him who died and was raised for them. From now on, therefore, we regard no one from a human point of view; even though we once knew Christ from a human point of view, we know him no longer in that way. So if anyone is in Christ, there is a new creation: everything old has passed away; see, everything has become new! All this is from God, who reconciled us to himself through Christ, and has given us the ministry of reconciliation; that is, in Christ God was reconciling the world to himself, not counting their trespasses against them, and entrusting the message of reconciliation to us. So we are ambassadors for Christ, since God is making his appeal through us; we entreat you on behalf of Christ, be reconciled to God. For our sake he made him to be sin who knew no sin, so that in him we might become the righteousness of God. (2 Cor 5:15-21)

All are made new, created again in the dying and rising of the Logos (reconciled to God after the ontological, social, personal devastation of sin); all are yet called to become new ("be reconciled"!) in the encounter. To receive the Spirit of the risen Christ is to be given the gift of reconciliation that we could never give ourselves, and to be called to the ministry and ambassadorship of this reconciliation. Our salvation bodies forth as we work the work of the one who sent the Son into the world.

In this sense we should speak of the aesthetics of the cross as central to its saving power. The story of hope's failure, of the loss of a life and the overcoming of a mission and of friendships by worldly power and incomprehension, becomes the rich and multilayered recapitulation of all of Israel's story, up to and including the expansion of healing beyond Jerusalem and out to the nations.[25] This good news calls all people, as the Law calls Israel, to a way of life that performs analogies to the holiness we see enacted in Jesus' life and death. It is this call to a new—and original—form of life that Paul speaks of through the liturgical appeals to eucharist and baptism. "As many of you as were baptized into Christ have clothed yourselves with Christ" (Gal 3:27); "For as often as you eat this bread and drink the cup, you proclaim the Lord's death until he comes" (1 Cor 11:26). The disciple is the one who desires to repeat in her body and habits the form she sees enacted when she encounters the risen crucified one. Christ is the one who lives otherwise: as if death has no hold on him, as if Cain were wrong about the scarcity of life and blessing, as if violence were an illogical (anti-Logos) act that is ultimately undone by forgiveness.

So the sacrifice of Christ is saving/healing because the Spirit moves within us and we find ourselves desiring to become what Paul calls "living sacrifices."[26] We can become a people who live a life of passionate utterance responding with transformed habits to God's gracious pursuit of the Adam, or God's beloved creation, into violence, sin, and death. The liturgical rhythm of baptism and eucharist are the form of a life that keeps time by this passionate utterance, the indwelling of the Spirit who brought Christ to the cross.

The "Sacrifice" in God

We can see, in this way, the fittingness of the cross and resurrection as a culminating event in Israel's devotion to YHWH. We can also name the ways that it is appropriate to the condition—ontological, social, personal—of a creation invaded by sin. The church fathers consistently draw attention to the humility of the cross and the glory of the resurrection as the antidote to the habits of sin: discipleship is about taking on his death and his resurrection, so that whether I am tempted to pride or despair, a life shaped by co-crucifixion and co-resurrection is a fitting means to overcoming these temptations.[27]

Still, there remains the question of how this act is appropriate to the eternal, loving, Triune God. The idea of crucified divine Logos inevitably raises difficult theological problems. Does God need a death in order to reconcile the world to himself? Does God die? Does part of God die? Is the death of the Logos real, so that for three days God is not a Trinity?

I have consistently invoked an analogical interval as a way of marking the difference between, for one way of putting it, what it sounds like for human language to describe God and what it might sound like for divine language to describe God. The same interval holds for our discussion of sacrifice, which, if it means anything for God, can only mean an act of holy-making that occurs in eternity, of which even the act at Golgotha itself is a temporal analog. "This, after all, is the truth of sacrifice: that behind the matter of Christ's offering up of himself lies the infinite truth of a God whose life is always already one of self-outpouring in another, as well as the response of love that that outpouring allows . . ."[28] The Father is, eternally, a "sacrifice" of being toward a Son; the Son is sacrificial love that returns; the Spirit is the Gift itself, "kenotic" in being nothing but the transference and celebration of this love. The mystery of the God incarnate, then, is the temporal acting out of a bloodless eternal sacrificial union.

Analogy, or we could say the participation of the temporal in the eternal, becomes the question driving the drama of the Incarnate Word: will the giving and receiving that makes God one in heaven hold even on earth? At his birth, when the child is given the figural name "God with us," the angel announces God the Father's recognition of the fleshly infant as a material and temporal icon of his heavenly Son. "He will be called Son of God" (Luke 1:35). This is the Logos, faithfully performed and lived in human history. It is theologically significant here that both Matthew and Luke insist that the Holy Spirit has come to Mary, overshadowing her as the power of God, making the Spirit the origin of this conception. As we saw above, this movement of the Spirit is what maintains the living unity of the Trinity: the Eternal Spirit rests upon the Son, and so the Son knows himself as Son and the Father recognizes the Son in this presence of the Spirit.[29] The annunciation affirms, theologically, the analogy of Incarnation: the heavenly pattern holds on earth, as the Logos takes shape in Mary through the resting presence of the Spirit.

Following this pattern, the baptism scene is the further insistence that the Father and Son continue to recognize the ontological strength of the analogy, or the integrity of their unity "on earth as it is in heaven." There is a kind of validation here: is it possible that the Father might recognize one who comes seeking a Jewish mikvah as a faithful sketch of his only begotten eternal Son? "Heaven was opened, and the Holy Spirit descended upon him in bodily form like a dove. And a voice came from heaven, 'You are my Son, the Beloved; with you I am well pleased'" (Luke 3:21-22). The scene is repeated deep into Jesus' ministry on the Mount Tabor, now validating a whole host of actions by the incarnate one. Jesus by this point in the story has blessed and cursed, responded to faith and doubt, has gotten angry and sad and grown tired; perhaps the analogy is strained here, as there is no direct mention of the Spirit, but rather a cloud that overshadows them on the mountaintop. Still, this Sinai-like presence must imply the resting of the Spirit, since the Father recognizes him and so affirms the integrity of the Trinitarian analogy. "This is my Son" (9:35)

It is the movement toward Jerusalem, though, that begins to strain the analogy in earnest. The powers of mistrust, betrayal, cowardice, and violence begin to mount against him, even as he turns his face toward the city where he will face trial and death. The invitation to avoid Jerusalem altogether becomes a fierce temptation, stirring up his passionate rebuke of Simon. Then, at the cross, though Jesus calls out now to his Father, the heavens are silent in return and there is no overshadowing Spirit or even cloud from which a voice of recognition comes. This is especially pronounced in Mark's Gospel, where Jesus for the first time calls on "God" in prayer, rather than his Father, as if without the Spirit's descent he himself has forgotten who he is, the beloved Son, and so appeals in the language of the Psalms as any Jewish believer might.[30]

With the resurrection we have a kind of delayed recognition: as if the story hesitates to suggest that the Father could even recognize in the tortured and dying body of this Galilean rabbi the temporal analog of his Son, and then proceeds to say exactly that.[31] In fact, Mark moves this suggestion forward in the narrative, putting it in the mouth of the Roman soldier who stood by watching him die. "Now when the centurion, who stood facing him, saw that in this way he breathed his last, he said, 'Truly this man was God's Son!'" (15:39). This parallels the dynamic traced in Endo's novel: even when silent, the Father speaks, because the Spirit bears witness within the lives of those who encounter him, who become the voice from the cloud: "This is God's Son." The execution itself becomes testimony, as did Eleazar's before him: Jesus' life (death, resurrection, ascension) is the word of the silent God.

Thus what the cross and resurrection reveal is that even in an act of sacrificial exchange, eternity and time are noncompetitively related. Shifting again to the Pauline language, it may look at first blush as if the form of God is directly opposite the form of a servant; in Christ though, we discover that it was not despite, but *because* he was so truly in the form of God that he could empty himself and take on the form of a servant.[32] Kenosis is how the true God acts, and this is as true in eternity as it is in time. Their kenotic deferral, or interpersonal exchange, is "sketched" in time as the Spirit-led life of Christ lived under the loving gaze of his Father. This sketch is both most complete and most surprising on Easter weekend, where the Spirit "finds" the dead Christ and announces the Father's recognition first in the passionate utterance of a guard, and then in the passionate utterance of the Son himself, who "responds" to the Father's rushing to meet him in the tomb by rising to a life beyond death. Easter morning is the ultimate telling of the parable of the prodigal son.

Violent sacrifice is what this eternal gift exchange looks like in a sinful world. No verse in the New Testament captures this more fully or movingly than John 13:1. "Now before the festival of the Passover, Jesus knew that his hour had come to depart from this world and go to the Father. Having loved his own who were in the world, he loved them to the end." "His own" here recalls from the prologue those who "knew him not." They do not know him because they live from the world's false origin, the ontological invasion that pollutes and revises epistemology. So Jesus prepares himself to perform the supra-cultic act of Eleazar and Isaiah's "man of suffering," now completing the analogy: it is divine love itself that binds the entire economy of sacrifice to the internal relations of the Triune God. Jesus' stubborn pursuit of "his own" will here demonstrate what divine love looks like.[33] The Logos made flesh is the Logos living a life in time that faithfully sketches the life of the Logos in eternity. Said otherwise, Jesus does in Roman-occupied Galilee in the first century what the Son does in eternity with his Father and Spirit: namely, he loves his own. For John the sacrifice of the cross is how the incarnate Logos loves to the end, since "greater love has no one than this" (John 15:13, NIV). To receive the Spirit that he breathes on his followers is to read the sign of his death as an indicator of love, and to desire the appropriate response: to want to be forgiven of our sins and to live a life of loving sacrifice and forgiveness.

Kenotically loving his Father and Spirit in Eternity means giving himself without remainder to the limitless joy of the Trinitarian dance; kenotically loving his Father and Spirit in Galilee means giving himself so fully to those ideas of the Father whom he has taken to calling "friends" that he is prepared to die so that the Spirit can rest on them, and draw them into the dance of the Triune Creator.

9

CHURCH

Leaving Emmaus

One never directly encounters God, even in the presence of the risen Jesus. This is, as Kierkegaard notes, as true for the disciples who followed him through Galilee and Judea as it is for those living millennia after them.[1]

The Emmaus disciples experience an epiphany simultaneous with an absence. "Then their eyes were opened, and they recognized him; and he vanished from their sight" (Luke 24:31). That is to say, they see him break the bread, and recall his exegesis of the Law and Prophets, especially the stubborn and loving pursuit of God through a sacrificial cult that atones for the sins and betrayals and limits of human faithfulness, and they connect the stranger to the story: this man is God's love for us, even exceeding the various layers of prescribed sacrifice. He is the ultimate sacrifice that atones not just for the sins of people, but for the oppressive dominion of sin itself, characterized as a world controlled by the powers and principalities of scarcity and death. Perhaps, having heard the story of the Syrophoenician woman and the crumbs, they even begin to imagine how this ultimate sacrifice is atoning and redemptive for the nations who live without the God of Israel. The Spirit moves within their burning hearts, they feel all of this in a brief and passing instant, and he is gone.

What a strange story. Strange and overwhelming: the entire narrative of the world, its birth, its meaning, its divine lover, told in a moment's encounter which turns out to be a nonencounter. If grace perfects and does not overwhelm or destroy its recipients, then those who receive this story must somehow become adequate to the epiphany, discovering a mode of reception that allows them to become a people who can take it in, so to speak. How is this possible? The following chapter will suggest that the answer is already given in the question: Christ's followers become a people adequate to the reception of grace by becoming "a people."

I might put it this way. It would take more than a person, more than two, more even than a panel, to begin to formulate a lived response to the encounter with the risen Christ. The story is strange enough that it would require the birth of a new cult, a new culture. The Emmaus story gives us indicators that this is, in fact, what it will take. First, the recognition scene occurs only after Jesus "took bread, blessed and broke it, and gave it to them." This likely suggests that in Luke's narrative Cleopas and his companion were with Jesus at the Passover feast, and so his actions here recall his prayers and distribution there. The connection of his death to the saving and forming event in Israel's history is not just, then, an exegetical discovery on the road to Emmaus, but already a ritualized recapitulation over a table in Emmaus. In Paul's language, finding ourselves in Christ as God's beloved children alongside God's Beloved Son is a discovery that goes beyond intellectual assent to his identity. It is a new form of life centered around shared prayers and sacrament. These strange, ritualized actions of blessing and breaking bread mediate to us this strange tale, that "in Christ God was reconciling the world to himself" (2 Cor 5:19). One cannot simply "accept" this story; one can only join in on an embodied and habitual retelling.

The other indicator in Luke 24 of the necessity of a cultic/cultural response to the experience of God in the risen Jesus is what happens next.

> That same hour they got up and returned to Jerusalem; and they found the eleven and their companions gathered together. They were saying, "The Lord has risen indeed, and he has appeared to Simon!" Then they told what had happened on the road, and how he had been made known to them in the breaking of the bread. (Luke 24:33-35)

Recall that this takes place in the evening. Though they have significant anxiety about being on the road after dark, they immediately depart on the seven-mile hike back to the city. This rash act emphasizes, first, the excessive "burning" of the Spirit's presence in these friends of Jesus, but also indicates that they experience this presence as a need to be with others. They discuss with one another what it was like slowly to come to know him through his exegetical and liturgical acts, and then they rush off to discern the meaning of this strange encounter with the other men and women who were Jesus' companions. The founding event of the reception of the risen Christ is not only, for Luke, the ritualized memory performed at the table in Emmaus, but the joining together of a body of witnesses that can only happen upon leaving Emmaus. One cannot receive this gospel on one's own, but only by leaving the home of a private experience and learning to listen to and live with an expansive body of witnesses.

Complexity

The experience of God is like the hearing of a periperformative utterance, like a dare or an insult, that motivates a response. It moves us, but the expression of this movement is varied and unpredictable. Creative, even. So immediately the question must arise: if this encounter is shared—the Lord has arisen and appeared to Simon, to the women who followed him from Galilee, to Cleopas, and soon, after the ascension, to Cornelius the Gentile and crowds in Jerusalem who never met him while he walked through the towns of Galilee—then what counts as an adequate or faithful response? Running seven miles after dark to be with friends? Proclaiming the resurrection despite the prohibitions of Rome? Sharing one's wealth with the poor (Acts 4:34-37)? Beginning a ministry that feeds the hungry and establishes tables as a place for the creation of bonds of friendship (Acts 6:1-6), parallel to the friendship Jesus shared with his followers? Risking shipwreck and stoning?

All of these and more are potential responses, as Luke's sequel makes clear. This also, though, demonstrates why discipleship is a communal venture. As varied as the periperformative responses are, some are inadequate to the Spirit of the risen Jesus. Keeping a portion of one's wealth and deceiving one's community follows an ethic of scarcity, thus of Cain's city, and fails to hear the invitation to become a new creation (Acts 5:1-11). The early church must discern the "Jewish shape" of the new messianic community, for instance, whether the new Gentile converts are committing themselves to circumcision and all the kosher laws (Acts 15). Other questions linger around the relative authority of the state—what to do if the response I am moved to make to the risen Jesus puts me in violation of the laws of a local or imperial governor (Acts 5, Rom 13)?

The limits and possibilities of Christian community will always have something conjectural about it, since it is the divine Spirit that shapes the witness of the gathered body.[2] This does not mean that no debates about doctrine of forms of life can ever be settled, but rather that the shape of the *ekklesia* and the language spoken within it ought to move forward through sharing of testimony, the building of consensus, and conciliar agreement. John Milbank has likened this to the construction of a medieval gothic cathedral, where, for instance, "a practical need for light may dictate the cutting of an extra window, irregularly positioned." Because the cathedral is not prefabricated or constructed all at once according to a single blueprint, it manages to incorporate the irregularities into its design as it evolves through the centuries of its construction. The ultimate manifestation of the term "church" would be the community in which a surprisingly coherent witness to the encounter with the risen Christ takes shape across irregularities that might have been thought incompatible, or destructive to the overall aesthetic. This unity of the Christian body is thus a complex and emergent unity: "In a 'complex space,' there is always room to adjust to the innovation made by free subjects, without thereby surrendering the quest for harmonic coherence."[3] In this way the church exists in the tension between periperformative innovation and consensus-shaped coherence. This tension has obviously not always governed the churches that have come to be through the ages, though we might pay attention to ways in which contemporary Christian communities who have spent long periods of time struggling for their own identity and integrity have managed to manifest this complexity.[4]

Shared discernment, then, is a key to the Christian faith. What happens back in Jerusalem, once the two from Emmaus have arrived, is the sharing of testimony in service of the crafting of a new language. Eventually this language will include the language disciplines that we now call Christology (who is Jesus?), Pneumatology (who is the Spirit that moves in us?), theology proper (who is the God revealed to us in the presence of Jesus and the Spirit?), and the doctrines of creation (what is the world, if the God who is revealed in the Christ is the one who called us to be out of nothing?), sin (what does this experience call us away from?), and more. It must also give birth to language about the identity of the community itself in which this language is spoken, and in which the culture surrounding it is embodied and practiced: this is ecclesiology, or the theological study of the church. The community that gathers to discern the shape of its many and variant experiences crafts a language for reality itself, a language that in turn shapes the lives and practices of those who speak it.

Thus we never directly experience the risen Christ: we only ever encounter him in the retelling, the listening, the gathering of testimony and repetition of an experience that allows, with Cleopas, Mary, and all the others who gathered around the tomb, who are saying, "The Lord has risen and appeared to . . . ," to craft a complex harmony of this disparate and "gothic" gathering of witnesses. The harmony emerges in tension with the openness to new witnesses. How can the Christian testimony maintain this harmonic openness?

Mediations of Sacrifice

Perhaps the most important answer to this question is "by faith," which in this case means by stubbornly asserting the strange belief that human bodies and human words can be recognizable as analogs to the eternal God. Recalling the movement through sin toward redemption traced in the previous chapters, we can see this faith as centered on sacrifice, which we can now redefine, with attention to the etymology of the term, as holy-making gifts. The church lives through bodily mediations of the sacrificial giving that is internal to the life of the Triune God.

This is true, first of all, in the way that human words can give themselves over, so to speak, as witnesses to something beyond oneself. The centrality of preaching in the books of Acts comes from this recognition. The apostles choose deacons to serve at tables so that the hungry will not be neglected even as the apostles remain free to devote themselves "to prayer and to serving the word" (6:4). The pun here seems intentional: the act of service performed in deferring my own bodily needs so that I can ensure that another has food becomes the pattern for the act of service in "feeding" human ears with the story of the risen Jesus. Human voices can speak truthfully of a deep mystery beyond telling, because this mystery is both within and beyond the experiences of any human witnesses. To preach, in the culture of Christianity, is to "serve the Logos" by means of humanly articulated logoi, in the wild hope that the analogy will hold between the word the preacher speaks in a particular moment and the Word that was with God in the beginning.

This is not to suggest that the apostles, or Luke, had the Johannine theology of the eternal Logos in mind when they spoke of "serving the word" in their preaching. Luke's "logology" is about Spirit-filled and Spirit-given testimony, first in the language Jesus himself uses and then in the language that this gives rise to in his disciples. When he appears to them after the cross, Jesus reminds them of "what you have heard from me" (Acts 1:4), and instructs them to wait for his own Spirit to move among them so that they too can be bearers of words, witnesses to all that his resurrection means for the world (1:8). When this happens in the second chapter, the great miracle of the event is the speaking itself: frightened, confused, sober humans can be filled with Christ's Spirit and become witnesses who speak and are understood across any apparent language barriers (2:4-11). Preaching in Acts is an appropriate response—a central response—to the encounter with the risen Jesus and the movement of the Spirit.

The appropriate response to the hearing of these many testimonies, in turn, is baptism. "Then Philip began to speak, and starting with this scripture, he proclaimed to him the good news about Jesus. As they were going along the road, they came to some water; and the eunuch said, 'Look, here is water! What is to prevent me from being baptized?'" (Acts 8:35-36). Baptism is the universal, or catholic, testimony of the human world to our participation in the life and death of Christ, universal in that there is no prerequisite to the rite other than the hearing of the testimony—recalling the first chapter, testimony of Scripture as well as of others past and present—the recognition of water, and the eunuch's "why not me?" observation. In this sense, baptism is how all humans can demonstrate a desire to find themselves as a new person "in Christ," and specifically in his dying and rising. Jesus in Mark had already made the connection between a Jewish ceremonial immersion and his own sacrificial death (10:38-39), a connection shown in ancient iconography through the sea monsters swimming around Jesus' feet in the Jordan: like the way of the cross, stepping into this water is an entrance into the terrors of sin and death. Paul makes the connection central to the new Christian version of the ritual: "We have been buried with him by baptism into death, so that, just as Christ was raised from the dead by the glory of the Father, so we too might walk in newness of life" (Rom 6:4).

In baptism the act of witness-bearing in words becomes an act of witness-bearing with one's body: to pass through water is to participate with Christ in the giving over of one's entire self—the memories and expectations, the desires and thoughts that accompany one's body—to a kind of ritual rebirth. In baptism the Christian is invited to "forget that you have a self to be shielded, reinforced, consoled, and lied to: hear the bitter truth that the cross enunciates, and accept the pain and disorientation of that enlightenment, in the trust that you are not hated or abandoned; and come up from the flood with a new person, 'alive to God' . . ."[5] The invitation to baptism is an invitation to repeat the sacrifice of Christ, an invitation so complete and radical that Paul sees it as the moment when we become Christ's own body. The church does not just represent or even celebrate the Incarnation, but becomes, through the Spirit's witness, the mediating Incarnation of the Logos.[6]

In and beyond: in the baptized community, the death and resurrection of the Logos and the descent of the Spirit become the nesting place of a language and testimony. Christ has died and risen, whether we manifest this sacrifice with our bodies and thus become faithful witnesses or not. This is the "Jeremiah point," in that the rite indicates a trust that God has already met us in a sacrifice that exceeds our broken desire to repeat it faithfully. But at the same time, this broken desire becomes the very excess it can only partially embody: there now exists on earth a community whose faithfulness corresponds to God's faithful pursuit of us, rather than only to our occasionally faithful but more often faithless pursuit of God.[7]

If "serving the word" is the community's initially appropriate response to the encounter with Christ, and baptism is the initially appropriate response to hearing the word, the eucharist is the initially appropriate response to "remembering your baptism." Like Cleopas, we encounter him in the breaking of the bread. Though teachings on this rite vary, and have been the cause of much of the division through church history, one organizing element across all traditions is the sense of the consumption of bread and wine as a regular participation in Christ's death and resurrection, a sort of baptism rendered habitual. "The Eucharist is the *site* where that same indissoluble bond between God and humanity accomplished in Christ becomes our food and drink, substance and sustenance for us, and where . . . through a bloodless sacrifice we partake of Christ, in regard to both his sufferings and his Godhead."[8]

To eat the bread and drink from the cup is, as Paul puts it, to "proclaim the Lord's death until he comes" (1 Cor 11:26). In this sense the eucharist makes a unity of the prior two mediations, the proclaiming of the word and the embodied act of baptism. The church forms its life around the regular embodied proclaiming of Christ's sacrifice by becoming living sacrifices.

To celebrate this "mystery of faith" through the rite of eucharist also draws together the two elements of salvation, connected to the original and actual layers of sin. We find our divine healing, Paul says, in an act of reconciliation that is accomplished once and for all in the death and resurrection of Christ; we find it as well, and not in opposition or competitive tension with this primary layer, in the habit-forming "ministry of reconciliation" which belongs to us. As with all sacraments—bodily signs of a bodiless God—the eucharist proclaims the astonishing compatibility of divine and human action.

Relatedly, the eucharist shows a correspondence between the Creator and creation that lies at the heart of things, and has been obscured through sin.[9] Though we tend to imagine the sacrality of what happens on the altar as a kind of divine intervention into an otherwise profane world, in fact the ancient theology of the eucharist suggests that here "alone," created things are invited to tell the truth about themselves.[10] This is, as we saw above, the surprising revelation of Christology: the form of the servant *is* the form of God, and so the finite creature is a just analog of—formed in harmony with—the infinite Creator. The natural elements of bread and wine are no more incompatible with the infinite nature of their Creator than is the flesh and blood of Jesus of Nazareth.[11] The idea that either the materiality of Jesus or of bread and wine is a contradiction to the heavenly Logos, and thus that Incarnational or eucharistic transformation could only be described as a paradox of opposites in unity, suggests something to us about the blindness brought on by the dominion of sin. Having lost a sense for the beautiful analogy of creature to Creator, we can imagine the arrival of God in time only as a kind of breaking and entering. It is fitting, then, that we have bread and wine to tell us the truth about ourselves, and so to become the center of an ecclesial life in which our sinful humanity finds itself in Christ, receiving and returning the love of the Father.

Receiving and returning: the mystery of the eucharist is that here, as we receive the broken body and spilled blood of Christ's sacrifice, we become the living sacrifices which his work invites us to become. We become what we were made to be, the ideas of God's Idea, the logoi of the Logos, that God imagined from all eternity.

Here especially the witness of the Spirit is essential to the transformation. John of Damascus, in a reflection on Isaiah 6, writes that the bringing of the sacrament to our lips is like the touching of the coal to the prophet's mouth: "The fire of the coal may be added to the desire within us to consume our sins and enlighten our hearts, and so that by this communion of the divine fire we may be set afire and deified."[12] The sacrament invites us, as God has always invited us, to move periperformatively toward this new creation, like those Emmaus disciples who acknowledge their burning desire to stay in the company of the risen Jesus and so become godlike in his presence. The beauty of the rite, from the audible prayers and readings to the visible elements and gathering of various communicants around the altar, is thus key to the transformative event itself: we are, we might say, compelled by what we see and hear and receive in our baptism to move toward our own transubstantiation, toward a deification that does not destroy but rather perfects our embodied existence.

Saint Anselm captures this aesthetics of the eucharist in his *Meditation on Human Redemption*. The bread and wine, if understood in their fullness, tell the entire story of creation and redemption, while also extending the invitation toward deification, an invitation which we accept not just with a decision or commitment or intellectual agreement, but primarily with joy:

> Christian soul, brought to life again out of the heaviness of death, redeemed and set free from wretched servitude by the blood of God,

rouse yourself and remember that you are risen, realize that you have been redeemed and set free. Consider again the strength of your salvation and where it is found. Meditate upon, delight in the contemplation of it. . . . Taste the goodness of your Redeemer, be on fire with love for your Saviour. Chew the honeycomb of his words, suck their flavor which is sweeter than sap, swallow their wholesome sweetness. Chew by thinking, suck by understanding, swallow by loving and rejoicing. Be glad to chew, be thankful to suck, rejoice to swallow.[13]

To "eat" this story, as Ezekiel ate the scroll, is to "hunger and thirst" for the righteousness of God that it invites us to enjoy. This communal mediation of God's saving work repeats and renews the work of salvation in Israel, where the Yom Kippur sacrifices are events of liturgical prayer and celebration. The public rejoicing is itself the evidence of and even the work of salvation: this movement from the isolation of beings broken by our sinfulness to the formation of a people characterized by the sound of ritual rejoicing is what biblical salvation looks like.

The joyfulness of a life in Christ is part of the invitation of the eucharist; at the same time, the regularity implies that the transformation of a human community into a collection of harmonizing living sacrifices is the work of a lifetime and more, and the moments of transfixed joyful contemplation are in many cases more an eschatological hope than a lived experience. The habitual return to the altar implies that one does not simply decide, in a moment of euphoria, to be in Christ; rather, one learns the practices of desiring to become a living sacrifice across a lifetime, thereby showing "how deeply Christian salvation seeks to be incorporated in history."[14]

This incorporation of salvation into history is itself the heart of the gospel. A God who could have reworked and recreated the world extrinsically sought instead to save it from within, by following the fallen creation through an initial "incarnate presence" in a people and their Law,[15] and by taking on flesh and dwelling among us. Ecclesiology reminds us that this incarnating presence does not end in the ascension of Christ, but that the Logos of God continues to body forth in the church. The embodied rites of eucharist, baptism, marriage, and the rest are at the center of this incorporation, but through them so too are the sharing of wealth, time, food, and clothing, the loving of strangers, the sacrificial and confrontational witness for justice alongside the vulnerable members of a community both inside and outside the church walls: these too are incorporations of God's salvation into history. For this reason we might say that the church itself is a sacrament, a living and material witness to God's grace at work in creation.

A Free People

Why, though, does salvation require this extension of Christ's work through a historical communion of disciples? For one thing, because God seems to be interested in human freedom.[16] God created humans who were free to love, and it is through a renewed freedom that God will recreate us. So Paul says, "It is for freedom that you have been made free," by which he seems to mean, again, that only in the work that Christ and his Spirit do within us do we discover the freedom for which God made us. So when Christ says from the cross, "It is finished," he cannot mean that the work of salvation is done, but rather that the work that he, as the incarnate Logos, came to do is done. The sending of the Spirit becomes then the invitation to his disciples to continue the work of salvation in the absence of his incarnate presence.

In this way the weekly gathering to celebrate the resurrection and to "proclaim the Lord's death until he comes" is the slow restoration of human freedom, allowing us to find ourselves in the one who gave himself in order to make us free. Christ's is the once and for all sacrifice, reconstructing and reaffirming the analogical interval between the love within God that is the Trinity and the love exchanged between God and a sinful world; our repetition of this sacrifice is the ongoing work of salvation, of becoming living sacrifices within the death and resurrection of the eternal Son of God. "We, in some real sense, taste and are nourished by the whole mystery of our redemption, our 'sacrificial' entry into the Trinity's life, and so in the drama of offering up and receiving, we gain some slight but true glimpse of the Trinity's infinite beauty."[17]

God demonstrates a stubborn prejudice for freedom not only in the refusal to remake creation without our consent (Genesis 3 and following), but also in the refusal to let Israel remain slaves in Egypt: the historical restoration of their freedom becomes the signature event of their eschatological communion with God. So the fourth commandment in Deuteronomy connects honoring Sabbath with rest for those who are no longer slaves—this is a holiness of free men and women that participates in the holiness of God. This also demonstrates the theological offense of the slavery that in many ways marks the transition to the modern world, where expansion of land holdings and the production of capital led so many Christians—Pope Nicholas V among them—to the acceptance of an economy built on racialized forced labor. The enslavement of one human being by another is so entirely at odds with the action of the God of Israel that it can only be seen as the construction of an oppositional culture to Israel and the church.[18] In the words of the Johannine literature, this is the domain of the Antichrist.

A restoration of freedom through kenotic giving helps us see why Mary is the traditional icon of this ecclesia. Gabriel's announcement to her of God's desire to take shape within her as the incarnate Logos takes the surprising form of God's work of salvation "waiting" on a human response. Mary's assent, "May it be unto me as you have said," shows the Christian narrative diverging from the Greek stories of a divine power that manifests, on occasion, in bodily assaults and overpowerings of weak human beings by deities.[19] Mary is the vulnerable virgin upon whom the Creator of the universe waits, so that her sacrificial assent to be God's can "catch up" to God's sacrificial desire to make Godself ours. She utters a periperfomative assent and Magnificat to the invitation to grow a new humanity within her womb, thus recapitulating, or reconstituting, Adam and Eve and Cain's false constitution of humanity.

We cannot, though, experience this reconstitution alone, any more than the Emmaus disciples could have experienced their reconstitution by the risen Christ had they not turned to one another, and then left Emmaus in search of the witness of others. Anselm gestures toward this in the same meditation, when he says, "I owe you as much more love than myself as you are greater than I . . . I pray you, Lord, make me taste by love what I taste by knowledge . . . I owe you more than my whole self, but I have no more, and by myself I cannot render the whole of it to you."[20] The inadequacy of any individual to experience the cross and resurrection of Jesus as "salving" is a direct consequence of an anthropology in which we are made for communion and conversation with the created world around us. To love requires not just a person willing to love, but another who can receive this love, whether this is a spouse, a sister, a pet, a spot in a garden, or an object that holds treasured memories. God's saving work perfects the humans God made; for this reason, as Vatican II's *Lumen Gentium* puts it, God "does not make men holy and save them merely as individuals, without bond or link between one another. Rather has it pleased Him to bring men together as one people, a people which acknowledges Him in truth and serves Him in holiness."[21] Not, of course, that all humanity or even creation together is adequate to the fullness of the divine mystery; rather, the entire catholic expression of creation is the fullest possible analogical rendering of the goodness of God, spoken into being as the "very good" cosmos.

Salvation in this case requires a church, because salvation is not an abstraction, as if it were simply a matter of stating or imagining that God's Spirit is now "with us." Rather, it occurs in a context, a place where a community belongs, where they find themselves in a familiar setting, among familiar faces. Church is the new humanity of Christ reconstituted through the time and space of a new community. To welcome a stranger, forgive a friend, fall in love and wed, share one's wealth and give of one's time: these are the human practices that, like bread and wine, show themselves as faithful analogies to the kenotic love that is the very form of God.

Sins of the Church

Churches are, of course, also places where humans sin, and show themselves to still be dominated by sin.[22] The twenty-first century has already brought this reality to light in the horrific revelations of long histories of the sexual abuses of children and cover-ups of those abuses by ordained priests, elders, and bishops. Here we ought to recall the words of Jeremiah, referenced in the previous chapter, in his condemnation of temple worshipers. "If you truly act justly one with another, if you do not oppress the alien, the orphan, and the widow . . . then I will dwell with you in this place." But if you carry on these oppressions, "and then come and stand before me in this house, which is called by my name," how will God respond? Pray your prayers in the holy place if you must: "I will not hear you" (7:5-16). To carry on the habits of Cain's city through willful acts of sinfulness against vulnerable and trusting creatures within the sanctuary is not simply to sin; it is rather to make God out to be a liar, and thus to erect a barricade to the very sacramental worship which proclaims and invites us into God's salvation. If Christ's sacrifices still exceed this sin, as it exceeds the sins against the covenant in Jeremiah's day, it will take many generations, and countless difficult relationships built around truth and reconciliation, to demonstrate what this excess looks like.

The formal response, too simplistic but yet perhaps still worth saying, is that a witnessing to the excess of Christ's sacrifice over the lies and abuses of Christians must take shape as the same ethic of "living sacrifices" that we have seen at the theological center of the church's preaching and sacramental existence. Emmanuel Katongole has written at length about such difficult work in African Christianity. He tells, for instance, of a Ugandan mother of a child kidnapped and forced into a guerrilla troupe—a troupe which professed faith in the Christian Bible—who discovered that she was unable to pray the lines from the Our Father, "as we forgive those who sin against us." She gathered other mothers like her to discuss this impasse. Eventually those prayers became intercessions for the warlords themselves. "Praying for those who had wronged us became our sacrifice," is the way that mother put it to Katongole.[23] To incorporate the saving work of Christ involves seeking justice, it involves the telling of hidden truth, and it also involves a half-mad and radical repetition of Jesus' gift of forgiveness.[24]

This is not to imply that the heavy lifting in the ministry of reconciliation belongs to those who have suffered rather than to those who have caused the suffering. The economy of forgiveness will always take place as a miracle of transformation, through intense work for all involved. It is often the offending one who lacks the courage to enter into this difficult work. Here we might recall Lewis's vignette in *The Great Divorce* of the "Big Man" who is too proud to be forgiven by one who once worked on his floor.[25] The telling of truths and the reconciling of wrongs is work to be taken on only with the care and wisdom of pastors, counselors, and in many cases legal support.

Still, it is work to be taken on. A community formed around the eucharist is a community that "locates itself in Gethsemane," which is to say in the founding memory of betrayal and cowardice, since this is the moment when Jesus' body is handed over.[26] The church is called to remember all of its violence and injustice if it is to fully experience the miracles of grace and renewal. Here we might recall Paul's repeated confession of his sins against Christ's followers, which leads him to add "by the grace of God I am what I am" (1 Cor 15:10).[27] The exchange of forgiveness is perhaps the central miracle in the life of the spirit-filled body of Christ.

This exchange is not even secondary to the saving work of God, since, as we have seen, salvation is noncompetitively both a divine gift and a human habit. What is bound on earth is bound in heaven (Matt 18:18), which ought to lead us to wonder what it means to enter into the divine presence bearing sins that our earthly companions have been unable to forgive. Perhaps the Triune God miraculously initiates and makes space for a difficult conversation among victims and abusers at the Last Judgment? It is no less a miracle, though, when we manage to embody generous practices of forgiveness on earth as a testimony to the superabundance of creative love.[28] In doing so we bear witness to the anarchy of our creation, our origin in a Giver with no origin, and heaven celebrates these anarchic exchanges as saving moments. Those who gather at the altar for Christ's atoning sacrifice become mutual atoners for one another,[29] "loosing" one another's sins through radical acts of personal and communal sacrifice.

If in Northern Uganda or Pennsylvania a new community comes into being and extends the historical life of Christ into new relationships and new events of healing, this will be a church that is, in the creedal language, "one, holy, catholic, and apostolic" despite its also being made of sinners, and despite being characterized by temptations to fragment, exclude itself from strangers, and isolate itself from the saving work to which Jesus commissioned the apostles. That is to say, the gift of God's work, in the Spirit who rested on Jesus, will provide the context and form that makes the church what it is, and the ongoing repetition of his life in the lives of Christians, as they interpret Scripture, pray, proclaim the gospel, and practice the sacramental saving ministries, will bring this work to its completion.

In a history flooded with accounts of injustice and domination, an authentic incorporating of Christ's history will always involve a conversion of the powerful toward the vulnerable. This is to say more than "Christians should be mindful of the vulnerable." Rather, Christians are those who recall that the Logos grows inside the body of a poor young virgin from Nazareth, and who recall that when the Spirit moves within her she recognizes that the story taking on a body within her womb is one that will scatter the proud, bring down the powerful, lift up the lowly, fill the hungry, and send the rich away empty (Luke 2:51-53). God's presence in the world meets us in this overturning and upheaval of a world made wrong-side up by sin. The periperformative utterance is the utterance of the Logos, and the performances it inspires are the works of the Spirit, only if the words discerned and the responses generated repeat among the ecclesial body the work begun in the body of Jesus of Nazareth. Said otherwise: a spirit who does not meet creation in the lifting of the vulnerable and "conversion" of the proud into the humble is not the Spirit of Christ, any more than a spirit who rested within creation somewhere other than upon the broken body of Jesus is his Spirit.

Circulating the Gift

All this work takes time: time to form habits and time to fail, time to grieve the actions and betrayals that call for our forgiveness.[30] The existence of the church is all the evidence we need that "one must not understand the saving effects of the Incarnation to be immediate."[31]

Perhaps it could have been otherwise. God the Father sends God the Spirit "to lead us into all truth," and while this leading no doubt happens in various ways throughout creation, the church is the community where this gift is named, celebrated, and intentionally incarnated into difficult historical habits.[32] Whether God could have saved us another way, "it pleased Him to bring men together as one people" as a means of our salvation. This is fitting, as Thomas might have put it, in that the church becomes the analog of the Triune God, the temporal and therefore messy space in which the Spirit comes to rest, gradually, on the broken body of the Son.

In this very gradualness, the Christian Church can identify itself as the people who, repeating ritually the sacrifice of Christ, form themselves as a community where friendships can be practiced, alms shared, and above all the gift of forgiveness can circulate. It will involve people unlike me, as well as people who will sin against me and against whom I will sin. Together we will become a people as we learn to practice atonement: to forgive and to be forgiven. The church is the community of salvation, and in it the healing work of God in Christ takes shape, takes on existential form, in the healing and loving and justice-seeking lives of those who are baptized into his death and thus await, with all creation, the day of his coming.

10

PRAYER

Language and Absence

The journey from Emmaus begins in an absence and a longing. How can they be with the one who made their hearts burn within them? Either they cannot, which seems an unacceptable response, or they can, but differently now.

Luke's Gospel does not end in grief over this absence, but in joy, and in the exchange of blessing:

> Then he led them out as far as Bethany, and, lifting up his hands, he blessed them. While he was blessing them, he withdrew from them and was carried up into heaven. And they worshipped him, and returned to Jerusalem with great joy; and they were continually in the temple blessing God. (Luke 24:50-53).

This is the same temple in which the Gospel opens, with the account of God hearing the prayer of Israel and promising joy, deliverance, and the turning of God and the people to one another (1:5-17). In the beginning of the Gospel the absence seems more tragic. The apparent barrenness of God's marriage to Israel finds a repetition in the barrenness of Zechariah and Elizabeth, and so we find the priest calling for aid from the God who is conspicuously un-present. Even these prayers, though, contain a memory hovering just under the surface, of Sarai and Hannah, the matriarchal metaphors of Israel's surprising and unlikely rebirths. The people are gathered outside the temple because they remember these stories, and their petitions are in this sense not initiated only by God's absence, but also by their ancient memories of his remarkable presence.

In the post-Easter trip to the temple, the worship is a response to all that has taken place, all that has been made present in Jesus' life, death, and resurrection, and also all its theological implications, including the radical notion of bringing into the temple itself the celebration of the extra-cultic sacrifice. "Worshiping" their friend suggests that they have begun, at least, to do some of this theological reflection.

Now, however, it is a more permanent absence that intervenes, since with his ascension they are "continually blessing" the one who is no longer there. Of course, in another sense the ascension changes nothing, since their prayers were shaped by an absence even prior to Jesus' ascension, when he taught them to pray to the one he called Father and who dwells beyond time and space.

Prayer is that strange practice in which we speak to, bless, and call on a God we never directly encounter. Christian prayer is a pattern of communication that locates itself in the intratrinitarian passionate utterance, and draws creatures in as participants in this dialogue.

Pragmatic and Fatalistic Praying

Why do Christ's followers pray? One temptation of a theology of prayer—and it is a very old temptation, one which the ancient Greek polytheists warned against[1]—is to begin with creaturely needs and then appeal to the Creator for their fulfillment. Prayer of course can include petitions of this sort, but problems arise, theologically speaking, when prayer begins here. For if prayer were primarily about petitions, what does this say about God? Augustine notes that we might petition God like one petitions a judge, attempting to influence God with our flattering praise.[2] In this case, praise would be a tool that we put to use for the higher end of getting our petitions heard. But this suggests a weakness in God, a neediness for approval and a vulnerability to flattery that is incompatible with the account of God's being sketched in these pages.

When God instructs Moses on Sinai regarding the proper orders of offerings for the consecration of priests, it seems at first as if something like this manipulative petitioning may be at work. They are to bring, among other things, two rams and a basket of yeastless bread to the doorway of the tabernacle. One of the rams should be slaughtered, then burned away entirely on the altar. "It is a burnt offering to the Lord; it is a pleasing odor, an offering by fire to the Lord" (Exod 29:18). What does this offering suggest about YHWH? Does God get hungry? Is God's stomach the way to God's heart? This recalls the conclusion of the story of the flood, when Noah builds an altar and makes an enormous burnt offering of every kind of clean animal and bird that had come through the waters with him. "And when the Lord smelled the pleasing odor, the Lord said in his heart, 'I will never again curse the ground because of humankind . . .'" (Gen 8:21).

Might we speculate, though, that Israel's scribes are cognizant of this theological challenge? These questions bring us close to the challenge issued to another god in Israel's story, the tauntings of Elijah to the prophets of Ba'al: "Cry aloud! Surely he is a god; either he is meditating, or he has wandered away, or he is on a journey, or perhaps he is asleep and must be awakened" (1 Kgs 18:27). It seems that the scribes of the Old Testament at some point develop a sophistication that issues in an internal critique of Yahweh-the-hungry.[3] In Exodus, they insist that the God of Israel is not manipulatable by food, and so alongside the burnt offering there is something quite different. Take the other ram, God says, and carefully prepare it to be eaten. Place it alongside the basket of bread, so that the two together form an irresistible aroma. Leave them there at the tent of meeting. Then Aaron and his sons, the priests, will return to the tent, finding the meal still there where they left it. "Aaron and his sons shall eat the flesh of the ram and the bread that is in the basket, at the entrance of the tent of meeting. They themselves shall eat the food by which atonement is made, to ordain and consecrate them" (29:32-33). Unlike the aging Isaac, they seem to be saying, God cannot be bought for a pot of stew.

Most Christians do not, perhaps, envision a God quite so given to corporeal manipulation as the gods of Canaan. Still, a version of this theology lies embedded in much popular Christian discussion around prayer, as though God waits to act until the prayers of Christians have achieved a certain unspecified quantity or quality. This is an interventionist view of prayer, in the sense that the world will go on as before—my mother will not forgive her aunt, war will never cease, the cancer will remain—unless praying people find the right words and achieve the critical mass that will motivate God into action. While it may not be an imagined weakness on God's part that calls for prayer, it still is the praying itself that acts as the primary cause, putting into effect a chain of events for which the petitioners have been praying.[4]

This is a popular theology that tends to manifest itself in pragmatic cultures such as the United States, where a tree is known by its fruit, and a fruit in turn by its usefulness. The mystical sense of prayer as "wasting time" with God is totally lacking here: praying is about effecting change, and the harder one works at it, the better the results are bound to be.

This may come in part from reading a text like James 5, which at first glance seems to suggest that praying is how Christ's followers make things happen.

> Are any among you suffering? They should pray. Are any cheerful? They
> should sing songs of praise. Are any among you sick? They should call
> for the elders of the church and have them pray over them, anointing

them with oil in the name of the Lord. The prayer of faith will save the sick, and the Lord will raise them up; and anyone who has committed sins will be forgiven. Therefore confess your sins to one another, and pray for one another, so that you may be healed. The prayer of the righteous is powerful and effective. (Jas 5:13-16)

"The prayer of faith will save the sick." The term "save" here is significant, in that it is identical in the Greek to the word for "heal." The New International Version loses this richness by translating "and the prayer offered in faith will make the sick person well," whereas the New Revised Standard Version goes back to the Authorized Version's option for "save." Salvation is, in the New Testament, a healing in the fullest sense of the word, and nowhere is that more evident than in James' text. God will save, raise up, the one who has fallen, and we are invited to suffer in prayer with the suffering, rejoice in prayer with the rejoicing. To pray in times of suffering and in times of cheer. To pray for the sick and for the sinner. In all, as the verses preceding repeat over and over, "Be patient." Pray like the farmer in Jesus' parable, who plants and waits, in full knowledge that he is taking part in a power that exceeds his own manipulation of soil and seed (Mark 4:26-29).

Often this pragmatic prayer theology ("our prayers move God to act") sits uncomfortably alongside another sense of prayer. In this understanding, God is willfully and directly behind each and every occurrence in the world. Here an overly simplistic reading of Jeremiah 29:11, "I know the plans I have for you," or Romans 8:28, "all things work together for good," might lead us to suppose that whatever happens is, in fact, God's will.

The passage from Romans comes at the end of Paul's treatment of resurrection, and so in context suggests that God will not be overcome by any power or any evil: in effect, that no "things" that happen can finally escape God's care-filled summoning of the world toward eschatological life and goodness. This, though, is some distance from a shrugging "everything happens for a reason" theology, as if God were the immediate motivational push behind each world event. Paul's theology here is informed by something close to an Aristotelian notion of final causality, since God's eschatological invitation of all things to the great resurrection "causes" events in the present to take the shape they do.[5]

Coupled with the interventionist account of prayer, this more fatalistic account of providence can function like a theological safety net, granting authority to God after the fact: after, for example, one's prayers have apparently not been answered. *God must have had good reason for vetoing our prayers.*

These images of God (interventionist agent, fatalist sovereign) seem deeply incompatible with the ones the New Testament develops in the theological light cast by Christ's resurrection. In Luke's Gospel, prayer is a response to God. Even the petitions of the Our Father begin with the recognition that God is a Father (and so knows how to give good gifts—11:13), is in heaven (and so is beyond the impoverishments of earth—6:20), and is holy (and so has power over even the spiritual forces of the world—4:34). This is the one whom we ask for daily bread: the asking is a response to the revelation of God as giver, as heavenly, and as holy.

If on the other hand petition is primary, then prayer is first and foremost a request to God. In requesting, the one asking takes control of the conversation, so that even if the petitioned refuses, he or she plays according to the rules established by the petitioner. This is what makes Oliver Twist's request for "more" such a deservedly famous subversion of power. He takes power away from the tyrannical governors of the orphanage by forcing them to choose one of two options: Yes you may, or No you may not. Even an exaggerated, abusive "no," like the one young Oliver gets, remains within the terms he himself established.

God is one whom we must first trust to be something other than a tyrant, which I take it is what James means by "the prayer offered in faith." God is like a father who knows how to give good gifts, and now one to whose generosity is added the attribute of consistency (Jas 1:17). God then is one whom we must trust to initiate the dialogue. A prayer that is primarily petitionary will not escape one of the problematic doctrines of God sketched above. We pray this way only because, at some deep and perhaps undiscovered level, we do not trust God to know what we need before we ask.

Excessive Metaphysics

This, of course, simply leads us to a larger question. Why pray if God knows what we need before we ask? Those disciples who bring Luke's Gospel to a conclusion by blessing God in the temple are not trying to accomplish something, nor do they seem particularly concerned about assigning God the role of efficient cause of all that they experience. What, though, are they doing?

Perhaps the most obvious response is that they are praying out of an excess of joy, or perhaps gratitude, or perhaps a mixture of the two. They have experienced something astonishing, and as they begin to sort through what this means for all of creation, they are moved to involve themselves in the language of blessing. "A metaphysics that begins in excess over lack correlates to prayer that begins in gratitude over petition."[6] Luke ends in praise because Luke ends in excess: the excess of a cosmos now centered in the resurrection of God's Son. The temple-going disciples here are like the dreamers of Psalm 126, who live to see Zion's fortunes restored: "Then our mouth was filled with laughter, and our tongue with shouts of joy" (v. 2).

To pray is to participate in divine excess. This participation connects to what I have said about sin, salvation, and the ministry of reconciliation above, since the work of saving/resurrecting is God's, and also work that God has shared with us.

Consider again the account of the consecration of priests in Exodus. Why do these two sets of instructions, one to burn something as a pleasing aroma, another to prepare a meal for God and then eat it themselves, remain side by side in the text? In these strangely mingled instructions we can find a clue to a theology of prayer. On the one hand, God is beyond need, beyond the rhythms of hunger and satiety, thirst and drunkenness, and especially beyond the lapses in judgment that these bring. God has no need of anything or anyone beyond God's own continuing life.

However, God does not say, in light of this transcendence, *I am beyond human manipulation, therefore disdain all offerings to me. I will give and forgive when and how and to what extent I choose, without your input.* Rather, God invites precisely this input. *Pleasant smells will not cause me to forgive or sanctify; they are a fitting response, though, to my holiness.* It is good for the people to make gifts of their best livestock and firstfruits to God, to prepare it with great care, to observe the highly detailed language of liturgy. In Paul's allegorical idiom, it is good for God's people to offer their bodies as a living sacrifice, an odor pleasing to God (Rom 12:1). It is good not because it moves God to action, but because it moves the church toward God. Prayer, in this sense, has what Augustine calls an enlarging capacity: "His gifts are very great, but we are small and straitened in our capacity of receiving."[7] Praying expands our desires, so that we can receive more of what God gives. This is why Thomas Aquinas insists that prayer does not change God, but rather changes us. "For we pray not that we may change the Divine disposition, but that we may impetrate that which God has disposed to be fulfilled by our prayers."[8] God's bountiful giving will always exceed our ability to impetrate, or request, God's grace. Prayer simply helps to close the gap.

Prayer then, like theology itself, begins in encounter. It is, in the words of Hans Urs von Balthasar, "dialogue, not man's monologue before God."[9] Prayer is a dialogue, and God opens the conversation. The basic form of prayer is a contemplative listening, a listening which may issue from reading, worshiping, attentive acts of service, meals with friends or strangers, or silence. It may take the form of remembering, as it often does in the psalms. Psalm 77, again, which wonders, "Has God forgotten to be gracious," replies to its own question with "I will remember your wonders of old." The petitions are then reframed as responses to God's past actions, calling God to be faithful to God's character displayed "of old." In various ways, and by means of various disciplines, the one praying can attempt to "keep silent" until God speaks.

This does not, though, imply something like a linear or temporal dialogue, as though the Christian should be attempting to hear a divine voice. Here we would do well to recall the Christology sketched above, and draw connections to the current theme. Jesus' divinity is never an isolated "someone," but rather the Logos surprisingly "analogizable" as, harmonious with, human action. In Maximus' account of the Gethsemane prayer, he notes the revelation of their noncompetitive cooperation at its fullest and most tense expression: "Clearly the negation here—Not what I will—absolutely precludes opposition and instead demonstrates harmony between the human will of the Savior and the divine will shared by him and his Father. . . ."[10] There is no voice of the Logos, because the Logos speaks with a human voice, and comes mediated through the coherence of a deified human will, which is to say a will prepared to desire all of what God is eternally desiring.

A God who perfects rather than destroying our nature speaks as a kind of call constructed—humanly, socially, prayerfully, with all the resources of the Bible and the historical community of faith and human reason at our disposal—in and through our response. That might be one way of putting it. Our response is saturated with the excess of the call it both names and presupposes. "Not what I will but what you will" implies a prior sense of who God is and what God desires, which only at this moment, in Jesus' human voice, comes to expression. "Has God forgotten to be gracious" is something like an angry petition that, on the page, appears to come first in the prayer. But the remembering of wonders of old then follows as the horizon in which the psalmist can make this petition, a horizon of bounty cobbled together from Israel's ancient testimonies of astonishment at the hand of their God. There is a "mutual embrace of call and response"[11] that allows us to name ourselves as creatures existing within the good and full creation of God.

If God speaks, or if in the silences we remember how God has spoken in the past, our petitions can become appropriate responses. Like Israel, who contemplates the holiness of a God beyond hunger and need by preparing pleasing aromas, we hear of or recall the boundless river of God's mercy, and then ask to stand in the current. The "purpose" here, if it is proper to speak of purpose in praying, is not to move God toward mercy, but to bring a harmony between our desire for grace and God's always greater desire to give it. The God whose mercies, as Sirach puts it, cannot increase or decrease, since they are beyond measure (18:5-6), invites us to ask for exactly this increase: it is perfectly acceptable, in the faiths of Israel and Christianity, to ask for "more" mercy, since the "more" will always be but a dim reflection of the surplus of mercy God gives. Prayer is a path to deification: we pray so that we can become the sort of people who desire for God to be the sort of god God always already is.

In this sense, we should perhaps reverse our thinking about prayers of petition. Intercessions and appeals to God are not prayers in search of an answer. They are already answers: our prayers are responses to God's petitions to us to receive the abundance of God's mercy. Moved by a biblical narrative or iconic image or a neighbor's witnessing of God's measureless mercy, we appeal to God to continue lavishing that bounty on a world in need.

In fact, if what I said before is correct about God's eternal knowledge of creation as a knowing and loving of God's own ideas, or Idea, then even our attempts to contemplate these infinite mercies is a response. We are in the position of Jesus, coming up out of the baptismal waters, only to find out, through the descent of the Spirit, that the Father has been actively dwelling on his love for him: "This is my Son, my beloved." To find ourselves in Christ through baptism is to be the ones who receive gladly the gracious news that God looks on us with the same active love with which the Father looked on Jesus that day, and indeed with which the Father has been looking on the Son from all eternity. This is prayer: to find ourselves standing where Christ stood, receiving the descending Spirit, hearing the Father call us his beloved child, and then to find ourselves moved to respond. Prayer is a "movement of divine reflexivity, a sort of answering of God to God in and through the one who prays."[12] In this sense prayer not only has a christological shape, it is a Trinitarian structure.

We could put it this way: we petition God as a response to the mercies revealed to us in contemplation of God's bounty, even when we experience this revelation as lack; we contemplate God as a response to the revelation that God has, from before all time, been contemplating us. "In the Son, the Father contemplates us from before all time, and is well pleased."[13]

Purpose and Prayer

Still, it is difficult to avoid a lingering purpose question. In the end, if God is already disposed to act, and cannot be changed by petitions, if prayer is our response that can never influence or affect the constant way in which God opens the conversation, why pray?

Prayer in the eternal Trinity is a dialogue of free Persons; prayer in the temporal cosmos is the work of free creatures. Praying binds us to a God who never desires that we be bound to God against our will. God is already loving the world, and God's invitation to me to pray is in effect an invitation to waste time in God's presence, contemplating/petitioning God's mercies. This changes me—indeed it changes us together, since as Cyprian of Carthage points out, we do not pray "my Father" but rather "our Father."[14] Praying together, and praying for one another, does have an effect: it binds us to one another in love, and, by allowing us to stand in the place of the one in whom "all things hold together" (Col 1:17), it binds us at the same time to our Creator's love.

There is, though, a further "purpose" to prayer, or perhaps aftereffect, since prayer itself is its own purpose in the same way that time spent with a friend must be, at its deepest level, accomplishing no other task than the spending of this time in her presence. In John's Gospel, as we have seen, Jesus is constantly saying that he is doing his Father's work, sharing in his Father's business. "Works" in this Gospel becomes a synonym for signs or miracles, and the reason for this is that Jesus is humanly acting in ways that seem more fitting for his Father in heaven to act: healing the sick, forgiving sins, multiplying food. In all of these things, "the Father who dwells in me does his works" (14:10). The great acts of saving, healing, forgiving, and making the world just are God's acts, God's works; yet central to the mystery of John's Gospel is that God the Father has shared these works with his Incarnate Son, so that there is no competition between the transcendent God accomplishing them and the enfleshed Jesus accomplishing them. The scribes and teachers of Israel insist that God alone can do these great acts of mercy; Jesus does not disagree, but says that the greatest of all mercies is that God has shared these works of mercy with him.

Further, this is precisely what it means in John's Gospel to receive Christ's Spirit. "Jesus said to them again, 'Peace be with you. As the Father has sent me, so I send you.' When he had said this, he breathed on them and said to them, 'Receive the Holy Spirit. If you forgive the sins of any, they are forgiven them; if you retain the sins of any, they are retained'" (John 20:21-23). The disciples will also "do the works that" Jesus does (14:12), healing broken bodies, condemning acts of injustice, forgiving sins, because the work that the Father has shared with him, he shares with us.

This is the great mystery of the power of prayer: God is working infinitely merciful acts toward creation, and therefore we finite creatures also work. We pray that our own sins and the sins of others will be forgiven not so that God will be motivated to forgive: God has always already been at work forgiving our sins, recreating us with the same loving appeal by which God first called us into existence. We pray, rather, as a response to the summons to join in the work. God does not need to become a forgiver of sins; we need to become a forgiven people, people shaped through habits as receivers of this gift. Through the working of God the Father and God the Son, and through the prayers of those disciples upon whom God the Spirit comes to rest, the work of salvation is being done. The one who lives as unforgiven can begin, ever so slowly, to reimagine herself as the forgiven one that God imagines her to be. Nations at war begin to receive grace from one another. The sick are saved—physically or in other ways—from the disease that attempts to claim them. The prayers of the righteous participate in the praying within God, and so are "powerful and effective."

Serving at God's Table

One of the oldest traditions in the iconography of the church, dating back to the time of Constantine, takes the three visitors to Abraham as allegories for the three Persons of the Trinity, and thus has come to be known as "The Old Testament Trinity." The various icons in this tradition show the three figures seated around a table under the oak of Mamre, with food and drink on the table before them. In most of the images, they sit around a four-sided table, so that one side, the side "nearest" the viewer, is open. The figures even turn slightly toward this opening, suggesting an invitation to the viewer: *God's table is open for you; come share in our feast.*[15]

While Andrei Rublev's famous icon shows this scene occurring near Abraham's house, some older strands of the tradition leave Abraham and Sarah in the scene along with the visitors.[16] They bear dishes for the feast, and so the icon has come to have an alternative name, "The Hospitality of Abraham." Now, as a depiction of an Old Testament story, it is clear enough why Abraham and Sarah would be bringing food and drink to the table: it is their house, and the story is about their hospitality in contrast to the coming inhospitality of Sodom. However, as an allegory of the Trinity, the image is surprising. We (the worshipers, standing in front of the icon) are invited to God's table, to partake of his generous feast as if we belonged there with the Persons of the Trinity, and yet the human characters in the image are providers, not just receivers. Why does God's feast need supplementing by the patriarchs and matriarchs? Why are humans not just feasters, in this image, but also the literal hands of providence?

But perhaps we have not yet taken seriously enough what it is to be included in God's work as though we ourselves were God. "I said," Jesus quotes to the Pharisees, "you are gods" (John 10:34). This means finding our place at God's table, but then also finding our place in God's kitchen. We are invited to pray for God's mercies: to "make more" of that which cannot possibly increase because it is boundless; to pray for the sick that God is not too blind to see nor too cold-hearted to love, but too generous to want to save all alone. God's greatest act of mercy is to invite us to come to the divine feast hungry, and then, once we are there, to teach us to cook.

It must be said, finally, that there is no magic to prayer, if we think of magic as an immediate act that bypasses the normal patterns of life in time and materiality. There was no rabbit in my hat, now there is a rabbit. In fact, the witness of the New Testament is the opposite of magic, since by sharing the reconciling work with humans God has slowed down the saving action in creation. "My Father is still working, and I also am working" (John 5:17). Regardless of the complex questions about what God *could* have done, incarnating mercies through the complexities of time and space is what God *has* done. I pray for the forgiveness of our sins, knowing that forgiveness must be embodied, and so will take time, grief, the changing of habits, the restoration of relationships. Perhaps death will intervene, and a sin will remain woefully unforgiven in this life—here we can rejoice that sharing the work with us does not imply that God is unable to work above and beyond our workings.

Likewise I pray for the sick, knowing that health is difficult. It is a process that requires the shared wisdom of friends, family, doctors, nurses, providers of food, industry, governments. Too often we find ourselves unable, for various reasons and for no reason at all, to live into this health. Children die, cancer wins, violence against bodies continues. Here again we can rejoice that God's ability to "save the sick" is not limited to our ability to maintain life. This is not to say that God chooses or wills sickness or death. God has an irrevocable prejudice for abundant life. But in a world scarred by sin and disease, God's graced healing does not come all at once. Even Lazarus eventually goes back to the tomb. God's mercies come to us mediated through one another, through the creaturely prayings and workings of God's praying and working. And beyond that, we can only throw ourselves on the mercy of a God whose grace is boundless, and hope that the cancer, the war, the hate, the loneliness that outlasts us so often on earth will never find a place in God's abundant kingdom.

11

LAST THINGS

Hope

The disciples watched as their rabbi was executed, when they "had hoped that he was the one to redeem Israel" (Luke 24:21). Humans are creatures who live by hope. We anticipate a future shaped by love, belonging, a home, rest, joy. We pray for the health of a sick child, for the sibling to overcome addiction, for barren soil to be renewed. And all the while we continue to live with a hope that is difficult to name, and not entirely fulfilled even when the health returns, the sibling comes home clean, or the rains and grasses return.

Barth's language of small hopes and great hope is not meant to suggest that these nameable things that we hope for are insignificant, but rather that they are "sized" for human experience. Hope that Jesus of Nazareth was Israel's redemption is indeed a large hope, yet one that the disciples were just beginning to enter and to feel. As such, they could deeply feel its end as well. What they find, when they announce the disappointment of this hope, is that what they had assumed was the great and consummating hope of Israel's faith, the survival of the one marked for the redemption of all lost tribes and the end of all unjust occupation, had in fact been a small hope, or rather, a hope still insufficiently formed by their Scriptures and the community of faith. With the surprising return of their Messiah, and especially his exegetical suggestion that an unjust execution is also at the same time a supra-liturgical sacrifice for all lands and peoples through all of creation, they discover that their "great hope" was not yet great enough. The Messiah who meets them beyond death changes what it means to hope, and so what it means to be a human, in both the small and the great moments. "If there is also a small hope for today and tomorrow, if there are also temporal, penultimate, provisional and detailed hopes for the immediate future, it is only because He is the future One who shows Himself in every future."[1] To see Christ in every future is to discover the

Spirit moving within, and to respond with periperformances that bear witness to the new great and small hopes to live within a world that bears the image of the risen Logos, God's eternal Son.

Eschatology is Christian theology's imagined intersection of the hope that creatures have with the goodness in which God made us and to which God calls us. The Bible often uses the language of marriage to speak of this intersection, casting Jesus in the role of the bridegroom and the church as the bride. It is the hoped-for end, though we should take care to note that the analogical interval is not thereby dissolved: we do not become the Creator, the Creator does not become a creature. Rather, the interval shows itself, sounds itself, as fully harmonic, with all dissonance gone. The story of salvation is the dramatic tension in the analogy, the tension between the movement or processions of the Persons in God and those movements extended as missions on the earth. Can the Father know and love the Son in the Spirit's descent even in the tomb? The ending of the story is the resounding affirmation of this noncontrastive harmony throughout the cosmos: the analogy between eternity and time holds not only in Christ's tomb, but in all created things, all the logoi made in the image and called to the likeness of Logos. Here the holy-making gift that took the form of a violent sacrificial death in time blooms again in an excessive and peace-making gift embodied in all creation. The manifestation of this analogy is the great hope of all Christian prayer, the essence of our gratitudes and intercessions. "Thy Kingdom come, thy will be done, on earth as it is in heaven."

Even here, though, grace perfects nature rather than destroying or replacing it. We want to hold the seahorses in our hand even while feeling saturated with their presence. In that sense, the great question of eschatology is not whether all of time can manifest its source and destiny in the eternal ideas, but whether we can experience this, whether we can go on being creatures when and as this happens. Would such a revelation still cause a human heart to burn with passion and the desire to know, love, and act in response? Or would this be the end of creaturely limit? Isaiah's vision of hope's fulfillment suggests that the establishment of YHWH's house will not, in fact, bring about the conclusion of human activity: nations shall stream toward God's mountain, and the people will continue learning God's ways and forming communities in need of arbitration and justice. How can we imagine creation in this ultimate expression, where activity is transformed but not silenced? A world in which human hands remain at work beating swords into plowshares (2:2-4), and mountains and hills burst into song at the unchecked abundance of all creation (55:12-13)?

Delay

It was a surprise within the Jewish Christian community of the first century that the messianic fulfillment of Israel's hopes and the hopes of all the nation entailed delay. The Emmaus disciples assumed they were wrong in thinking that Jesus was the Messiah, since their hopes were not fulfilled. Even, though, as the spreading news of resurrection gave them cause to rethink this expectation, what they experience is not an uncomplicated fulfillment of all hope. Even at Emmaus, as I have said, the risen Jesus is mostly absent. So "Christian" became the term for those who "are expecting" (Phil 3:20) the return of Jesus, and the transformation of bodies and souls, along with all creation, that this return entails.

The notion that the ascended Jesus will come again a second time catches up the prophetic texts about the coming Day of the Lord—when kings and nations and all people will be judged (Zeph 1), the harvests will overflow (Amos 9:13), the dead will rise (Isa 26:19), and peace will reign from God's mountain through the earth (Isa 2, Mic 4)—and integrates this into the messianic faith in Jesus. What was coming in ancient times has both come already and is still to come in the advent of Jesus of Nazareth. It is not so much that the great and terrible Day of the Lord is equated with his ultimate return, as that the Day "has come" in Jesus' incarnation, and simply extends until the last day, when "the Lord himself, with a cry of command, with the archangel's call and with the sound of God's trumpet, will descend from heaven, and the dead in Christ will rise first" (1 Thess 4:16).

This extension is a pneumatological surprise. The God who "made you without you . . . does not justify you without you," as Augustine put it,[2] and so the "long" Day of the Lord is the delay in which creatures receive the invitation to act in accord with the just passion that the Spirit pours into their hearts. Saint Paul calls this an invitation to creatures "to work out their own salvation with fear and trembling" (Phil 2:12). Barth's language here is that those who initially may "correspond" or answer back to God's summons to join in the work will ultimately experience a grace that allows us to "cooperate" with the work.[3] For God, of course, the work of creating us and making us just does not actually take time; but God graciously shares the latter work with timely creatures. The working of the Incarnate Jesus is the Father's work "lasting," as is the work of the Spirit-filled church throughout the generations.

This work, again, involves human experience, and so if life in time involves loss, the "making right of all things" entails a faith in the return or resurrection of all that is lost. So Robinson's novel notes the connection between the limited memories we retain, and the fullness that we long for.

> There is so little to remember of anyone—an anecdote, a conversation at the table. But every memory is turned over and over again, every word, however chance, written in the heart in the hope that memory will fulfill itself, and become flesh, and that the wanderers will find a way home, and the perished, whose lack we always feel, will step through the door finally and stroke our hair with dreaming, habitual fondness, not having meant to keep us waiting long.[4]

"Wanderers" here suggests not just the persons missing, but the fullness of their presence, all that we missed when they were here or forgot after they were gone: the whole seahorse. Here the consummate hope of temporal beings is for the end of loss itself, the accrual of all the moments and encounters and loves that, limited beings that we are, we simply cannot hold in our hands forever as we wish.

In the New Testament's idiom, the Spirit that moves within us is sufficient to overcome loss, whether the loss be brought on by death, betrayal, injustice, fear, or a combination of these interruptions. If the Spirit of the risen Jesus is alive in us, then "neither death, nor life, nor angels, nor rulers, nor things present, nor things to come, nor powers, nor height, nor depth, nor anything else in all creation, will be able to separate us from the love of God in Christ Jesus our Lord" (Rom 8:38-39). If, by extension, all things hold together in Christ (Col 1:17), then to be unseparated from God's love in Christ means that nothing will in fact separate us from the loves and hope that form our experience as human creatures in time. The presence of the risen Messiah invites us to find ourselves in him, in his dying and in his rising, so that "he who raised Christ from the dead will give life to your mortal bodies also through his Spirit that dwells in you" (Rom 8:11). The Spirit that bears witness with our spirits, and in and through the communion of creatures that surrounds us, will not stop this witness-bearing, even at death. The Spirit leads us through our hopes both great and small, to the return of all that is lost.

The deep message of Christology, as we have seen, is that those who are not only reliant on the body's senses for what they know and love, but further dominated by sin in the ways that they know and love, are invited to "taste and see" the bodily, sin-ruined body of Jesus. This thoroughly human experience of the divine Logos becomes an invitation to find ourselves in Christ's supra-cultic offering, and so be "rapt up" in communion-relationship with the Creator of all things.[5] For this reason, it is essential to this faith in a second coming that Jesus "will come again in the same way," which is to say bodily. The delayed Day of the Lord is not the end of human bodies or creaturely materiality, and so we will not see God without the analogical mediation of the Incarnate One. When Paul calls the bodies which will rise by the awkward name "spiritual bodies," he is suggesting not immateriality but rather an embodiment that stretches the limits of our imagination. What would it be to have this body that I now live with, and yet not experience sickness and pain? Or to live in this body in such a way as to no longer fear human cruelty or fear the grief of an unbearable loss? Or again to live in my body even as I share its molecules with all organic beings from which it has grown, and all which will make use of my body after I am dead? Our present bodies could only be something like "a bare seed" (1 Cor 15:37) of the bodies that will grow from them to meet the risen Christ.

We hope to see God in the risen Christ, that is to say, as Dante's pilgrim saw the Logos: as the human body inviting us into an indescribable experience of the fullness of the divine presence. Thomas Aquinas calls this the beatific vision: "In heaven . . . we shall see Him by a form which is His essence, and we shall be united to Him as to something known."[6] In this case we will look first at the body of Jesus, who is the personal presence of the Logos giving shape to a human life, and then through him at the creatures around us,[7] from the friend to the heron to the bit of sediment and finally to ourselves, and see clearly and without the filtering of a dark glass (1 Cor 13:12), the Logos in whose image all is made. We will see the human body, mediated though our own human bodies, and see also the Logos: "no distinction between them can be perceived; for whatever one can see of the Son is divinity, wisdom, power, holiness, and impassibility."[8]

Judgment

The delay of the recreation of all things, as God defers to bodies and temporality, shows why Christian theology insists that the second coming, or ultimate "marriage" between the holy and just God and God's correspondingly and cooperatively holy and just creatures, will also be a day of judgment. If God had no pattern of attending to creaturely responses to the divine invitation to be, there would be no need to talk about creation under judgment, as God could simply provide the holiness and justice for us all. But a God who creates not by decree but by invitation, a letting-be, and who follows us out of Eden, a God who waits on Mary's response, who does not overpower our spirits but instead bears witness within us to the passionate utterances of God's love and faithfulness, is a God who respects the limited and historical and material paths that creatures actually choose. So every "thought, word, and deed" of humans, every instinct and operation of God's created things throughout the cosmos, matters. God will consider them all, will "weigh" them in light of the eternal idea of creation—not that their weight should be "equal" of course, since the creature is not identical to but an analog of the Logos. God delights in our bodily limits: we know this already, since God saw them and declared them "very good," or filled with holiness and justice sufficient to remind God of God's own holiness and justice. Are there elements of creaturely histories that will not remind God of God's own holiness and justice? These sins are not ones that a loving God will ignore or pretend not to see; rather, God will name and condemn all that does not belong to God's creative idea, even as God names and celebrates all that does.

Andrei Tarkovsky's film *Andrei Rublev*, about the life and work of the fifteenth-century Russian iconographer, contains a pivotal scene in which the iconographer reimagines Christ's final act of judging the world. Rublev has been commissioned to paint frescoes on the walls of a church in Vladimir, depicting iconography of the Last Judgment. As he hesitates, puts his assistants on hold, and seeks inspiration, he receives news of a violent attack on his painters by the private soldiers of a nearby duke. He responds to the news with violence of his own: he grabs paint in his hands and begins glopping it and smearing it on the white walls. Then, while a young acolyte reads from the Epistles, a "holy fool" enters, a woman who has until then hovered around the church and stared mutely at the iconographers, occasionally laughing without observable cause. Here, though, her mood is different. She sees the mess of paint and begins to weep loudly, smelling it, looking around as if unable to believe they are not troubled as she is. It is as if the woman can feel the madness of violent acts of murder and torture in the paint that Rublev threw there.

At this moment, the iconographer knows what to do. He had been imagining scenes of torture and punishment, but something about her response has reminded him of the hope that Christ's coming will bring. The fallen world is the story of violence and cruelty. Christ's judgment is our only hope that these violences will not stand, finally, before the holy Creator. "It's a holiday!" Rublev cries. "They are celebrating!" He then fills the church, as well as the rest of his paintings through his life, with images of celebratory feasting. These images serve to reimagine human life and human experience as beyond the pain of blindness, starvation, and warfare—not as if these never existed, exactly, but rather as if they were themselves "nothing" beyond moments of lack in a creation saturated with abundance. Even as churches burn and he and his companions endure more violence and hatred, Rublev becomes a kind of resistance figure, a "holiday" iconographer bearing witness to the celebration of abundance for which God created us.[9]

God's final judgment is a key moment in the theological story, since it reminds us that God desires to celebrate with all creation God's embodied ideas and their periperformances throughout all of time. And, consistent with all we have seen so far, God grants creatures participation in judgment as well. Jesus tells his disciples that they too will be involved in the final judgment, sitting on twelve thrones alongside him (Matt 19:28). While the New Testament's apocalyptic imagery is quite difficult to interpret, here we may notice a new element of participation in the Gospel account of our ultimate end. Those whose lives are transformed by the witness of the Spirit to the resurrected presence of the Son do not simply receive judgment, but share in the act. They serve at God's table, they participate in the ministry of reconciliation—they cook in God's kitchen—*and* they sit in seats of judgment.

Something like a human act of judgment is already apparent in the church's personal and communal work of discernment, what 1 John calls "testing the spirits," where human beings make judgments about what does and does not fit with the divine idea that they can only see through shared and trusted testimonies. The image of disciples sitting in eschatological chairs of judgment suggests that, surprisingly, our judgment will continue to matter to God, and will not be waved away for the divine word that supersedes it. God will not only respect the various ways that creatures responded to his gracious "let there be," but God will also respect the church's judgments on the patterns of life that fit and do not fit as appropriate to God's loving invitation.

Temporality remains important for these acts of discernment, since the communal sense of what fits and what does not will change through time, as new material for discernment enters the church's vision.[10] It will also diverge from community to community as evidence and arguments and contexts are weighed differently.[11] Which patterns of economic exchanges fit, and which do not, within the historical incorporation of Christ's body into the world? Which patterns of sexuality and desire? Which responses to military inscription? As William Cavanaugh writes, the Catholic Church in Chile was able to say that celebration and cooperation with the reign of terror of General Pinochet did not fit, and so the declaration of excommunication for all those who supported his government became their vocalized witness of a judgment rendered from the throne of the apostles: this is not the life and witness of one of God's very good creatures, and so this pattern of life has no place in the risen creation we celebrate in the Mass.[12] We can imagine and perhaps hope for a similar witness from the churches of Northern Uganda, or Boston, Pennsylvania, Ireland, the U.S. border, and wherever sexual abuse or the active abuse and neglect of children and refugees and others coexists with the blessing and accepting of the Christian sacraments. The disciples within these communities belong in seats of judgment, bearing witness to God's final judgment with human declarations of what fits and what does not in God's holy communion on earth.

Because the church is not hypostatically one with God, but a community of humans working out their salvation together, our judgment will never be final. God will respect and invite and include our discernment, honor the excommunications and condemnations, but not be held captive to them. God's judgment is the final judgment that exceeds all ours, just as the coming of God in Christ is the coming of the great hope that exceeds the small hopes. The early church literature captures this idea with the common use of "anathema." The term is found in Paul for those who preach another gospel (Gal 1:8), and is used through the first centuries of the church as an ecclesial pronouncement of separation of someone or a group of people from not just the eucharist (excommunication) but from the life of the church as a whole. It is, though, itself not a final statement of the destiny for those cut off, but, as the Greek term suggests, a suspending of judgment, or better a "sending up" of judgment toward a higher court.[13] Every effort of the body of Christ through the ages to discern what does and what does not belong is in this sense "anathema;" some practices though are declared as such as the church's way of saying, in effect, *for all we can tell, this life is so far from the shape of the life you created, God, that its presence among us will only bring harm; still, we render the final judgment, as in all things, to you.*

Heaven and Hell

What we call heaven, then, is the Christian way of imagining the full and excessive experience of created life. Perhaps we should say the transcendent heaven of the eschaton, since what we are talking about now is not the heaven created in Genesis 1, but part of "a new heaven and a new earth." Still, as this new creation descends, if heaven takes shape as the resurrected life of abundance, then in a sense the "heavenly" experience is the deep reality that has always been the truth of creation. C. S. Lewis expresses this idea in *The Great Divorce*, where heaven is not ethereal, but instead overwhelming in its substantiality. The saints and angels are "Solid People," and the grass and wildflowers and even drops of water seem to be made of a heavier material than pilgrims "on holiday" there.[14] Lewis' contemporary Charles Williams explores a similar idea in his novel *The Place of the Lion*, where incarnations of the divine ideas appear within and around a small English village. Responses to these appearances vary, from the frightened to the intellectually skeptical. A butterfly collector enters a state of catatonic rapture when he catches a glimpse of the "form of butterfly" hovering over a garden, attracting all the local specimens into a kind of metaphysical consummation.

Heaven is the excess itself, we might say: the excess of God's gift over and beyond our desires. So the New Testament likens it to a feast, to finding what was lost, to yeast or a seed that grows and expands improbably so that it can feed and give shade. The man who lives to enjoy butterflies both has and has not yet imagined the truth of his desire; similarly, humans who live for a joyful experience of all that we long for, from the seahorses to lost family and friends, have not yet fully imagined what it is to stand in the presence of all that we love. This is a joy beyond earthly language, requiring words that, while still human, are also divine: to be filled with the "good things" not just that we wish for, but that are our true desires. The term heaven, or kingdom of heaven, or reign of God, serves as a marker of the transcending remainder, the excess of human hope that would shape a true and everlasting abundance of life.

Indeed, our wishes may compete with our truest desires: "Now, if we are made for heaven, the desire for our proper place will be already in us, but not yet attached to the true object, and will even appear as the rival of that object."[15] It may be, like the narrator in Lewis' parable, that we learn to let go of the things we thought we wanted—personal recognition, national security, a Messiah resistant to execution—so that we can experience ourselves as newly created by our deepest desires. As creatures do this they begin to find, like the disciples leaving Emmaus or the woman who finds the lost coin, that they have never desired more nor less than the experience of themselves as joyful creaturely analogies of the eternal Logos.

This imagined excess is not separate from, but really just an expression of, the Christology sketched above. Jesus is the divine Idea, the Logos, living a human life. To find ourselves in Christ is to meet this life with our own existential and anarchic performances of unscripted life. Gregory of Nyssa's comments about the ascending Son—"for whatever one can see of the Son is divinity, wisdom, power, holiness, and impassibility"—suggests in fact that heaven is the idea imagined from this vision of Christ, or perhaps the intersection of that vision with my own existential discovery of divinity, wisdom, power, holiness and impassibility. In other words, I discover what I mean when I say the word "heaven" only as I contemplate the heavenly Logos, and find myself being made like the heavenly Logos even in the midst of my earthly life.

A God who comes in judgment, honoring the paths that creatures have taken rather than forcing those creatures into conformity with the divine will, is also a God who rejects as unholy and sinful those paths and habits in which God can no longer acknowledge God's image. Hell is the most common name the New Testament gives to the negative side of divine judgment.

Here, though, contradictions abound: To the extent that a creature still is, that creature is good. If what I want is in fact destroying me and everything I love, do I in fact want this, or I have ensnared myself in my own perversions of desire? How could I actually glimpse an experience of the fullness of joy and love in God, and desire anything else? Is the freedom to turn from God not in some way still marked as an image of God's own freedom, implying that in some deep metaphysical sense, we can never really rebel against God?[16]

At the base of hell, Dante the pilgrim finds Lucifer, frozen in a lake of ice, which he has created by the flapping of his angelic wings in his very attempt to flee the presence of God. He is, in this sense, "marked" for survival like Cain, as though Satan's ontology itself were the last waystation of God's grace, and nothing but the hand of God keeps him in existence even as the very trajectory of his life careens toward nothingness. The darkness and terror of hell—the gnashing of teeth, perhaps—is in finding oneself fighting the very gift of life and being, as one so twisted around as to imagine that nothingness is good (a senseless desire which itself makes nothingness, as I suggested earlier, into evil).

If divine condemnation is thus full of ironies, is it appropriate to call hell eternal? In some sense, first of all, we must recognize this as a theologically nonsensical question, or at least one with a simple answer: only God is eternal, and those beings which God has made have "eternal life" as they find themselves transformed in the Spirit into the manifold refracted images of the Son. Hell is neither God nor a godly transformation of created reality, so cannot be eternal.

Still, this reasoning does not make hell temporary in the same way that life within creation is temporary. If we allow ourselves to be guided here by the notion that salvation is both a divine act and a human experience, then the essential question is whether it is possible to never experience ourselves in the light of the divine imagination, and thus to "miss" heaven.

Here there is perhaps a surprising amount of hesitation in the theological tradition. Many of the Greek church fathers speculate on what they call *apocatastasis*, or the eventual enjoyment of God by all God's creatures. Gregory of Nazianzus suggests, perhaps with a undertone of humor, that part of the saints' vision is to see, beyond what he himself can imagine, a just treatment of sinners that does not involve an endless hell, "a way that is more humane and worthier of God."[17] Augustine is more sure of the metaphysical reality of hell than most, but his reasoning is, oddly, rather rushed, especially when he brushes past the counter-argument that an eternal punishment hardly seems appropriately measured to a temporal sin.[18]

There is some reasonability to the idea that hell should "last." Here we might consider the risk Shakespeare takes in his late romance *The Winter's Tale*, when he breaks with what was considered the rules of good drama and inserts a gap of sixteen years between Acts 3 and 4.[19] The opening scenes of the play dramatize King Leontes' spiral into a senseless jealous rage, a rage which eventually destroys his family and nearly ruins the kingdom. He is so unrecognizable as the king and father he once was that when he receives news of the deaths of his wife and his children, he continues to pour verbal abuse on the former and to scoff at the idea that the latter are even his offspring.

The question that the audience must ask, as the king shifts out of his rage at last and begins to realize what he has done, is not how much punishment the king deserves, since there is no obvious unit of measurement or fitting equivalence for a jealousy which becomes hate and causes death. The question, perhaps, is what it would take for a man so consumed by untruth to repent, to feel the weight of his sins, and to bear witness to those who were there for his downfall that he is no longer the man who did those things. How could a court—and the audience here serves also as court—discern "true repentance" in King Leontes?

At least part of the playwright's answer to this implied question is "time." Time itself enters as a character, in fact, and begs the audience's pardon for the gap of years, "As you had slept between" acts.[20] The long gap between these acts occurs, apparently, so that we can see the king fulfill his promise to "once a day . . . visit/ The chapel where they lie, and tears shed there." This, he says, "shall be my recreation."[21] Hell is in a sense the place—the life—he lives for all these intervening years, a life of loveless loss, of living with the reality that was apparently what he wanted and chose in his sin-sick state of mind. Moreover, this is the hell in which he will have to stay if he cannot learn to practice penitence and to practice as well a receiving of a gift of forgiveness. A simple passage from the "earth" of his daily court to the "heaven" of a resurrection would be aesthetically inadequate, because it would be humanly inadequate.[22] The sinner must give an account of the way he has destroyed elements of God's creation. And this account giving must take time. Hell must last.

Lewis' language here is worth considering, that the loveless existence of a life without God is hell only if one stays; it is purgatory if one moves from there toward the new creation. Of course, part of the difficulty is attempting to imagine what "taking time" and "moving toward" look like beyond death. But perhaps this is part of the idea of God's final judgment that also needs revising. The language of hope tends to invoke the future, and so heaven and hell take on a mythological construct, something like an "after-life," that strange near oxymoron that sounds as if we imagine that life has no after, just more living, but really simply reminds us that we have no idea what comes next.

Perhaps, though, God's final judgment, an event in which the church participates, is not an event that takes place in that imagined gap between death and the kind of living that comes next, but rather is God's loving summons that saturates all of time, every present, with God's own eternal presence. In this sense, eschatological is not only, or even primarily, a future-orientation, but more like a "transcendental future"[23] that is also a transcendent past and present. Here again it is important to keep in mind the analogical interval. An imagined and longed-for return to health, a making of peace between members of opposing tribes, or other hopes are a human way of experiencing, in time, something like what it is to enjoy the fullness of God's eternal presence. The Christian hope in a future resurrection of bodies and souls, alongside all the creatures that ever issued from the divine imagination, is essential to the ethic and proclamation of faith.[24] And it is also the case that the resurrection is not simply "to come," but is already active in those "small" instances of overcoming addiction and restoring broken relationships and discovering life on the other side of enslavement. And in this respect, "tomorrow's" resurrection may only be fuller and more profound versions of the resurrections already occurring today. After all, as Jesus points out, to God all are already alive (Luke 20:38), and the resurrection is in this sense a way of finally matching our way of knowing ourselves and one another to the way that the eternal God knows and experiences us.

Since the centuries of late antiquity, Christians have found ways of distinguishing cosmic history, with the events of origin that natural science seeks evidence for, from theological beginnings when God speaks all things into being. (This is why we do not need to hypothesize about the coexistence of dinosaurs with the patriarchs and matriarchs of Genesis in order to believe that God created the world.) In the same way, we can suggest that "the end" of history, in the gradual entropy, for instance, of the cosmic energy generated in the Big Bang, is not in competition with the telos of all creation in the presence of God. God's imagination of our beginning, or existence, and our end is, to use another analogy, operative in a different dimension than the cosmic and temporal beginning and endings.[25] Or perhaps, more appropriately, it is this dimension, but experienced excessively.

Thus our future in God is as much a transcending present as a transcending past, since these distinctions are themselves only analogs for the eternity enjoyed by God. Eastern Orthodox liturgy shows this idea in the invocation of the place of worship as a little heaven on earth. Not simply as a picture or representation, but as an actual participatory experience of communal life in the loving and caring presence of our creator. Liturgy is not so much an imagining of a hoped-for future, as a celebration of what "was in the beginning, is now, and ever shall be."

To return to the question of hell, then, we do not have to imagine a purgatory as a holding place after we die, from which we can go on changing our desires for an indefinite amount of "time" (whatever time means to us after we die), in order to integrate Shakespeare's insight about the necessity of humanly recognizable truth-telling and contrition. Rather, as God is eternal, thus full of time, God's judgment on a life can determine whether something like an adequate human desire for God and hatred of sin has come to expression. We can—and the church must—"anathematize" those sins outside and especially inside of the community which we consider to be utterly oppositional to the divine ideas; in doing so, though, we do not condemn anyone to an everlasting hell, but rather make our judgments as we are able, and send the final judgment up to the higher court where it belongs.[26]

What God's judgment will be, of course, is beyond us, and we rightly have no more control or insight into this than Jonah had into the judgment on Nineveh. (Of course, we can sulk at the injustice of a God who chooses to act mercifully rather than to destroy, as Jonah did!) We invite confession and administer last rites because it is entirely appropriate to our roles as ministers of reconciliation to invite one other to "enter the judgment hall affirming their fundamental choice for God."[27] When God looks at a person's entire life, not simply what they said and choices they made, not simply the last thoughts or feelings—God is not an executor bound by the final draft of a last will and testament—but the entire life, will God find there some trace of desire for "heaven," or the truth of oneself in God? That is the real theological question around an everlasting hell.

And the answer may be no—no, in some cases, God may look at an entire life and not see the Logos there. Von Balthasar calls this a "borderline case,"[28] a life that bears no trace of its creator even to God. One could build a life that is an utter refusal of faith, hope and love, and this life would, in the end, be unrecognizable to the God who called us into being.

But it is also possible that even the life that is utterly unrecognizable to me, to us, to readers of Scripture devoted to like-mindedness with the humble servant Christ, would be recognizable to God. Perhaps even those forms of life appropriately excommunicated and "anathematized" are lives in which God can see resonances of the Logos. Again, Jeremiah's excessive covenant language points us in the direction of a God of remarkable excess: God makes the sacrifice that undermines our refusal of sacrifice; correspondingly, God makes the judgment that sees in our form of life a denial of the very thing we actively pursue—*this hating, this lying, this destroying, is a twisted expression of the creature's true desire to love, to be immersed only in truth, to create herself anew within my life.* "Sin is not a seeking of things evil by nature but an abandonment of the better things."[29] Perhaps God will see what even others cannot, in my actions: traces of the better things I turned from, even as I sought them in disordered ways.

Hell will, in this case, always exist only in the sense that the sins that are perverted expressions of true human desire can never enter, as these perversions, into heaven. My selfish ambition will always be excluded from heaven even as God recognizes it, as I hope God does, as Logos-centered desire for deification. If, on the other hand, God looks on my entire life and sees there nothing but a heart turned in on itself, with no desire for God at all, then I myself in my entire personal being will always be excluded, cut off from the divine idea of which my life is a unique expression.

World without End

I said above that eschatology is not exactly about our future, but something more like God's transcendent future that is also, mysteriously, as present now as it one day will be. This may help to reframe some of our theological confusion over the line between our participation in God's work and God's initiative in that work, which seems most acute in conversations about ecology and eschatology. Do new farming practices, for instance, attuned to local ecosystems and sustainability, create the peaceable kingdom of Isaiah's vision, or does God bring the kingdom to earth despite what we do? The answer, which I hope will by now be more or less clear, is that neither of these alternatives is an adequate expression of the way the God of Scripture pursues, invites, and waits for us. The work of God is not dependent on what we do, and yet our participation in God's work of healing ourselves and the world around us is how this saving work happens within and around us.

The way the habits we form in our treatment of the planet on which we live share in God's work is identical to the way our habit-forming treatment of human beings shares in God's work. Without ever imagining that it is our job to keep someone alive forever, we also prohibit murder and manslaughter, and call the treating of another with charity and justice the highest of Christian virtues. God is the source of my neighbor's life and the agent of her resurrection; my interactions with her form a part of the path to my salvation, as well as of hers. Someone who insists on using, abusing, raping, or murdering another human being has not experienced even the first manifestations of God's salvation, such that they might see the other person as God created her. Such a vision would in effect prohibit the sinful act, since "the dullest and most uninteresting person you talk to may one day be a creature which, if you saw it now, you would be strongly tempted to worship . . ."[30] The same holds, then, for someone who is complicit with the abuse of nonhuman creatures, the devouring of forests, the raising and warming of ocean waters. We might imagine the perspective of the saints and angels, looking on us in these practices: what they see is us attacking the divine idea of the butterfly, the seal, the polar bear, the rainforest. Ideas that, if we could see them as the collector in Williams' novel saw them, we would be tempted to worship. Only those blinded and dominated by sin would do such a thing: only the unsaved.

And so God waits, as Gabriel waited on Mary. Perhaps the angels of the Amazon wait for us to cease refusing to let the Logos grow in ourselves, and so in the trees and waters and air around us. Creation groans, Paul says, while waiting for us to live as generous children of the generous God of our planet. The resurrection of the ancient trees we kill and the mountains we strip will be God's excessive Spirit-filled act that goes beyond any care we could take of them, just as the crossing of Jordan was once God's gift for those who hoped for safe passage over the Ohio River. And yet the care of those trees matters, just as the courage of finding a way to the river mattered. Our habits of care are deifying, and so God waits.

The waiting itself is an excessive surprise, in these last days of the messianic age, when creation itself longs for us to take on our inheritance as God's children, and live within it as those enraptured, passionately moved, by the Word of being that God utters to us from the dawn of time.

NOTES

Preface

1   Oscar A. Romero, *Voice of the Voiceless: The Four Pastoral Letters and Other Statements* (Maryknoll, N.Y.: Orbis, 1985), 133–35, quoting from 135.

2   See especially "Against the Dead Consensus," *First Things*, March 2019, https://www.firstthings.com/web-exclusives/2019/03/against-the-dead-consensus.

3   "Amazon Rainforest Fires: Here's What's Really Happening," *New York Times*, August 28, 2019, https://www.nytimes.com/2019/08/23/world/americas/amazon-fire-brazil-bolsonaro.html.

4   Pope Francis VI, *Laudato si'* 116, http://www.vatican.va/content/francesco/en/encyclicals/documents/papa-francesco_20150524_enciclica-laudato-si.html.

5   Emmanuel Katongole and Jonathan Wilson-Hartgrove, *Mirror to the Church: Resurrecting Faith after Genocide in Rwanda* (Grand Rapids: Zondervan, 2009), 34.

6   Rowan Williams, *On Christian Theology* (Oxford: Blackwell, 2000), 16.

7   See Willis Jenkins' description of a Christian community working through the challenges of depleted fisheries on the Chesapeake Bay in *The Future of Ethics: Sustainability, Social Justice, and Religious Creativity* (Washington, D.C.: Georgetown University Press, 2013), 173–74.

8   "Cardinal Tobin Leads Hundreds of Catholics in Protest against ICE in Newark," *National Catholic Reporter*, September 6, 2019, https://www.ncronline.org/news/justice/cardinal-tobin-leads-hundreds-catholics-protest-against-ice-newark.

9   "Black Parishioners in Louisiana Pray on Easter for Alleged Racist Who Burned Down Their Church," *Daily Beast*, April 21, 2019, https://www.thedailybeast.com/louisiana-church-fires-black-parishioners-pray-for-holden-matthews-accused-of-burning-down-church-in-hate-crime.

10 *Martyrdom of Polycarp* 11, in *The Ante-Nicene Fathers*, vol. 1, ed. Alexander Roberts and James Donaldson (New York: Christian Literature Company, 1885). Subsequent references will be to this edition.

11 "White Man Accused in Church Killings Told Black Friend He Planned Mass Shooting at SC College," *U.S. News & World Report*, June 20, 2015, https://www.usnews.com/news/us/articles/2015/06/20/man-accused-of-church-killings-spoke-of-attacking-college.

12 Donald B. Kraybill, Steven M. Nolt, and David Weaver-Zercher, *Amish Grace: How Forgiveness Transcended Tragedy*, 1st ed. (San Francisco: Jossey-Bass, 2007).

13   "Mother Emanuel Survivors Visit Tree of Life, Offer Strength, Solidarity," *Pittsburgh Jewish Chronicle*, May 10, 2019, https://jewishchronicle.timesofisrael.com/mother -emanuel-survivors-visit-tree-of-life-offer-strength-solidarity/.

14   Katongole, *Mirror*, 143.

15   *Martyrdom of Polycarp* 22.

16   "What the Notre-Dame Fire Reveals about the Soul of France," *New York Times*, April 16, 2019, https://www.nytimes.com/2019/04/16/world/europe/france-notre -dame-religion.html.

Introduction

1   Thomas Aquinas, *Summa Theologiae*, 2nd rev. ed., trans. Fathers of the English Dominican Province (London: Burns, Oates and Washbourne, 1920), preface. Rev. and ed. for New Advent by Kevin Knight. https://www.newadvent.org/summa/. All subsequent references will be to this edition. Hereafter *S.T.*

2   Willie Jennings, in *After Whiteness: An Education in Belonging* (Grand Rapids: Eerdmans, 2020), calls the *disputatio* "a beautiful discursive practice, a useful method for organizing ideas, and an able guide into certain kinds of conceptual frames." Kindle edition, chap. 2.

3   Albert Schweitzer, *The Quest of the Historical Jesus*, ed. John Bowden, 1st complete ed. (Minneapolis: Fortress, 2001), 4.

4   See Henri De Lubac's exegetical project in *Medieval Exegesis*, vols. 1–3 (Grand Rapids: Eerdmans, 1998–2008), along with his critical reading of Augustine in *Augustinianism and Modern Theology* (London: G. Chapman, 1969). See also Hans Urs von Balthasar's reading of Maximus in *Cosmic Liturgy: The Universe according to Maximus the Confessor*, trans. Brian Daley (San Francisco: Ignatius, 2003), and of Gregory of Nyssa in *Presence and Thought: An Essay on the Religious Philosophy of Gregory of Nyssa* (San Francisco: Ignatius, 1995). More recently, Kathryn Tanner's *Christ the Key* (Cambridge: Cambridge University Press, 2010), or the early John Milbank's "Postmodern Critical Augustinianism: A Short Summa in Forty Two Responses to Unasked Questions," *Modern Theology* 7, no. 3 (1991): 225–37.

5   See Leonid Kishkovsky, "Russian Theology after Totalitarianism," in *The Cambridge Companion to Orthodox Christian Theology*, ed. Mary B. Cunningham and Elizabeth Theokritoff (Cambridge: Cambridge University Press, 2008), 261–75.

6   Hans Urs von Balthasar, *First Glance at Adrienne von Speyr* (San Francisco: Ignatius, 1981), along with von Speyr's own *The Cross, Word and Sacrament* (San Francisco: Ignatius, 1983). I owe my awareness of von Speyr to Gene Rogers. See also von Balthasar's *Two Sisters in the Spirit: Thérèse of Lisieux & Elizabeth of the Trinity* (San Francisco: Ignatius, 1992); Rowan Williams, *Teresa of Avila* (London: G. Chapman, 1991); and idem, *The Wound of Knowledge: Christian Spirituality from the New Testament to St. John of the Cross*, 2nd rev. ed. (Cambridge, Mass.: Cowley Publications, 1991).

7   The work of Stanley Hauerwas, among others, brought reflection on practice into the theological mainstream. Sarah Coakley has taken this a step further, and joined systematic theology with field research in her *God, Sexuality, and the Self: An Essay 'On the Trinity'* (Cambridge: Cambridge University Press, 2014).

8   Michael De La Bedoyere, *The Cardijn Story: A Study of the Life of Mgr. Joseph Cardijn and the Young Christian Workers' Movement Which He Founded* (London: Longmans, Green and Co., 1958).

9   Ernesto Cardenal, *El Evangelio En Solentiname* (Madrid: Editorial Trotta, 2006). Many thanks to my colleagues Jen Owens-Jófre and Mariana Sabino-Salazar and

the *Platica* students of Seminary of the Southwest for many insightful conversations on this book.

10   Wabash Center, https://www.wabashcenter.wabash.edu/syllabi-topic/theology/.

11   Rebecca S. Copp, "Theology and the Poetics of Testimony," in *Converging on Culture: Theologians in Dialogue with Cultural Analysis and Criticism*, ed. Delwin Brown, Sheila Greeve Davaney, and Kathryn Tanner (Oxford: Oxford University Press, 2001), 58. Thanks to my student Lize Burr for bringing this important essay to my attention.

12   Jean-Yves Lacoste, *From Theology to Theological Thinking*, trans. W. Chris Hackett (Charlottesville: University of Virginia Press, 2014), 88.

13   Kathleen M. Fisher, "Look before You Leap: Reconsidering Contemplative Pedagogy," *Teaching Theology & Religion* 20, no. 1 (2017): 4–21.

14   Coakley, *God, Sexuality and the Self*, 41 and 43.

15   Serene Jones and Paul Lakeland, *Constructive Theology: A Contemporary Approach to Classical Themes* (Minneapolis: Fortress, 2005), 19, 45.

16   I use the adjectives "constructive" and "systematic" interchangeably, which will perhaps surprise some. In doing so, I am attempting to emphasize the "built" aspect of any attempt to say who God is. My thoughts here about the necessary distinction between two legitimate disciplines are influenced by a panel discussion on the future of systematic theology at the American Academy of Religion's annual meeting, especially the reflections of Vincent Lloyd and Sarah Coakley. I take this distinction to be in line with what Katherine Sonderegger calls for in an interview about her ongoing systematic theology project (Fortress Catalogue, Winter 2020), with what Willie Jennings (*After Whiteness*, chap. 1) describes as the need for intimacy among various theological contexts, and also with the reflections of Carlos Mendoza-Álvarez, *La Resurrección como Anticipación Mesiánica* (Mexico, D.F.: Universidad Iberoamericana A.C., 2020), Kindle edition, 56ff., describing the new movement of liberation theology beyond the formation of subjectivities and into the generous formation of intersubjectivity.

17   Anthony D. Baker, "Arguing the Mystery: Teaching Critical Thinking in the Theology Classroom," *Wabash Center Journal on Teaching* 1, no. 1 (2020): 37–45.

1   Theology

1   Eliezer Berkovits, *God, Man, And History* (Middle Village, N.Y.: Jonathan David, 1979), 18.

2   John Behr, *The Mystery of Christ: Life in Death* (New York: St. Vladimir's Seminary Press, 2006), 27.

3   Translation from Kendal Soulen, *The Divine Name(s) and the Holy Trinity* (Louisville: Westminster John Knox, 2011), 7-23.

4   Jeffrey Stackert, *A Prophet Like Moses: Prophecy, Law, and Israelite Religion* (Oxford: Oxford University Press, 2014).

5   Berkovits, *God, Man, And History*, 43.

6   Mendoza-Álvarez, *Resurrección*, 200.

7   From his "Funeral Homily for Msgr. Luigi Giussani," reprinted in *Joseph Ratzinger in Communio*, vol. 2, *Anthropology and Culture* (Grand Rapids: Eerdmans, 2013), 184–87.

8   Aristotle, *Nicomachean Ethics* 2.1.1103a.

9   Abraham Joshua Heschel, *Between God and Man; an Interpretation of Judaism* (New York: Harper, 1959), 82.

10   Israël Knohl, *The Sanctuary of Silence: The Priestly Torah and the Holiness School* (Minneapolis: Fortress, 1995), 180–86.

11   Jorge Luis Borges, *The Book of Sand, and Shakespeare's Memory*, trans. Andrew Hurley (London: Penguin Books, 2001), 36–38.

12   Marilynne Robinson, *Gilead* (New York: Farrar, Straus & Giroux, 2005), 65.

13   Bonaventure, *On the Reduction of the Arts to Theology*, trans. Zachary Hayes (New York: Franciscan Institute, 1996), 26.

14   This image of interpretation as a fusing of horizons comes from Hans-Georg Gadamer, *Truth and Method*, 2nd rev. ed. (New York: Continuum, 2004), and has been put to use for theology and biblical interpretation by Anthony Thiselton in *The Two Horizons: New Testament Hermeneutics and Philosophical Description* (Grand Rapids, Eerdmans, 1980) and *Hermeneutics: An Introduction* (Grand Rapids: Eerdmans, 2009).

15   Augustine, *The Trinity* 8.6, trans. Edmund Hill (Hyde Park, N.Y.: New City Press, 1990). Subsequent references will be to this edition.

16   Coakley, *God, Sexuality, and the Self*, 43.

17   Peter Ochs, "Morning Prayer as Redemptive Thinking," in *Liturgy, Time, and the Politics of Redemption*, ed. Randi Rashkover and C. C. Pecknold (Grand Rapids: Eerdmans, 2006), 64–65.

18   Berkovitz on occasion speaks this way, as if the encounter with God at Sinai were clear and obvious, and the difficulty of theology lies in the later moments where it is less so. I am challenging the non-ambiguity of even the Sinai encounter, since Exodus presents us with a divine presence there accompanied by clouds, symbols, and thunder-like rumblings. In a related but different way, Christian theologian William J. Abraham suggests that epistemological ambiguity ceases when Christians accept "once for all" the efficacy of the revelation accounts (*Crossing the Threshold of Divine Revelation* [Grand Rapids: Eerdmans, 2006], 53). Though with both of these theologians it would take more detail and engagement to fully demonstrate my point, it seems to me these accounts move beyond ambiguity by making the encounter with God too much like an encounter with a discrete and embodied dialogue partner. God, I am suggesting throughout this book, does not meet us like that.

19   Jean Yves Lacoste explores the way theology can be shaped by "inexperience" of God (*Experience and Absolute: Disputed Questions on the Humanity of Man*, trans. Mark Raftery-Skehan [New York: Fordham University Press, 2004]).

20   Anna Estany and David Casacuberta, "Contributions of Socially Distributed Cognition to Social Epistemology: The Case of Testimony," *Eidos* no. 16 (2012): 41.

21   The example of the cockpit as a "system of distributed cognition" comes from Edwin Hutchins and Tove Klausen, "Distributed Cognition in an Airline Cockpit," in *Cognition and Communication at Work*, ed. Y. Engeström and D. Middleton (Cambridge: Cambridge University Press, 1996), 15–34.

22   Coakley, *God, Sexuality, and the Self*, 45.

23   Catherine Pickstock, *Repetition and Identity* (Oxford: Oxford University Press, 2013), chap. 3.

24   Karl Barth, *Dogmatics in Outline* (New York: Harper, 1959), chap. 2.

25   For the story of a community built around friendships among persons with and without disabilities, see Jean Vanier, *Community and Growth*, 2nd rev. ed (New York: Paulist Press, 1989).

26   This is why Wittgenstein argued that there is no such thing as a private language (*Philosophical Investigations*, trans G. E. M. Anscombe [New York: Macmillan, 1953], 88–93 [paras. 243–261]).

27 Augustine, *Confessions* 3.6, trans. Maria Boulding, The Works of Saint Augustine: A Translation for the 21st Century (Hyde Park, N.Y.: New City Press, 2002), 11. Subsequent references will be to this edition.

28 Alice Walker, *The Color Purple* (Orlando: Harcourt, 1982), 17.

29 Walker, *Color Purple*, 192–95. Shug's theology, which is not to say Walker's, is post-incarnational, and therefore different from the one sketched in these pages.

30 Again, see Lacoste on lack of experience as a source of theological reflection (n. 19, above).

31 Walker, *Color Purple*, 285.

32 Howard W. Stone and James O. Duke, *How to Think Theologically* (Minneapolis: Fortress, 2013), 13–16.

33 Fisher, "Contemplative Pedagogy," 4–21.

2 Spirit

1 Jean-Louis Chrétien, *The Ark of Speech*, trans. Andrew Brown (London: Routledge, 2004), 111.

2 See Martin Luther's harsh handling of Aristotle in *Address to the German Nobility Concerning Christian Liberty* (Champaign, Ill.: Project Gutenberg), http://search .ebscohost.com/login.aspx?direct=true&AuthType=ip,sso&db=nlebk&AN=1085290 &site=eds-live&scope=site. See also Karl Barth's argument in *Church Dogmatics*, vol. 2.1, *The Doctrine of God*, trans. G. W. Bromiley et al. (Edinburgh: T&T Clark, 1957), that Christianity is not a religion because it begins not in human categories but in divine revelation.

3 J. L. Austin, *How to Do Things with Words* (Oxford: Oxford University Press, 2009).

4 Stanley Cavell, *Philosophy the Day after Tomorrow* (Cambridge, Mass.: Harvard University Press, 2005), 15.

5 Both examples are from Cavell, *Day after Tomorrow*, 17–21.

6 "*Boris Godunov*; Opera in Four Acts, Based on Pushkin," libretto translation by John Guttman for the Metropolitan Opera, act 4, scene 1, Archive.Org, last modified 2020, accessed July 22, 2020, https://archive.org/stream/borisgodunovopera00muss/ borisgodunovopera00muss_djvu.txt.

7 Eve Kosofsky Sedgwick, *Touching Feeling* (Durham, N.C.: Duke University Press, 2014), 68.

8 Sedgwick, *Touching Feeling*, 68.

9 Sedgwick, *Touching Feeling*, 70.

10 Sedgwick, *Touching Feeling*, 74.

11 Sedgwick, *Touching Feeling*, 76.

12 I am using the term in a sense analogous to its use in Mendoza-Álvarez, *Resurrección*, 154–55 and 254ff. In his text, the word denotes an origin that is itself without origin, or a generative gift that arrives from beyond temporality.

13 Combining insights from Erich Przywara, *Analogia Entis: Metaphysics: Original Structure and Universal Rhythm*, trans. John R. Betz and David Bentley Hart (Grand Rapids: Eerdmans, 2014), and Jean-Luc Marion, *Givenness and Revelation*, trans. Stephen E. Lewis (Oxford: Oxford University Press, 2016). See also Andrew Davison, *Participation in God: A Study in Christian Doctrine and Metaphysics* (Cambridge: Cambridge University Press, 2019), chap. 7.

14 So it is for instance inadequate to say, as Kelly Brown Douglas says, "Theology is God talk. But it is not God doing the talking. Rather, it is human beings talking about the meaning of God in their lives" ("Theological Method and the Jesus Movement

through the Work of F. D. Maurice and Vida Scudder," *Anglican Theological Review* 102, no. 1 [2020]: 7).

15   See Wesley Hill, *Paul and the Trinity: Persons, Relations, and the Pauline Letters* (Grand Rapids: Eerdmans, 2015), 149–53.

16   Quoted in Hans Urs von Balthasar, *Theological Aesthetics*, vol. 1, *Seeing the Form*, trans. Erasmo Leiva-Merikakakis (San Francisco: Ignatius, 1982), 23.

17   Chrétien, *Ark of Speech*, 11.

18   Maximus the Confessor, *Chapters on Knowledge* 1.17, in *Maximus Confessor: Selected Writings*, trans. George C. Berthold (New York: Paulist Press, 1985), 131.

19   Peter Lombard, *The Sentences*, trans. Giulio Silano (Toronto: Pontifical Institute of Mediaeval Studies, 2007), 42–43, 45, 48. See also Elizabeth Hastings, "Augustine of Hippo and William of Saint-Thierry on the Relation between the Holy Spirit's Personal Identity (Rom 5:5) and His Sovereign Freedom Ad Extra," *Studia Patristica* 48 (2010): 361–66.

20   Aquinas, *S.T.* 2-1.70.3, resp.

21   Aquinas, *S.T.* 1.1.8, ad. 2.

22   Ben Quash, *Found Theology: History, Imagination and the Holy Spirit* (London: T&T Clark, 2013), 276.

23   See Teresa of Avila's moving reflection on the intimate companionship of Simon and Christ after the crucifixion in her concluding chapter of *The Interior Castle*.

24   Williams, *On Christian Theology*, 138.

25   Harumi Murakami, *Killing Commendatore*, trans. Philip Gabriel and Ted Goossen (New York: Penguin Books, 2018), 567.

26   Davison, *Participation*, 192.

27   Ignacio Ellacuría, *Ignacio Ellacuria: Essays on History, Liberation, and Salvation*, trans. Michael Edward Lee (Maryknoll, N.Y.: Orbis, 2013), 279.

28   Dumitru Staniloae, *Theology and the Church*, trans. Robert Barringer (New York: Saint Vladimir's Seminary Press, 1980), chap. 1.

3   Trinity

1   See Aristotle, *Metaphysics* 7, and David Bradshaw, *Aristotle East and West: Metaphysics and the Division of Christendom* (Cambridge: Cambridge University Press, 2005).

2   Gregory of Nyssa, *On Not Three Gods, to Ablabius*, trans. William Moore, in *Nicene and Post-Nicene Fathers*, series 2, vol. 5 (Buffalo, N.Y.: Christian Literature Company, 1892), 335. Subsequent references will be to this edition.

3   See Nonna Verna Harrison, "Gregory of Nyssa on Knowing the Trinity," in *The Holy Trinity in the Life of the Church*, ed. Khaled Anatolios (Grand Rapids: Baker Academic, 2014), 55ff.

4   On this point, see Rowan Williams, *Christ the Heart of Creation* (London: Bloomsbury, 2018), chap. 1.

5   Ellacuría, *Essays*, 278.

6   See Lewis Ayres, *Nicaea and Its Legacy: An Approach to Fourth Century Trinitarian Theology* (Oxford: Oxford University Press, 2004).

7   See Hill, *Paul and the Trinity*, 65ff.

8   Soulen, *Divine Name(s)*, chap. 2.

9   Gregory of Nyssa, *On Not Three Gods*, 334.

10   Augustine, *Confessions* 13.29, 44.

11   Augustine, *The Trinity* 5.16–17.

12 Athanasius, Letter 1.9, in *The Letters of Saint Athanasius concerning the Holy Spirit*, trans. C. R. B. Shapland (New York: Epworth Press, 1951).

13 See Khaled Anatolios, "Personhood, Community, and Trinity in Some Patristic Texts," in *The Holy Trinity in the Life of the Church*, ed. Khaled Anatolios (Grand Rapids: Baker Academic, 2014).

14 See Frederick Bauerschmidt, *Thomas Aquinas: Faith, Reason, and Following Christ* (Oxford: Oxford University Press, 2013), 160–65.

15 Sergius Bulgakov, *The Comforter*, trans. Boris Jakim (Grand Rapids: Eerdmans, 2004), 184.

16 Augustine, *The Trinity* 7.11.

17 See Eugene F. Rogers, Jr., *Sexuality and the Christian Body: Their Way into the Triune God* (Cambridge: Blackwell, 1999).

18 David Bentley Hart, *The Beauty of the Infinite: The Aesthetics of Christian Truth* (Grand Rapids: Eerdmans, 2004), 294.

19 John Milbank, *The Word Made Strange* (Oxford: Blackwell, 1997), chap. 7.

20 Augustine, *The Trinity* 8.12.

21 See Staniloae, *Theology and the Church*, chap. 3.

22 Kathleen McVey, "Syriac Christian Tradition and Gender in Trinitarian Theology," in *The Holy Trinity in the Life of the Church*, ed. Khaled Anatolios (Grand Rapids: Baker Academic, 2014), 199ff. See also Eugene F. Rogers, Jr., *Elements of Christian Thought: A Basic Course in Christianese* (Minneapolis: Fortress, 2021), 114.

23 Jarena Lee, "My Call to Preach the Gospel," in *Religious Experience* (Philadelphia, 1849), https://pluralism.org/african-religion-in-america.

24 Tanner, *Christ the Key*, 145.

25 This is, again, consistent with Mendoza-Álvarez's use of the term. See chap. 2, n. 12, above.

4 Creation

1 Using here David Bentley Hart's translation: *The New Testament* (New Haven, Conn.: Yale University Press, 2017).

2 This is one of the many theological insights I owe to my first professor, Craig Keen.

3 Thomas, *S.T.* 1.1.8, reply 2.

4 See, for instance, Maximus the Confessor, *Ambiguum* 7, in *On Difficulties in the Church Fathers: The Ambigua*, trans. Nicholas Constas (Cambridge, Mass.: Harvard University Press, 2014), 75–141. Subsequent references will be to this edition.

5 Athanasius, *On the Incarnation of the Word* 1.1, in *Christology of the Later Fathers*, trans. Edward Rochie Hardy (Philadelphia: Westminster, 1954). Subsequent references will be to this edition.

6 Ochs, "Morning Prayer," 65.

7 William Desmond, *Being and the Between* (Albany, N.Y.: SUNY Press, 1995), 322.

8 Desmond, *Being and the Between*, 321.

9 Augustine, *Confessions* 10.6, 8–10.

10 Quoted in Mark McIntosh, "The Maker's Meaning: Divine Ideas and Salvation," *Modern Theology* 28, no. 3 (2012): 365–84.

11 Augustine, *The Trinity* 1.2.

12 Nicholas of Cusa, *De docta ignorantia* 104, in *Selected Spiritual Writings: Nicholas of Cusa*, trans. H. Lawrence Bond (New York: Paulist Press, 1997), 134.

13   The notion of a revelation within God is the principle of Bulgakov's sophiological theology. See Sergius Bulgakov, *The Wisdom of God: A Brief Summary of Sophiology*, trans. Patrick Thompson, O. Fielding Clarke, and Xenia Braikevitc (New York: The Paisley Press, 1937).

14   See Davison, *Participation*, 104–5.

15   See Rowan Williams, "The Deflections of Desire: Negative Theology in Trinitarian Disclosure," in *Silence and the Word: Negative Theology and Incarnation*, ed. Denys Turner and Oliver Davies (Cambridge: Cambridge University Press, 2002), 128.

16   Davison, *Participation*, 23ff.

17   David G. Horrell, Cherryl Hunt, and Christopher Southgate, *Greening Paul: Rereading the Apostle in a Time of Ecological Crisis* (Waco, Tex.: Baylor University Press, 2010), chap. 4.

18   See David Bentley Hart, *The Hidden and the Manifest: Essays in Theology and Metaphysics* (Grand Rapids: Eerdmans, 2017), 6.

19   Here I am developing analogy as used in mathematics in the direction of Thomas' analogy of proportion. See Przywara, *Analogia Entis*, 231–32, and Betz's introduction.

20   Davison's explanation (*Participation*, 182ff.) is especially precise.

21   David H. Kelsey, *Eccentric Existence: A Theological Anthropology* (Louisville: Westminster John Knox, 2009), 161ff.

22   John of the Cross, *Romances* 3, in *The Collected Works of Saint John of the Cross*, rev. ed., trans. Kieran Kavanaugh and Otilio Rodriguez (Washington, D.C.: ICS Publications, 1991), 62.

23   See my *Shakespeare, Theology, and the Unstaged God* (London: Routledge, 2020).

24   https://allpoetry.com/Black-Rook-In-Rainy-Weather.

25   Rogers, *Elements*, 120.

26   See Catherine Keller, *Face of the Deep: A Theology of Becoming* (London: Routledge, 2003). For a more nuanced critique, see Karen Baker-Fletcher, "Something or Nothing: An Eco-Womanist Essay on God, Creation, and Indispensability," in *This Sacred Earth: Religion, Nature, Environment*, 2nd ed, ed. Roger S. Gottlieb (London: Routledge, 2004).

27   Kathryn Tanner, *God and Creation in Christian Theology: Tyranny or Empowerment* (Minneapolis: Fortress, 2005), 38.

28   Augustine, *The Trinity* 5.15.

29   Ellacuría, *Essays*, 151.

5   Human Beings

1   Sergius Bulgakov, *The Friend of the Bridegroom: On the Orthodox Veneration of the Forerunner*, trans. Boris Jakim (Grand Rapids: Eerdmans, 2003), 32.

2   Augustine, *Confessions* 3.6, 11.

3   Wolfhart Pannenberg, *Jesus—God and Man*, trans. Lewis L. Wilkins and Duane A. Priebe (Philadelphia: Westminster John Knox, 1977), 205.

4   Karl Barth, *Church Dogmatics*, vol. 4.2, *The Doctrine of Reconciliation*, trans. G. W. Bromiley (Edinburgh: T&T Clark, 1958), 119.

5   Maximus the Confessor, *Ambiguum* 7.21–27.

6   Maximus the Confessor, *Ambiguum* 7.19.

7   Maximus the Confessor, *Ambiguum* 7.15.

8   Sergius Bulgakov, *The Bride of the Lamb*, trans. Boris Jakim (Grand Rapids: Eerdmans, 2001), 53.

9   W. H. Auden, "After Reading a Child's Guide to Modern Physics," https://allpoetry
    .com/After-Reading-A-Child's-Guide-To-Modern-Physics.

10 Barth, *Church Dogmatics* 4.2, 120

11 Martin Heidegger, *Being and Time*, ed. and trans. Joan Stambaugh and Dennis J.
    Schmidt (Albany: SUNY Press, 2010), 205.

12 G. K. Chesterton's argument in *The Everlasting Man* (London: Hodder & Stough-
    ton, 1936), chap. 1, that our human uniqueness manifested itself in the first drawing
    on a cave wall is still worth consideration. The argument needs updating, though,
    with discoveries of visual artistry from earlier eras throughout central Africa. See
    Ed Yong, "A Cultural Leap at the Dawn of Humanity," *Atlantic*, March 2018, https://
    www.theatlantic.com/science/archive/2018/03/a-deeper-origin-of-complex-human
    -cultures/555674/.

13 Willie James Jennings, *The Christian Imagination: Theology and the Origins of Race*
    (New Haven, Conn.: Yale University Press, 2010), 286. This corresponds with an
    emerging critique of nineteenth- and twentieth-century readings of Israel's his-
    tory and theology as culminating in a sublation of the priestly law and its relation
    to place—as if Israel were most herself when she loses her connection to particular
    farming, ranching, and sacrificial practices. See Stackert, *Prophet Like Moses*, chap. 1.

14 Marilynne Robinson, *Housekeeping: A Novel* (New York: Picador, 1980), 194–95.

15 Marilynne Robinson, *When I Was a Child I Read Books: Essays* (New York: Farrar,
    Straus and Giroux, 2012), 93.

16 Robinson, *When I Was a Child*, 21.

17 Jennings, *Christian Imagination*, esp. 248–49.

18 James H. Cone, *God of the Oppressed* (Maryknoll, N.Y.: Orbis, 1997), 146.

19 Mendoza-Álvarez, *Resurrección*, 15ff.

20 Celia Deane-Drummond, "In Adam All Die? Questions at the Boundary of Niche
    Construction, Community Evolution and Original Sin," in *Evolution and the Fall*, ed.
    William T. Cavanaugh and James K. A. Smith (Grand Rapids: Eerdmans, 2017).

21 Robinson, *Housekeeping*, 12–13.

22 James H. Cone, *The Spirituals and the Blues: An Interpretation* (Maryknoll, N.Y.:
    Orbis, 1992), 78–96.

23 Przywara, *Analogia Entis*, 160.

24 I owe this way of putting things to my friend and colleague Dusty McDonald.

25 Alfred North Whitehead, *Process and Reality*, ed. David Ray Griffin and Donald W.
    Sherburne, corrected ed. (New York: Free Press, 1978), 47–48.

26 See Michael J. Gorman, *Inhabiting the Cruciform God: Kenosis, Justification, and The-
    osis in Paul's Narrative Soteriology* (Grand Rapids: Eerdmans, 2009).

6   The God-Human

1   Rowan Williams, *Resurrection: Interpreting the Easter Gospel*, rev. ed. (Cleveland: Pil-
    grim Press, 2002), 75.

2   Mendoza-Álvarez, *Resurrección*, 202.

3   Williams, *Resurrection*, chap. 2.

4   Mendoza-Álvarez, *Resurrección*, 248. Translation is mine. See also Milbank, *Word
    Made Strange*, chap. 5.

5   Dante, *Inferno* 1.35, in *The Portable Dante*, ed. and trans. Mark Musa (New York:
    Penguin Books, 2003). Subsequent references will be to this edition.

6   Dante, *Inferno* 1.90–93.

7   Dante, *Inferno* 2.31–35.

8   My reading of Dante is influenced by Vittorio Montemaggi's remarkable book, *Reading Dante's Commedia as Theology: Divinity Realized in Human Encounter* (Oxford: Oxford University Press, 2018), as well as by conversations with my former student and current—and future, I hope—friend Daniel Strandlund.

9   Augustine, Exposition of Psalm 96.2, in *Expositions of the Psalms*, vol. 4, trans. Maria Boulding, The Works of Saint Augustine: A Translation for the Twenty-First Century (Hyde Park, N.Y.: New City Press, 2001).

10   Rowan Williams, *On Augustine* (London: Bloomsbury, 2016), chap. 2.

11   Augustine, Exposition of Psalm 9.14, in *Expositions of the Psalms*, vol. 1, trans. John E. Rotelle, The Works of Saint Augustine: A Translation for the Twenty-First Century (Hyde Park, N.Y.: New City Press, 2000).

12   See Augustine, *City of God* 20.18.

13   Pannenberg, *Jesus—God and Man*, 196.

14   Willis Jenkins, *Ecologies of Grace: Environmental Ethics and Christian Theology* (Oxford: Oxford University Press, 2008).

15   This is the thesis of Mendoza-Álvarez's book, namely, that an increasingly intersubjective community among survivors is the formation of a catholic hope in a universal resurrection. See *Resurrección*, 242ff.

16   Lancelot Andrewes, "Sermon 4 Of the Holy Ghost, Whit-Sunday 1611," in *Lancelot Andrewes: Sermons*, ed. George Morley Story (Oxford: The Clarendon Press, 1967), 253. I have modernized the spelling.

17   Maximus the Confessor, *Opusculum* 6, in *On the Cosmic Mystery of Jesus Christ*, trans. Paul M. Blowers and Robert Wilken (Crestwood, N.Y.: St. Vladimir's Seminary Press, 2003), 174. Subsequent references will be to this edition.

18   Maximus the Confessor, *Opusculum* 6, 176.

19   Paul in Rom 5, and Irenaeus in *Against Heresies* 3, in *The Ante-Nicene Fathers*, vol. 1, ed. Alexander Roberts and James Donaldson (Buffalo, N.Y.: Christian Literature Company, 1885).

20   Jennings, *Christian Imagination*, 252–53.

21   For more on the theme of God's pursuit of creation, see my *Diagonal Advance* (London: SCM Press, 2011).

22   *Origen of Alexandria, Commentary on the Gospel according to John* 1.22, in *Commentary on the Gospel according to John: Books 1–10*, trans. Ronald E. Heine (Washington, D.C.: Catholic University of America Press, 1989). Subsequent references will be to this edition.

23   Williams, *On Christian Theology*, chap. 6.

24   Rowan Williams, "The Body's Grace," in *Theology and Sexuality: Classic and Contemporary Readings*, ed. Eugene F. Rogers, Jr. (Oxford: Blackwell, 2002), 311–12.

25   The main thesis of Williams, *Christ the Heart of Creation*.

26   Gorman, *Inhabiting*, chap. 1.

27   Origen, *Commentary on the Gospel according to John* 1.231.

28   Gregory of Nyssa, *Ad Theophilus*, in *Anti-Apollinarian Writings*, trans. Robin Orton (Washington, D.C.: Catholic University of America Press, 2015), 267. Subsequent references will be to this edition.

29   Dante, *Paradise* 33.130–132, in Musa, *Portable Dante*. Subsequent references will be to this edition.

30   Dante, *Paradise* 33.143–145.

7 Sin

1   Augustine, *Confessions* 12.11, 11.

2   Augustine, *The Trinity* 4.2, 153.

3   An important argument of Reinhold Niebuhr's in *The Nature and Destiny of Man: A Christian Interpretation* (New York: Scribner, 1949). I am grateful to my student Joel McAlister for pointing this out to me.

4   See Joy Ann McDougall, "The Bondage of the Eye/I? A Transnational Feminist Wager for Reimagining the Doctrine of Sin," in *Reimagining with Christian Doctrines: Responding to Global Gender Injustices*, ed. Grace Ji-Sun Kim and Jenny Daggers (New York: Palgrave-MacMillan, 2014), 105–25.

5   Ellacuría, *Essays*, 152.

6   Ellacuría, *Essays*, 152.

7   The classic account of this theology is Anselm's *The Fall of Satan*, in *Theological Treatises*, trans. and ed. Jasper Hopkins and Herbert Warren Richardson (Cambridge, Mass.: Harvard Divinity School Library, 1965).

8   Gorman, *Inhabiting*, chap. 2.

9   Augustine, *City of God* 15.2, in *The City of God (De Civitate Dei): Books 11–22*, trans. William S. Babcock (Hyde Park, N.Y.: New City Press, 2014).

10 Athanasius, *On the Incarnation* 4.

11 Paul J. Griffiths, *Decreation: The Last Things of All Creatures* (Waco, Tex.: Baylor University Press, 2014).

12 Hill, *Paul and the Trinity*, 55ff.

13 Jacob Milgrom, *Studies in Cultic Theology and Terminology* (Leiden: Brill, 1983).

14 Barth, *Church Dogmatics* 2.1, 505.

15 Bulgakov, *Bride of the Lamb*, 147.

16 Mary Wollstonecraft Shelley, *Frankenstein, or, The Modern Prometheus* (London: Sever, Francis, & Company, 1869), 131.

17 Shelley, *Frankenstein*, 96.

18 Shelley, *Frankenstein*, 85.

19 See Bulgakov, *Bride of the Lamb*, 189, for whom Prometheus becomes a figure of the deifying impulse within the Kingdom of God. See also my arguments about the myth in *Diagonal Advance*.

20 Augustine, *Confessions* 7.12, 18.

21 See Davison, *Participation*, chap. 10.

22 Bulgakov, *Bride of the Lamb*, 153.

23 Gregory of Nyssa, *Ad Theophilus*, 264.

24 Gorman, *Inhabiting*, chap. 2.

25 Ellacuría, *Essays*, 152.

26 Frederick Douglass, *My Bondage and My Freedom* (Buffalo, N.Y.: Miller, Orton & Mulligan, 1855), 194.

27 Douglass, *My Bondage*, 200.

28 Frederick Douglass, *The Life and Times of Frederick Douglass* (Mineola, N.Y.: Dover, 2012), 442–44.

29 Augustine, Exposition of Psalm 5.7, in Rotelle, *Expositions of the Psalms*, vol. 1.

30 See James Alison, *The Joy of Being Wrong: Original Sin through Easter Eyes* (New York: Crossroad, 1998).

8 Sacrifice

1 With this reference to character consistency in fiction, I am thinking especially of Flannery O'Connor's story of her neighbor's assessment of her own writing, retold by Anne Lamott: "Them stories," the neighbor said, "just gone and shown you how some folks would do" (Anne Lamott, *Bird by Bird: Some Instructions on Writing and Life* [New York: Random House, 1994], 51).

2 Thomas, *S.T.* 3.46.1, resp.

3 "The Lamentations Service for Holy Saturday Matins," Orthodox Christianity, https://orthochristian.com/78602.html.

4 I owe this connection to conversation with my first theology professor, Craig Keen.

5 David P. Wright, "Azazel," in *Anchor Bible Dictionary*, vol. 1, ed. David Noel Freedman (New York: Doubleday, 1992), 536–37. My debts to my colleague Steve Bishop are extensive in this section.

6 Knohl, *Sanctuary of Silence*, 129ff. This is increasingly noted by Hebrew Bible scholars, especially since Hubert and Mauss. See Gary Anderson, "Sacrifice and Sacrificial Offerings (OT)," in *Anchor Bible Dictionary*, vol. 5, ed. David Noel Freedman (New York: Doubleday, 1992), 878.

7 Irenaeus, *Against Heresies* 5.19.1, in Roberts and Donaldson, *Ante-Nicene Fathers*, vol. 1, 547.

8 See Knohl, *Sanctuary*. I am reading here the fourth commandment from Exodus together with the version from Deuteronomy.

9 Milgrom, *Cultic Theology*.

10 Jacob Milgrom, *Cult and Conscience: The Asham and the Priestly Doctrine of Repentance* (Leiden: Brill, 1976).

11 Stackert, *Prophet Like Moses*, introduction.

12 Davison, *Theology of the Old Testament*, cited in Anderson, "Sacrifice," 882.

13 Cited in Anderson, "Sacrifice," 887.

14 This is a central theme throughout Pannenberg, *Jesus—God and Man*.

15 Participation as involvement: this is Andrew Davison's way of putting my account of atonement (*Participation*, 276).

16 Shusaku Endo, *Silence: A Novel*, trans. William Johnson (New York: Picador Modern Classics, 2016), 64.

17 Endo, *Silence*, 187.

18 Endo, *Silence*, 204.

19 Kenosis of the Spirit is Bulgakov's language. See *Comforter*, 220ff.

20 Gorman, *Inhabiting*, 81ff.

21 Ellacuría, *Essays*, 208ff.

22 I am revising Gorman here, who stays with Austin's "performative" category and thus misses the opening for Spirit-led response. *Inhabiting*, 101.

23 Augustine, *The Trinity* 13.

24 See Jane Lancaster Patterson, *Keeping the Feast: Metaphors of Sacrifice in 1 Corinthians and Philippians* (Atlanta: SBL, 2015), especially chap. 7.

25 Mendoza-Álvarez, *Resurrección*, 174ff.

26 Anderson, "Sacrifice," 890.

27 Augustine, among others, in *The Trinity* 4.2.

28 David Bentley Hart, *Hidden and Manifest*, 215.

29 Hans Urs von Balthasar, *The Action*, vol. 4 of *Theo-Drama: Theological Dramatic Theory*, trans. Graham Harrison (San Francisco: Ignatius, 1988), 323.

30 See Hart, *Hidden and Manifest*, 196.

31 Delayed recognition rather than "trinitarian inversion," as Balthasar has it. See *The Dramatis Personae: The Person in Christ*, vol. 3 of *Theo-Drama: Theological Dramatic Theory*, trans. Graham Harrison (San Francisco: Ignatius, 1992), 188ff.

32 Gorman, *Inhabiting*, chap. 1.

33 See Origen, *Commentary on the Gospel according to John* 1.231.

9 Church

1 Søren Kierkegaard, *Philosophical Fragments*, trans. Howard V. Hong and Edna H. Hong (Princeton: Princeton University Press, 1985).

2 John Milbank, *Being Reconciled: Ontology and Pardon* (London: Routledge, 2003), chap. 7.

3 Milbank, *Word Made Strange*, 277.

4 Christopher Hancock, "Complexity Theory and the Chinese Church," *International Journal for the Study of the Christian Church* 15, no. 4 (2015): 261–74.

5 Williams, *Resurrection*, 54.

6 Williams, *Resurrection*, 52–56.

7 Echoing Barth's translation of *pistis* as God's faithfulness in *The Epistle to the Romans*, trans. Edwyn Clement Hoskyns (Oxford: Oxford University Press, 1933).

8 Hart, *Hidden and Manifest*, 200.

9 See Hart, *Hidden and Manifest*, 210.

10 Ellacuría, *Essays*, chap. 9.

11 The central argument in Williams, *Christ the Heart of Creation*.

12 Quoted in Hart, *Hidden and Manifest*, 199.

13 Anselm, *Meditation on Human Redemption* 1–12, in *The Prayers and Meditations of St. Anselm*, trans. Sister Benedicta Ward (London: Penguin Books, 1973), 230. Subsequent references will be to this edition. Anselm is commonly associated with a transactional view of salvation in which Christ's death is God's way of satisfying our debt. This meditation complicates this picture by demonstrating the centrality of our involvement in the work of redemption through desire and joy. On this, see David Bentley Hart, "A Gift Exceeding Every Debt: An Eastern Orthodox Appreciation of Anselm's Cur Deus Homo," *Pro Ecclesia* 7, no. 3 (1998): 333–49.

14 Ellacuría, *Essays*, 233.

15 See Michael Wyschogrod, "Incarnation," *Pro Ecclesia* 2, no. 2 (1993): 208–15.

16 See Aaron Riches, "Sacrifice and Freedom: On Mystagogy and the Way of Atonement," *Communio* 45, no. 1 (2018): 54–84.

17 Hart, *Hidden and Manifest*, 215.

18 The key argument of Jennings, *Christian Imagination*.

19 Riches, "Sacrifice and Freedom," 62.

20 Anselm, *Meditation on Human Redemption*, 248–54.

21 Pope Paul VI, *Lumen Gentium* 2.9, https://www.vatican.va/archive/hist_councils/ii _vatican_council/documents/vat-ii_const_19641121_lumen-gentium_en.html.

22 My thoughts here have been influenced by the research of my student Lize Burr.

23 Emmanuel Katongole, *The Sacrifice of Africa: A Political Theology for Africa* (Grand Rapids: Eerdmans, 2011), 156.

24 Katongole, *Sacrifice*, 193, on forgiveness as a kind of madness.

25 C. S. Lewis, *The Great Divorce* (London: Geoffrey Bles, 1946), chap. 4.

26 Williams, *Resurrection*, 51.

27 Williams, *Resurrection*, 51.

28 Mendoza-Álvarez, *Resurrección*, 254ff.

29 Milbank, *Word Made Strange*, 160ff.

30 On grief as necessary for forgiveness, see Brené Brown, *Rising Strong: How the Ability to Reset Changes the Way We Live, Love, Parent, and Lead* (New York: Random House, 2015). I owe this insight and reference to the Reverend Miles Brandon.

31 Tanner, *Christ the Key*, 260.

32 Williams, *Resurrection*, 55.

10 Prayer

1 *The Epistle of Porphyry to the Egyptian Anebo*, http://www.tertullian.org/fathers/porphyry_anebo_02_text.htm.

2 Augustine, *On the Sermon on the Mount according to Matthew* 2.12, in *Nicene and Post-Nicene Fathers*, vol. 6, trans. William Findlay and Phillip Schaff (Buffalo, N.Y.: Christian Literature Company, 1888), 37–38.

3 See Knohl, *Sanctuary of Silence*.

4 See the insights on secondary causality and interventionist theology in Davison, *Participation*, 232.

5 Davison, *Participation*, 113ff.

6 Desmond, *Being and the Between*, 231.

7 Augustine, Letter 130.17, https://www.newadvent.org/fathers/1102130.htm.

8 Thomas, *S.T.* 2-2.83.2, resp.

9 Hans Urs von Balthasar, *Prayer*, trans. Graham Harrison (San Francisco: Ignatius, 1986), 14.

10 Maximus the Confessor, *Opusculum* 6, 176.

11 Jean-Louis Chrétien, *The Call and the Response*, trans. Anne A. Davenport (New York: Fordham University Press, 2004), 5.

12 Coakley, *God, Sexuality, and the Self*, 113.

13 Von Balthasar, *Prayer*, 51.

14 Cyprian of Carthage, *Treatise on the Lord's Prayer*, trans. Robert Ernest Wallis, in *The Ante-Nicene Fathers*, vol. 5, ed. Alexander Roberts, James Donaldson, and A. Cleveland Coxe (Buffalo, N.Y.: Christian Literature Company, 1886). Rev. and ed. for New Advent by Kevin Knight, http://www.newadvent.org/fathers/050704.htm.

15 See Rowan Williams, *The Dwelling of the Light: Praying with Icons of Christ* (Norwich: Canterbury Press, 2003), 45–63.

16 Vladimir Lossky and Leonid Ouspensky, *The Meaning of Icons* (Boston: Boston Book and Art Shop, 1969), 202. My thinking about these two versions has been informed by Gene Rogers.

11 Last Things

1 Karl Barth, *Church Dogmatics*, vol. 4.1, *The Doctrine of Incarnation*, trans. G. W. Bromiley (Edinburgh: T&T Clark, 1953), 121.

2 Augustine, Sermon 169.13, in *Sermons* (148–183) *on the New Testament*, trans. and ed. Edmund Hill, The Works of Saint Augustine: A Translation for the 21st Century (Hyde Park, N.Y.: New City Press, 1992), 231.

3 Barth, *Church Dogmatics*, vol 4.1, 113.

4 Robinson, *Housekeeping*, 194–95.

5 Hans Urs von Balthasar, *Glory of the Lord*, vol. 1, 120ff.

6 Thomas, *S.T.* 3, Supplement, 93.1, reply 3.

7 Augustine, *City of God* 20.

8   Gregory of Nyssa, *Ad Theophilus*, 267.

9   I am indebted to Eduardo Muñoz for reminding me of the theological subtleties of *Tarkovsky*.

10   This relates to Thomas' insistence, in *S.T.* 3.59.5, that an initial judgment precedes a final judgment, so that the effects of human action through time can be taken into account. God does not need this new information, so it only makes sense if human acknowledgement of the justness of God's judgments matters.

11   I am referring here to the ecclesiological principles, especially important in Anglicanism, of adiaphora and subsidiarity.

12   William T. Cavanaugh, *Torture and Eucharist: Theology, Politics, and the Body of Christ* (Oxford: Blackwell, 1998).

13   Elizabeth A. Livingstone and Frank Leslie Cross, "Anathema," in *The Oxford Dictionary of the Christian Church* (Oxford: Oxford University Press, 2005).

14   Lewis, *Great Divorce*, chap. 4.

15   C. S. Lewis, *The Weight of Glory* (New York: HarperCollins, 2001), 29.

16   See the cryptic and unexplained note in Pavel Florensky, *At the Crossroads of Science & Mysticism: On the Cultural-Historical Place and Premises of the Christian World-Understanding*, trans. Boris Jakim (Kettering, Ohio: Semantron Press, 2014), 55: "At the time of the arrival of the Last Judgment there will be perfect freedom: there will be no obstacles to believing or not believing. A time favorable for eschatological ideas is approaching."

17   Hans Urs von Balthasar, *Dare We Hope "That All Men Be Saved"? With a Short Discourse on Hell*, trans. David Kipp and Lothar Krauth (San Francisco: Ignatius, 1988), 63.

18   Augustine, *City of God* 20.1.11.

19   Marjorie Garber, *Shakespeare after All* (New York: Anchor, 2005), 842.

20   William Shakespeare, *The Winter's Tale* 4.1.17, in *The Oxford Shakespeare*, 2nd ed, ed. John Jowett et al. (Oxford: Oxford University Press, 2005).

21   William Shakespeare, *Winter's Tale* 3.2.237–239.

22   This alternative, in fact, is closer to the plot of *Much Ado about Nothing*. We might read *Winter's Tale* as a revision of *Much Ado*, now making an aesthetic experiment with appropriate-time-taking confession.

23   Cone, *Spirituals and the Blues*. See chap. 5, above.

24   A central theme throughout Mendoza-Álvarez, *Resurrección*.

25   Kathryn Tanner, *Jesus, Humanity and the Trinity: A Brief Systematic Theology* (Minneapolis: Fortress, 2001), chap. 4.

26   While I find Hart's arguments, in *That All Shall Be Saved: Heaven, Hell, and Universal Salvation* (New Haven, Conn.: Yale University Press, 2019), in favor of universal salvation to be persuasive in many respects, it seems to me that in insisting that "not only is an eternal free rejection of God unlikely, it is a logically vacuous idea" (178), he collapses the important analogical distance between our share in the Logos and the being of the Logos itself. There is, that is to say, a necessary agnosticism to the question of what judgments any creature's life is finally making regarding God, as there is a necessary agnosticism about God's ultimate judgment about any creature. This is precisely why Gregory hopes that the saints can see the divine logic that he himself cannot.

27   Von Balthasar, *The Last Act*, vol. 5 of *Theo-Drama: Theological Dramatic Theory*, trans. Graham Harrison (San Francisco: Ignatius, 1998), 296.

28   Von Balthasar, *Last Act*, 298.

29   Augustine, *Nature of the Good* 34, in *Augustine: Earlier Writings*, ed. and trans. J. H. S. Burleigh (Philadelphia: Westminster, 1952), 337.

30   Lewis, *Weight of Glory*, 45.

BIBLIOGRAPHY

Abraham, William J. *Crossing the Threshold of Divine Revelation*. Grand Rapids: Eerdmans, 2006.

"Against the Dead Consensus." *First Things*, March 2019. https://www.firstthings.com/web-exclusives/2019/03/against-the-dead-consensus.

Alison, James. *The Joy of Being Wrong: Original Sin through Easter Eyes*. New York: Crossroad, 1998.

"Amazon Rainforest Fires: Here's What's Really Happening." *New York Times*, August 28, 2019. https://www.nytimes.com/2019/08/23/world/americas/amazon -fire-brazil-bolsonaro.html.

Anatolios, Khaled. "Personhood, Community, and Trinity in Some Patristic Texts." In *The Holy Trinity in the Life of the Church*, edited by Khaled Anatolios. Grand Rapids: Baker Academic, 2014.

Anderson, Gary. "Sacrifice and Sacrificial Offerings (OT)." In *Anchor Bible Dictionary*, vol. 5, edited by David Noel Freedman, 870–86. New York: Doubleday, 1992.

Andrewes, Lancelot. "Sermon 4 Of the Holy Ghost, Whit-Sunday 1611." In *Lancelot Andrewes: Sermons*, edited by George Morley Story. Oxford: Clarendon, 1967.

Anselm. *The Fall of Satan*. In *Theological Treatises*, translated and edited by Jasper Hopkins and Herbert Warren Richardson. Cambridge, Mass.: Harvard Divinity School Library, 1965.

———. *Meditation on Human Redemption*. In *The Prayers and Meditations of St. Anselm*, translated by Sister Benedicta Ward. London: Penguin Books, 1973.

Athanasius. Letter 1. In *The Letters of Saint Athanasius concerning the Holy Spirit*. Translated by C. R. B. Shapland. New York: Epworth Press, 1951.

———. *On the Incarnation of the Word*. In *Christology of the Later Fathers*, translated by Edward Rochie Hardy. Philadelphia: Westminster, 1954.

Auden, W. H. "After Reading a Child's Guide to Modern Physics." https://allpoetry.com/After-Reading-A-Child's-Guide-To-Modern-Physics.

Augustine. *The City of God (De Civitate Dei): Books 11–22*. Translated by William S. Babcock. Hyde Park, N.Y.: New City Press, 2014.

———. *Confessions*. Translated by Maria Boulding. The Works of Saint Augustine: A Translation for the Twenty-First Century. Hyde Park, N.Y.: New City Press, 2002.

———. Exposition of Psalm 9. In *Expositions of the Psalms*, vol. 1, translated by John E. Rotelle. The Works of Saint Augustine: A Translation for the Twenty-First Century. Hyde Park, N.Y.: New City Press, 2000.

———. Exposition of Psalm 96. In *Expositions of the Psalms*, vol. 4, translated by Maria Boulding. The Works of Saint Augustine: A Translation for the Twenty-First Century. Hyde Park, N.Y.: New City Press, 2001.

———. Letter 130. https://www.newadvent.org/fathers/1102130.htm.

———. *Nature of the Good*. In *Augustine: Earlier Writings*, edited and translated by J. H. S. Burleigh. Philadelphia: Westminster, 1952.

———. *On the Sermon on the Mount according to Matthew*. In *Nicene and Post-Nicene Fathers*, vol. 6, translated by William Findlay and Phillip Schaff. Buffalo, N.Y.: Christian Literature Company, 1888.

———. Sermon 169. In *Sermons (148–183) on the New Testament*, translated and edited by Edmund Hill. The Works of Saint Augustine: A Translation for the Twenty-First Century. Hyde Park, N.Y.: New City Press, 1992.

———. *The Trinity*. Translated by Edmund Hill. The Works of Saint Augustine: A Translation for the Twenty-First Century. Hyde Park, N.Y.: New City Press, 1990.

Austin, J. L. *How to Do Things with Words*. Oxford: Oxford University Press, 2009.

Ayres, Lewis. *Nicaea and Its Legacy: An Approach to Fourth Century Trinitarian Theology*. Oxford: Oxford University Press, 2004.

Baker, Anthony D. "Arguing the Mystery: Teaching Critical Thinking in the Theology Classroom." *Wabash Center Journal on Teaching* 1, no. 1 (2020): 37–45.

———. *Diagonal Advance*. London: SCM Press, 2011.

———. *Shakespeare, Theology, and the Unstaged God*. London: Routledge, 2020.

Baker-Fletcher, Karen. "Something or Nothing: An Eco-Womanist Essay on God, Creation, and Indispensability." In *This Sacred Earth: Religion, Nature, Environment*, edited by Roger S. Gottlieb, 2nd ed., 428–37. London: Routledge, 2004.

Barth, Karl. *Church Dogmatics*. Vol. 2.1, *The Doctrine of God*. Translated by G. W. Bromiley et al. Edinburgh: T&T Clark, 1957.

———. *Church Dogmatics*. Vol. 4.1, *The Doctrine of Incarnation*. Translated by G. W. Bromiley. Edinburgh: T&T Clark, 1953.

———. *Church Dogmatics*. Vol. 4.2, *The Doctrine of Reconciliation*. Translated by G. W. Bromiley. Edinburgh: T&T Clark, 1958.

———. *Dogmatics in Outline*. New York: Harper, 1959.

———. *The Epistle to the Romans*. Translated by Edwyn Clement Hoskyns. Oxford: Oxford University Press, 1933.

Bauerschmidt, Frederick. *Thomas Aquinas: Faith, Reason, and Following Christ*. Oxford: Oxford University Press, 2013.

Behr, John. *The Mystery of Christ: Life in Death*. New York: St. Vladimir's Seminary Press, 2006.

Berkovits, Eliezer. *God, Man, And History*. Middle Village, N.Y.: Jonathan David, 1979.

"Black Parishioners in Louisiana Pray on Easter for Alleged Racist Who Burned Down Their Church." *Daily Beast*, April 21, 2019. https://www.thedailybeast.com/louisiana-church-fires-black-parishioners-pray-for-holden-matthews-accused-of-burning-down-church-in-hate-crime.

Bonaventure. *On the Reduction of the Arts to Theology*. Translated by Zachary Hayes. New York: Franciscan Institute, 1996.

Borges, Jorge Luis. *The Book of Sand, and Shakespeare's Memory*. Translated by Andrew Hurley. London: Penguin Books, 2001.

Bradshaw, David. *Aristotle East and West: Metaphysics and the Division of Christendom*. Cambridge: Cambridge University Press, 2005.

Brown, Brené. *Rising Strong: How the Ability to Reset Changes the Way We Live, Love, Parent, and Lead*. New York: Random House, 2015.

Bulgakov, Sergius. *The Bride of the Lamb*. Translated by Boris Jakim. Grand Rapids: Eerdmans, 2001.

———. *The Comforter*. Translated by Boris Jakim. Grand Rapids: Eerdmans, 2004.

———. *The Friend of the Bridegroom: On the Orthodox Veneration of the Forerunner*. Translated by Boris Jakim. Grand Rapids: Eerdmans, 2003.

———. *The Wisdom of God: A Brief Summary of Sophiology*. Translated by Patrick Thompson, O. Fielding Clarke, and Xenia Braikevitc. New York: The Paisley Press, 1937.

Cardenal, Ernesto. *El Evangelio En Solentiname*. Madrid: Editorial Trotta, 2006.

"Cardinal Tobin Leads Hundreds of Catholics in Protest against ICE in Newark." *National Catholic Reporter*, September 6, 2019. https://www.ncronline.org/news/justice/cardinal-tobin-leads-hundreds-catholics-protest-against-ice-newark.

Cavanaugh, William T. *Torture and Eucharist: Theology, Politics, and the Body of Christ*. Oxford: Blackwell, 1998.

Cavell, Stanley. *Philosophy the Day after Tomorrow*. Cambridge, Mass.: Harvard University Press, 2005.

Chesterton, G. K. *The Everlasting Man*. London: Hodder & Stoughton, 1936.

Chrétien, Jean-Louis. *The Ark of Speech*. Translated by Andrew Brown. London: Routledge, 2004.

———. *The Call and the Response*. Translated by Anne A. Davenport. New York: Fordham University Press, 2004.

Coakley, Sarah. *God, Sexuality, and the Self: An Essay 'On the Trinity.'* Cambridge: Cambridge University Press, 2014.

Cone, James H. *God of the Oppressed*. Maryknoll, N.Y.: Orbis, 1997.

———. *The Spirituals and the Blues: An Interpretation*. Maryknoll, N.Y.: Orbis, 1992.

Copp, Rebecca S. "Theology and the Poetics of Testimony." In *Converging on Culture: Theologians in Dialogue with Cultural Analysis and Criticism*, edited by Delwin Brown, Sheila Greeve Davaney, and Kathryn Tanner, 56–70. Oxford: Oxford University Press, 2001.

Cyprian of Carthage. *Treatise on the Lord's Prayer*. Translated by Robert Ernest Wallis. In *Ante-Nicene Fathers*, vol. 5, edited by Alexander Roberts, James Donaldson, and A. Cleveland Coxe. Buffalo, N.Y.: Christian Literature Company, 1886. Revised and edited for New Advent by Kevin Knight. http://www.newadvent.org/fathers/050704.htm.

Dante. *Divine Comedy*. In *The Portable Dante*, edited and translated by Mark Musa. New York: Penguin Books, 2003.

Davison, Andrew. *Participation in God: A Study in Christian Doctrine and Metaphysics*. Cambridge: Cambridge University Press, 2019.

Deane-Drummond, Celia. "In Adam All Die? Questions at the Boundary of Niche Construction, Community Evolution and Original Sin." In *Evolution and the Fall*, edited by William T. Cavanaugh and James K. A. Smith, 23–47. Grand Rapids: Eerdmans, 2017.

De La Bedoyere, Michael. *The Cardijn Story: A Study of the Life of Mgr. Joseph Cardijn and the Young Christian Workers' Movement Which He Founded*. London: Longmans, Green and Co., 1958.

De Lubac, Henri. *Augustinianism and Modern Theology*. London: G. Chapman, 1969.

———. *Medieval Exegesis*. 3 vols. Grand Rapids: Eerdmans, 1998–2008.

Desmond, William. *Being and the Between*. Albany, N.Y.: SUNY Press, 1995.

Douglas, Kelly Brown. "Theological Method and the Jesus Movement through the Work of F. D. Maurice and Vida Scudder." *Anglican Theological Review* 102, no. 1 (2020): 7–30.

Douglass, Frederick. *The Life and Times of Frederick Douglass*. Mineola, N.Y.: Dover, 2012.

———. *My Bondage and My Freedom*. Buffalo, N.Y.: Miller, Orton & Mulligan, 1855.

Ellacuría, Ignacio. *Ignacio Ellacuria: Essays on History, Liberation, and Salvation*. Translated by Michael Edward Lee. Maryknoll, N.Y.: Orbis, 2013.

Endo, Shusaku. *Silence: A Novel*. Translated by William Johnson. New York: Picador Modern Classics, 2016.

The Epistle of Porphyry to the Egyptian Anebo. http://www.tertullian.org/fathers/porphyry_anebo_02_text.htm.

Estany, Anna, and David Casacuberta. "Contributions of Socially Distributed Cognition to Social Epistemology: The Case of Testimony." *Eidos* no. 16 (2012): 40–68.

Fisher, Kathleen M. "Look before You Leap: Reconsidering Contemplative Pedagogy." *Teaching Theology & Religion* 20, no. 1 (2017): 4–21.

Florensky, Pavel. *At the Crossroads of Science & Mysticism: On the Cultural-Historical Place and Premises of the Christian World-Understanding.* Translated by Boris Jakim. Kettering, Ohio: Semantron Press, 2014.

Gadamer, Hans-Georg. *Truth and Method.* 2nd rev. ed. New York: Continuum, 2004.

Garber, Marjorie. *Shakespeare after All.* New York: Anchor, 2005.

Gorman, Michael J. *Inhabiting the Cruciform God: Kenosis, Justification, and Theosis in Paul's Narrative Soteriology.* Grand Rapids: Eerdmans, 2009.

Gregory of Nyssa. *Ad Theophilus.* In *Anti-Apollinarian Writings,* translated by Robin Orton. Washington, D.C.: Catholic University of America Press, 2015.

———. *On Not Three Gods, to Ablabius.* Translated by William Moore. In *Nicene and Post-Nicene Fathers,* series 2, vol. 5. Buffalo, N.Y.: Christian Literature Company, 1892.

Griffiths, Paul J. *Decreation: The Last Things of All Creatures.* Waco, Tex.: Baylor University Press, 2014.

Hancock, Christopher. "Complexity Theory and the Chinese Church." *International Journal for the Study of the Christian Church* 15, no. 4 (2015): 261–74.

Harrison, Nonna Verna. "Gregory of Nyssa on Knowing the Trinity." In *The Holy Trinity in the Life of the Church,* edited by Khaled Anatolios. Grand Rapids: Baker Academic, 2014.

Hart, David Bentley. *The Beauty of the Infinite: The Aesthetics of Christian Truth.* Grand Rapids: Eerdmans, 2004.

———. *The Hidden and the Manifest: Essays in Theology and Metaphysics.* Grand Rapids: Eerdmans, 2017.

———. *That All Shall Be Saved: Heaven, Hell, and Universal Salvation.* New Haven, Conn.: Yale University Press, 2019.

Hastings, Elizabeth. "Augustine of Hippo and William of Saint-Thierry on the Relation between the Holy Spirit's Personal Identity (Rom 5:5) and His Sovereign Freedom Ad Extra." *Studia Patristica* 48 (2010): 361–66.

Heidegger, Martin. *Being and Time.* Edited and translated by Joan Stambaugh and Dennis J. Schmidt. Albany, N.Y.: SUNY Press, 2010.

Heschel, Abraham Joshua. *Between God and Man: An Interpretation of Judaism.* New York: Harper, 1959.

Hill, Wesley. *Paul and the Trinity: Persons, Relations, and the Pauline Letters.* Grand Rapids: Eerdmans, 2015.

Horrell, David G., Cherryl Hunt, and Christopher Southgate. *Greening Paul: Rereading the Apostle in a Time of Ecological Crisis.* Waco, Tex.: Baylor University Press, 2010.

Hutchins, Edwin, and Tove Klausen. "Distributed Cognition in an Airline Cockpit." In *Cognition and Communication at Work,* edited by Y. Engeström and D. Middleton, 15–34. Cambridge: Cambridge University Press, 1996.

Irenaeus. *Against Heresies.* In *Ante-Nicene Fathers,* vol. 1, edited by Alexander Roberts and James Donaldson. Buffalo, N.Y.: Christian Literature Company, 1885.

Jenkins, Willis. *Ecologies of Grace: Environmental Ethics and Christian Theology.* Oxford: Oxford University Press, 2008.

———. *The Future of Ethics: Sustainability, Social Justice, and Religious Creativity.* Washington, D.C.: Georgetown University Press, 2013.

Jennings, Willie James. *After Whiteness: An Education in Belonging.* Grand Rapids: Eerdmans, 2020.

———. *The Christian Imagination: Theology and the Origins of Race.* New Haven, Conn.: Yale University Press, 2010.

John of the Cross. *Romances.* In *The Collected Works of Saint John of the Cross*, translated by Kieran Kavanaugh and Otilio Rodriguez, rev. ed. Washington, D.C.: ICS Publications, 1991.

Jones, Serene, and Paul Lakeland. *Constructive Theology: A Contemporary Approach to Classical Themes.* Minneapolis: Fortress, 2005.

Katongole, Emmanuel. *The Sacrifice of Africa: A Political Theology for Africa.* Grand Rapids: Eerdmans, 2011.

Katongole, Emmanuel, and Jonathan Wilson-Hartgrove. *Mirror to the Church: Resurrecting Faith after Genocide in Rwanda.* Grand Rapids: Zondervan, 2009.

Keller, Catherine. *Face of the Deep: A Theology of Becoming.* London: Routledge, 2003.

Kelsey, David H. *Eccentric Existence: A Theological Anthropology.* Louisville: Westminster John Knox, 2009.

Kierkegaard, Søren. *Philosophical Fragments.* Translated by Howard V. Hong and Edna H. Hong. Princeton: Princeton University Press, 1985.

Kishkovsky, Leonid. "Russian Theology after Totalitarianism." In *The Cambridge Companion to Orthodox Christian Theology*, edited by Mary B. Cunningham and Elizabeth Theokritoff, 261–75. Cambridge: Cambridge University Press, 2008.

Knohl, Israël. *The Sanctuary of Silence: The Priestly Torah and the Holiness School.* Minneapolis: Fortress, 1995.

Kraybill, Donald B., Steven M. Nolt, and David Weaver-Zercher. *Amish Grace: How Forgiveness Transcended Tragedy.* 1st ed. San Francisco: Jossey-Bass, 2007.

Lacoste, Jean-Yves. *Experience and Absolute: Disputed Questions on the Humanity of Man.* Translated by Mark Raftery-Skehan. New York: Fordham University Press, 2004.

———. *From Theology to Theological Thinking.* Translated by W. Chris Hackett. Charlottesville: University of Virginia Press, 2014.

"The Lamentations Service for Holy Saturday Matins." Orthodox Christianity. https://orthochristian.com/78602.html.

Lamott, Anne. *Bird by Bird: Some Instructions on Writing and Life.* New York: Random House, 1994.

Lee, Jarena. "My Call to Preach the Gospel." In *Religious Experience.* Philadelphia, 1849. https://pluralism.org/african-religion-in-america.

Lewis, C. S. *The Great Divorce.* London: Geoffrey Bles, 1946.

———. *The Weight of Glory.* New York: HarperCollins, 2001.

Livingstone, Elizabeth A., and Frank Leslie Cross. "Anathema." In *The Oxford Dictionary of the Christian Church.* Oxford: Oxford University Press, 2005.

Lossky, Vladimir, and Leonid Ouspensky. *The Meaning of Icons.* Boston: Boston Book and Art Shop, 1969.

Luther, Martin. *Address to the German Nobility Concerning Christian Liberty.* Champaign, Ill.: Project Gutenberg. http://search.ebscohost.com/login.aspx?direct=true&AuthType=ip,sso&db=nlebk&AN=1085290&site=eds-live&scope=site.

Marion, Jean-Luc. *Givenness and Revelation.* Translated by Stephen E. Lewis. Oxford: Oxford University Press, 2016.

Martyrdom of Polycarp. In *Ante-Nicene Fathers*, vol. 1, edited by Alexander Roberts and James Donaldson. New York: Christian Literature Company, 1885.

Maximus the Confessor. *Ambiguum.* In *On Difficulties in the Church Fathers: The Ambigua*, translated by Nicholas Constas, 75–141. Cambridge, Mass.: Harvard University Press, 2014.

———. *Chapters on Knowledge.* In *Maximus Confessor: Selected Writings*, translated by George C. Berthold. New York: Paulist Press, 1985.

———. *Opusculum*. In *On the Cosmic Mystery of Jesus Christ*, translated by Paul M. Blowers and Robert Wilken. Crestwood, N.Y.: St. Vladimir's Seminary Press, 2003.

McDougall, Joy Ann. "The Bondage of the Eye/I? A Transnational Feminist Wager for Reimagining the Doctrine of Sin." In *Reimagining with Christian Doctrines: Responding to Global Gender Injustices*, edited by Grace Ji-Sun Kim and Jenny Daggers, 105–25. New York: Palgrave-MacMillan, 2014.

McIntosh, Mark. "The Maker's Meaning: Divine Ideas and Salvation." *Modern Theology* 28, no. 3 (2012): 365–84.

McVey, Kathleen. "Syriac Christian Tradition and Gender in Trinitarian Theology." In *The Holy Trinity in the Life of the Church*, edited by Khaled Anatolios. Grand Rapids: Baker Academic, 2014.

Mendoza-Álvarez, Carlos. *La Resurrección como Anticipación Mesiánica*. Mexico, D.F.: Universidad Iberoamericana A.C., 2020.

Milbank, John. *Being Reconciled: Ontology and Pardon*. London: Routledge, 2003.

———. "Postmodern Critical Augustinianism: A Short Summa in Forty Two Responses to Unasked Questions." *Modern Theology* 7, no. 3 (1991): 225–37.

———. *The Word Made Strange: Theology, Language, Culture*. Oxford: Blackwell, 1997.

Milgrom, Jacob. *Cult and Conscience: The Asham and the Priestly Doctrine of Repentance*. Leiden: Brill, 1976.

———. *Studies in Cultic Theology and Terminology*. Leiden: Brill, 1983.

Montemaggi, Vittorio. *Reading Dante's Commedia as Theology: Divinity Realized in Human Encounter*. Oxford: Oxford University Press, 2018.

"Mother Emanuel Survivors Visit Tree of Life, Offer Strength, Solidarity." *Pittsburgh Jewish Chronicle*, May 10, 2019. https://jewishchronicle.timesofisrael.com/mother -emanuel-survivors-visit-tree-of-life-offer-strength-solidarity/.

Murakami, Haruki. *Killing Commendatore*. Translated by Philip Gabriel and Ted Goossen. New York: Penguin Books, 2018.

The New Testament. Translated by David Bentley Hart. New Haven, Conn.: Yale University Press, 2017.

Nicholas of Cusa. *De docta ignorantia*. In *Selected Spiritual Writings: Nicholas of Cusa*, translated by H. Lawrence Bond. New York: Paulist Press, 1997.

Niebuhr, Reinhold. *The Nature and Destiny of Man: A Christian Interpretation*. New York: Scribner, 1949.

Ochs, Peter. "Morning Prayer as Redemptive Thinking." In *Liturgy, Time, and the Politics of Redemption*, edited by Randi Rashkover and C. C. Pecknold, 50–87. Grand Rapids: Eerdmans, 2006.

Origen of Alexandria. *Commentary on the Gospel according to John*. In *Commentary on the Gospel according to John: Books 1–10*. Translated by Ronald E. Heine. Washington, D.C.: Catholic University of America Press, 1989.

Pannenberg, Wolfhart. *Jesus—God and Man*. Translated by Lewis L. Wilkins and Duane A. Priebe. Philadelphia: Westminster John Knox, 1977.

Patterson, Jane Lancaster. *Keeping the Feast: Metaphors of Sacrifice in 1 Corinthians and Philippians*. Atlanta: SBL, 2015.

Peter Lombard. *The Sentences*. Translated by Giulio Silano. Toronto: Pontifical Institute of Mediaeval Studies, 2007.

Pickstock, Catherine. *Repetition and Identity*. Oxford: Oxford University Press, 2013.

Pope Francis. *Laudato si'*. http://www.vatican.va/content/francesco/en/encyclicals/ documents/papa-francesco_20150524_enciclica-laudato-si.html.

Pope Paul VI. *Lumen Gentium*. https://www.vatican.va/archive/hist_councils/ii_vatican _council/documents/vat-ii_const_19641121_lumen-gentium_en.html.

Przywara, Erich. *Analogia Entis: Metaphysics: Original Structure and Universal Rhythm*. Translated by John R. Betz and David Bentley Hart. Grand Rapids: Eerdmans, 2014.

Quash, Ben. *Found Theology: History, Imagination and the Holy Spirit*. London: T&T Clark, 2013.

Ratzinger, Joseph. "Funeral Homily for Msgr. Luigi Giussani." Reprinted in *Joseph Ratzinger in Communio*, vol. 2, *Anthropology and Culture*, 184–87. Grand Rapids: Eerdmans, 2013.

Riches, Aaron. "Sacrifice and Freedom: On Mystagogy and the Way of Atonement." *Communio* 45, no. 1 (2018): 54–84.

Robinson, Marilynne. *Gilead*. New York: Farrar, Straus & Giroux, 2005.

———. *Housekeeping: A Novel*. New York: Picador, 1980.

———. *When I Was a Child I Read Books: Essays*. New York: Farrar, Straus and Giroux, 2012.

Rogers, Eugene F., Jr. *Elements of Christian Thought: A Basic Course in Christianese*. Minneapolis: Fortress, 2021.

———. *Sexuality and the Christian Body: Their Way into the Triune God*. Cambridge: Blackwell, 1999.

Romero, Oscar A. *Voice of the Voiceless: The Four Pastoral Letters and Other Statements*. Maryknoll, N.Y.: Orbis, 1985.

Schweitzer, Albert. *The Quest of the Historical Jesus*. Edited by John Bowden. 1st complete ed. Minneapolis: Fortress, 2001.

Sedgwick, Eve Kosofsky. *Touching Feeling*. Durham, N.C.: Duke University Press, 2014.

Shakespeare, William. *The Winter's Tale*. In *The Oxford Shakespeare*, ed. John Jowett et al., 2nd ed. Oxford: Oxford University Press, 2005.

Shelley, Mary Wollstonecraft. *Frankenstein, or, The Modern Prometheus*. London: Sever, Francis, & Company, 1869.

Soulen, Kendal. *The Divine Name(s) and the Holy Trinity*. Louisville: Westminster John Knox, 2011.

Stackert, Jeffrey. *A Prophet Like Moses: Prophecy, Law, and Israelite Religion*. Oxford: Oxford University Press, 2014.

Staniloae, Dumitru. *Theology and the Church*. Translated by Robert Barringer. New York: Saint Vladimir's Seminary Press, 1980.

Stone, Howard W., and James O. Duke. *How to Think Theologically*. Minneapolis: Fortress, 2013.

Tanner, Kathryn. *Christ the Key*. Cambridge: Cambridge University Press, 2010.

———. *God and Creation in Christian Theology: Tyranny or Empowerment*. Minneapolis: Fortress, 2005.

———. *Jesus, Humanity and the Trinity: A Brief Systematic Theology*. Minneapolis: Fortress, 2001.

Thiselton, Anthony. *Hermeneutics: An Introduction*. Grand Rapids: Eerdmans, 2009.

———. *The Two Horizons: New Testament Hermeneutics and Philosophical Description*. Grand Rapids: Eerdmans, 1980.

Thomas Aquinas. *Summa Theologiae*. Translated by Fathers of the English Dominican Province. 2nd rev. ed. London: Burns, Oates and Washbourne, 1920. Revised and edited for New Advent by Kevin Knight. https://www.newadvent.org/summa/.

von Balthasar, Hans Urs. *The Action*. Vol. 4 of *Theo-Drama: Theological Dramatic Theory*. Translated by Graham Harrison. San Francisco: Ignatius, 1988.

———. *Cosmic Liturgy: The Universe according to Maximus the Confessor*. Translated by Brian Daley. San Francisco: Ignatius, 2003.

———. *Dare We Hope "That All Men Be Saved"? With a Short Discourse on Hell*. Translated by David Kipp and Lothar Krauth. San Francisco: Ignatius, 1988.

———. *The Dramatis Personae: The Person in Christ*. Vol. 3 of *Theo-Drama: Theological Dramatic Theory*. Translated by Graham Harrison. San Francisco: Ignatius, 1992.

———. *First Glance at Adrienne von Speyr*. San Francisco: Ignatius, 1981.

——. *The Last Act.* Vol. 5 of *Theo-Drama: Theological Dramatic Theory.* Translated by Graham Harrison. San Francisco: Ignatius, 1998.

——. *Prayer.* Translated by Graham Harrison. San Francisco: Ignatius, 1986.

——. *Presence and Thought: An Essay on the Religious Philosophy of Gregory of Nyssa.* San Francisco: Ignatius, 1995.

——. *Seeing the Form.* Vol. 1 of *Theological Aesthetics.* Edited by Joseph Fessio, S.J., and John Riches. Translated by Erasmo Leiva-Merikakakis. San Francisco: Ignatius, 1982.

——. *Two Sisters in the Spirit: Thérèse of Lisieux & Elizabeth of the Trinity.* San Francisco: Ignatius, 1992.

von Speyr, Adrienne. *The Cross, Word and Sacrament.* San Francisco: Ignatius, 1983.

Walker, Alice. *The Color Purple.* Orlando: Harcourt, 1982.

"What the Notre-Dame Fire Reveals about the Soul of France." *New York Times,* April 16, 2019. https://www.nytimes.com/2019/04/16/world/europe/france-notre-dame-religion.html.

Whitehead, Alfred North. *Process and Reality.* Edited by David Ray Griffin and Donald W. Sherburne. Corrected ed. New York: Free Press, 1978.

"White Man Accused in Church Killings Told Black Friend He Planned Mass Shooting at SC College." *U.S. News & World Report,* June 20, 2015. https://www.usnews.com/news/us/articles/2015/06/20/man-accused-of-church-killings-spoke-of-attacking-college.

Williams, Rowan. "The Body's Grace." In *Theology and Sexuality: Classic and Contemporary Readings,* edited by Eugene F. Rogers, Jr. Oxford: Blackwell, 2002.

——. *Christ the Heart of Creation.* London: Bloomsbury, 2018.

——. "The Deflections of Desire: Negative Theology in Trinitarian Disclosure." In *Silence and the Word: Negative Theology and Incarnation,* edited by Denys Turner and Oliver Davies, 115–35. Cambridge: Cambridge University Press, 2002.

——. *The Dwelling of the Light: Praying with Icons of Christ.* Norwich: Canterbury Press, 2003.

——. *On Augustine.* London: Bloomsbury, 2016.

——. *On Christian Theology.* Oxford: Blackwell, 2000.

——. *Resurrection: Interpreting the Easter Gospel.* Rev. ed. Cleveland: Pilgrim Press, 2002.

——. *Teresa of Avila.* London: G. Chapman, 1991.

——. *The Wound of Knowledge: Christian Spirituality from the New Testament to St. John of the Cross.* 2nd rev. ed. Cambridge, Mass.: Cowley Publications, 1991.

Wright, David P. "Azazel." In *Anchor Bible Dictionary,* vol. 1, edited by David Noel Freedman, 536–37. New York: Doubleday, 1992.

Wyschogrod, Michael. "Incarnation." *Pro Ecclesia* 2, no. 2 (1993): 208–15.

Yong, Ed. "A Cultural Leap at the Dawn of Humanity." *Atlantic,* March 2018. https://www.theatlantic.com/science/archive/2018/03/a-deeper-origin-of-complex-human-cultures/555674/.

INDEX OF SUBJECTS AND AUTHORS

INDEX OF SCRIPTURE